T0192387

Jumpstart Tableau

A Step-By-Step Guide to Better
Data Visualization

Arshad Khan

Apress®

Jumpstart Tableau: A Step-By-Step Guide to Better Data Visualization

Arshad Khan
California
USA

ISBN-13 (pbk): 978-1-4842-1933-1   ISBN-13 (electronic): 978-1-4842-1934-8
DOI 10.1007/978-1-4842-1934-8

Library of Congress Control Number: 2016941342

Managing Director: Welmoed Spahr
Acquisitions Editor: Susan McDermott
Developmental Editor: Douglas Pundick
Technical Reviewer: Girija Chavan
Editorial Board: Steve Anglin, Pramila Balen, Louise Corrigan, James DeWolf, Jonathan Gennick, Robert Hutchinson, Celestin Suresh John, Nikhil Karkal, James Markham, Susan McDermott, Matthew Moodie, Douglas Pundick, Ben Renow-Clarke, Gwenan Spearing
Coordinating Editor: Rita Fernando
Copy Editor: Kim Burton-Weisman
Compositor: SPi Global
Indexer: SPi Global
Cover image designed by Freepik.com.

Distributed to the book trade worldwide by Springer Science+Business Media New York, 233 Spring Street, 6th Floor, New York, NY 10013. Phone 1-800-SPRINGER, fax (201) 348-4505, e-mail orders-ny@springer-sbm.com, or visit www.springer.com. Apress Media, LLC is a California LLC and the sole member (owner) is Springer Science + Business Media Finance Inc (SSBM Finance Inc). SSBM Finance Inc is a Delaware corporation.

For information on translations, please e-mail rights@apress.com, or visit www.apress.com.

Apress and friends of ED books may be purchased in bulk for academic, corporate, or promotional use. eBook versions and licenses are also available for most titles. For more information, reference our Special Bulk Sales–eBook Licensing web page at www.apress.com/bulk-sales.

Any source code or other supplementary materials referenced by the author in this text is available to readers at www.apress.com. For detailed information about how to locate your book's source code, go to www.apress.com/source-code/.

Printed on acid-free paper

Contents at a Glance

Contents

About the Author

Arshad Khan is a versatile IT business intelligence and SAP software professional with over 30 years of experience. He has extensive consulting experience in business intelligence/analytics and SAP. He has consulted for such leading companies as Accenture, PricewaterhouseCoopers, Deloitte, Pacific Gas & Electric Co., Bose Corporation, DaimlerChrysler, Home Depot, Genentech, Chevron, Textron, PepsiCo, Polycom, Unisys, and Hitachi America. Since 2014, Mr. Khan has been consulting for the US Navy as a business intelligence architect. At Juniper Networks (a four-billion-dollar company), he led the Tableau-based analytics development team.

Mr. Khan, who has fifteen books on diverse subjects to his credit, previously authored five books on BI/data warehousing. He has also taught at seven universities, including the University of California (Berkeley, Santa Cruz, and San Diego), since 1995. Mr. Khan has a graduate degree in engineering and an MBA.

About the Technical Reviewer

Girija Chavan is a data analysis and data visualization evangelist who has provided professional consulting to companies such as Juniper Networks, Hewlett-Packard, and Accept Software. Girija has been invited to teach Tableau at UCSC Extension and at Santa Clara University. She was a guest speaker at the 2014 Annual Tableau Conference. She has completed advanced Tableau Desktop and Server training, Jedi training, and Stephen Few's workshops for data visualization, and she continues to pursue studies in the fields of data science and predictive analytics.

Girija holds a bachelor's degree and an MBA in IT. She currently works as a lead BI analyst and Tableau server administrator at Juniper Networks.

Acknowledgments

I would like to take this opportunity to thank Girija Chavan, a seasoned Tableau expert, for reviewing the manuscript and providing very useful feedback. I would also like to thank Barry Pierce, Mayra Lopez, and Natalie Wade for reviewing the manuscript and providing very useful feedback from a novice developer perspective.

Introduction

Jumpstart Tableau aims to teach novices the basics of Tableau software so that they can quickly develop simple reports and visualizations. Tableau is a very powerful software with a very rich set of features and functionality. However, to get started, users need to learn only a few key functions, which are widely used in every type of business. This book aims to teach those basic functions through a series of exercises, which are based on step-by-step instructions. Learning these exercises will not make anyone an expert. However, they will provide enough knowledge and hands-on capability to novices so that they can quickly develop powerful and professional-looking visualizations.

Jumpstart Tableau contains 40 exercises. Of these, one explains the Tableau interface, while the others provide step-by-step instructions for performing various functions. Functions covered include swapping, sorting, drill down, grouping, hierarchies, aggregation, filtering, formatting, and trending. The exercises show how to delete, copy, and save workbooks, export the data/results to Excel or PDF, and display the detailed underlying data. They also demonstrate analysis functions, including Top N and forecasting.

Jumpstart Tableau also contains step-by-step exercises that demonstrate how to create a dashboard, incorporate quick filters in dashboards, and use layout formatting, as well as how to cascade worksheet changes in a dashboard.

The exercises in this book are based on two sample data files provided by Tableau Software. These files can be downloaded from www.apress.com/9781484219331.

CHAPTER 1

Log on to Tableau

Objective: This exercise demonstrates how to launch Tableau and connect to an Excel spreadsheet data source

- Launch the **Windows Start menu**, as displayed in Figure 1-1

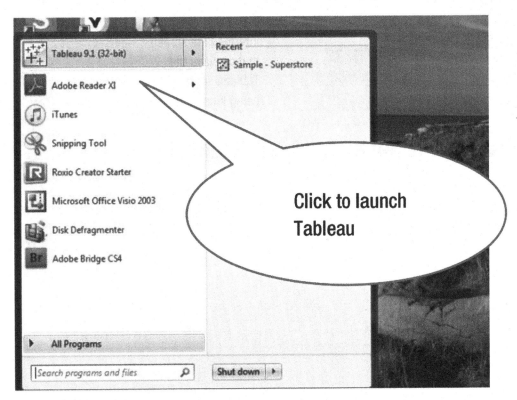

Figure 1-1. *Launching Tableau*

- Click Start ➤ All Programs ➤ **Tableau 9.1 (32-bit)**, which leads to the intermediate screen displayed in Figure 1-2

Electronic supplementary material The online version of this chapter (doi:10.1007/978-1-4842-1934-8_1) contains supplementary material, which is available to authorized users.

© Arshad Khan 2016
A. Khan, *Jumpstart Tableau*, DOI 10.1007/978-1-4842-1934-8_1

Figure 1-2. Intermediate screen

The intermediate screen, which flashes and then disappears, is followed by the **Welcome** screen displayed in Figure 1-3.

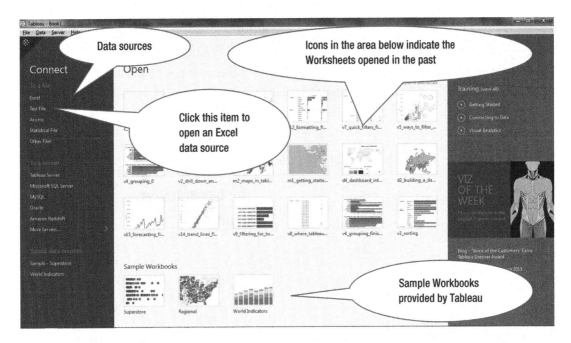

Figure 1-3. *Tableau Welcome window*

The left-hand pane is called the **Connect** pane; it lists the various data sources that you can connect to. These sources include relational databases, online data sources, text files, as well as Excel. An Excel sheet is considered a database table. It is possible to join one or multiple tables (or sheets) in Tableau.

The middle section of the window with the light background, under **Open**, lists the workbooks that were used recently. A workbook in this area can be launched by just clicking it. The three items listed under **Sample Workbooks** are provided by Tableau and show up by default.

The right section, **Discover**, contains links for getting started in Tableau.

In our exercise, we will connect to an Excel spreadsheet:

- Click **Excel**, as shown in Figure 1-3, which pops up the window displayed in Figure 1-4

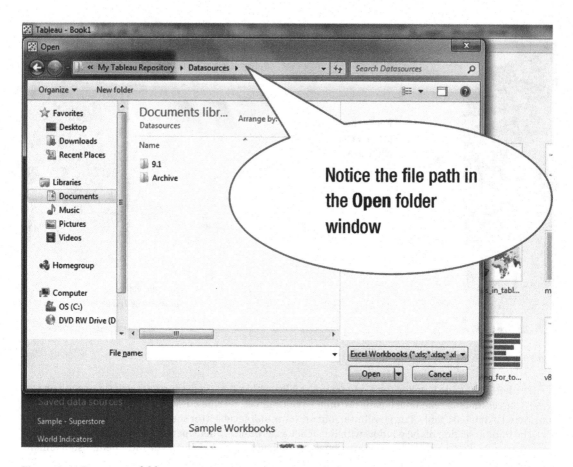

Figure 1-4. *Datasource folder*

The file that you want to connect to is at a lower level. Therefore, you need to drill down into the folder structure until the desired file is displayed.

Navigate to the desired spreadsheet as follows:

- **My Tableau Repository ➤ Datasources ➤ 9.1 ➤ en_US-US**

When the drilldown has completed, the display is as shown in Figure 1-5.

4

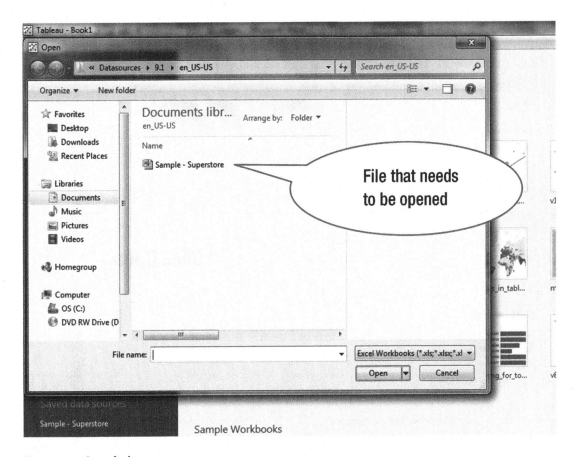

Figure 1-5. *Sample data source*

The Sample – Superstore file is now displayed in Figure 1-5.

- Click the **Sample – Superstore** file, which highlights it, as shown in Figure 1-6

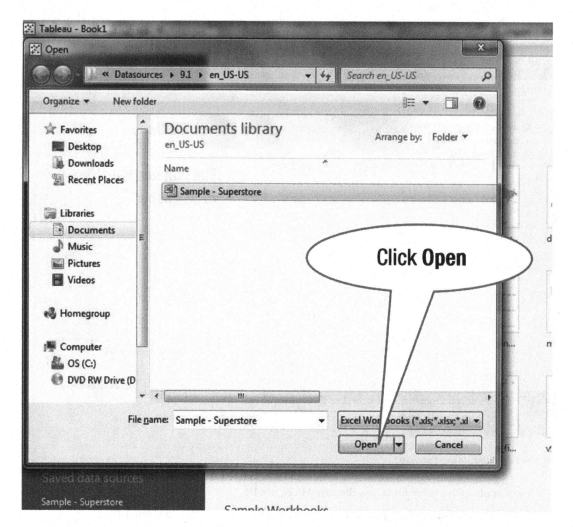

Figure 1-6. *Data source Excel spreadsheet*

- Click the **Open** button, as shown in Figure 1-6, which opens the
  Sample – Superstore spreadsheet and leads to the display shown in Figure 1-7

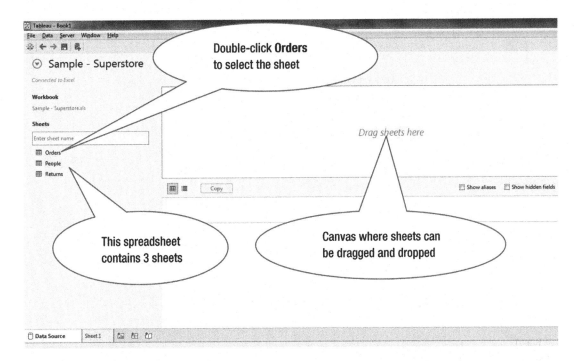

Figure 1-7. *Data Connection window*

This spreadsheet has three sheets: Orders, People, and Returns. We can connect to one or more of the sheets or tables, such as Orders.

The Orders sheet can be opened for analysis using one of two methods:

- Double-clicking the **Orders** sheet

- Dragging and dropping **Orders** onto the canvas

To drag and drop:

- Click the **Orders** sheet, as shown in Figure 1-8

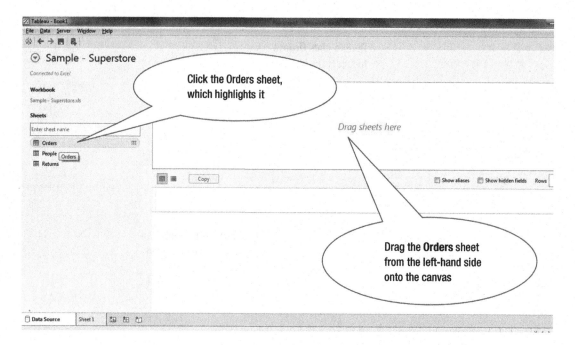

Figure 1-8. *Selecting the dataset*

- Drag **Orders** onto the blank canvas area, as shown in Figure 1-8, which leads to the display shown in Figure 1-9

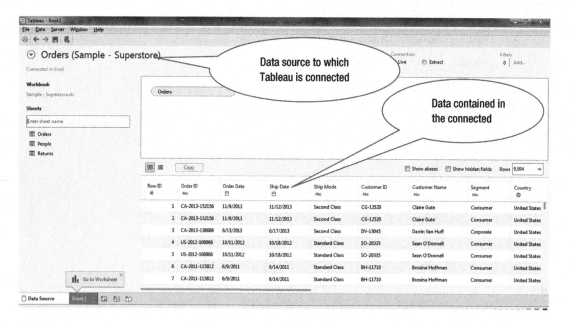

Figure 1-9. *Data imported from the Orders sheet*

Figure 1-9 shows that the **Orders** sheet of the **Sample – Superstore** data source (Excel spreadsheet) is connected to Tableau. The lower section of the display shows the data contained in the selected sheet (Orders). The first row contains the column headers. The table itself contains sales data for customers buying specific products.

The exercises in this book are primarily based on the Sample – Superstore spreadsheet, which is a subset of the **Global Superstore** spreadsheet, which has also been used in some exercises. However, the Global Superstore has been used in most of the Tableau sample workbooks.

CHAPTER 2

■ ■ ■

Connecting to Two Data Sources

Objective: This exercise demonstrates how to connect to two data sources

Figure 2-1 shows the Tableau Welcome screen after it is launched. The left-hand pane, under **Connect**, lists the various data sources to which Tableau can connect. These are split into three groups of data sources:

- To a file

- To a server

- Saved data sources

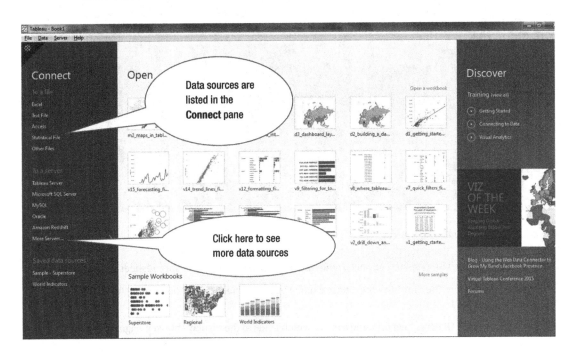

Figure 2-1. *Tableau Welcome screen*

For this exercise as well as subsequent exercises, we will only use the first option, **To a file**, because the Excel data source we will use is available there. The second option can be used when we need to connect to external data sources, which primarily are databases.

© Arshad Khan 2016
A. Khan, *Jumpstart Tableau*, DOI 10.1007/978-1-4842-1934-8_2

To display more data sources:

- Click **More Servers**, as shown in Figure 2-1, which leads to Figure 2-2, where the additional data sources are listed

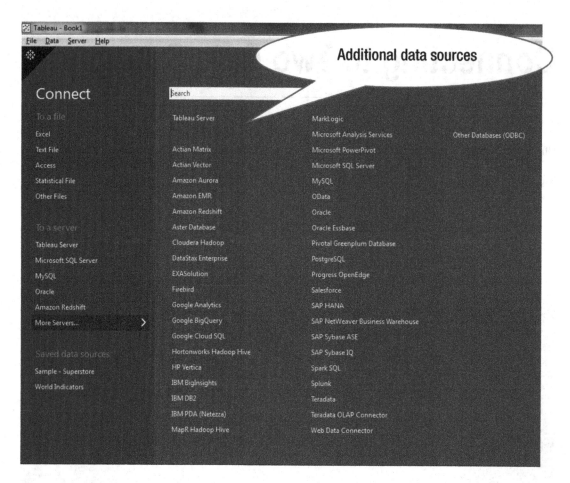

Figure 2-2. *Additional data sources*

For this exercise, you need to connect to the **Sample – Superstore** Excel spreadsheet data source:

- Connect to the **Sample - Superstore** data source, using the method demonstrated in Chapter 1

- Drag the **Orders** sheet onto the canvas, which leads to the display shown in Figure 2-3

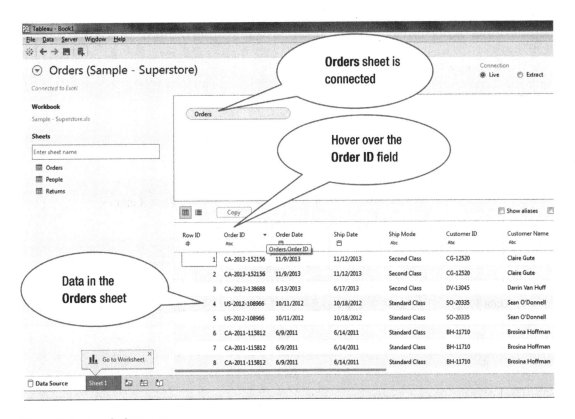

Figure 2-3. *Sample data source*

The source data can be used as-is. However, in some cases, data may need to be prepared so that it can enable better and/or easier analysis. For example, field names can be renamed so that they are easily understood by the business users. In some cases, a complex field may need to be split.

To rename the **Order ID** field:

- Hover over the **Order ID** field, as shown in Figure 2-3, which displays the pull-down arrow (shown next to the field name)

- Click the pull-down arrow for the **Order ID** field, which pops up the menu tree displayed in Figure 2-4

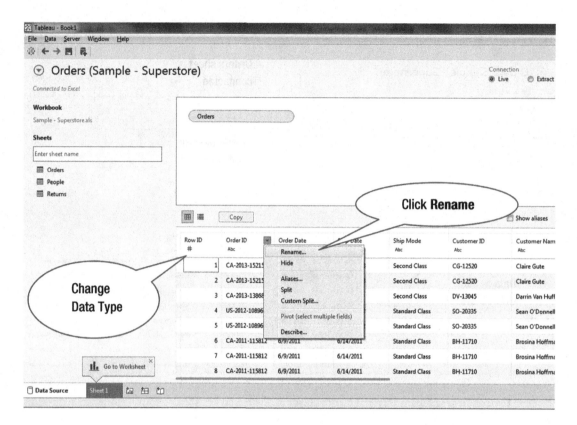

Figure 2-4. *Renaming or changing data type for a field*

- Click **Rename**, as shown in Figure 2-4, which pops up the **Rename Field** window displayed in Figure 2-5

- If the data type needs to be changed in a column, click the icon below the column header, as indicated in Figure 2-4

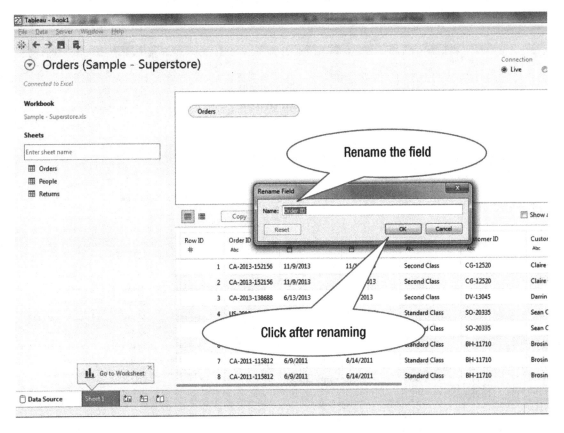

Figure 2-5. *Rename popup window*

- Enter the new field name in the **Name** field in the **Rename Field** popup box, as shown in Figure 2-5

- Click **OK**, which renames the field

There are two ways in which data can be accessed and used by Tableau. In **Connect Live**, a direct connection is made with the data source. In this mode, if the source data changes, it is immediately reflected in the visualizations and any analysis being performed.

Tableau also supports the **Extract** mode, in which data is pulled into the Tableau data engine, which takes the data offline. No live connection is maintained with the source system (from which the querying load is offloaded). However, in Extract mode, analysis can only be performed up to the time when the extract was pulled. When real-time data needs to be analyzed, this option will not work.

In Figure 2-6, the **Extract** mode is selected.

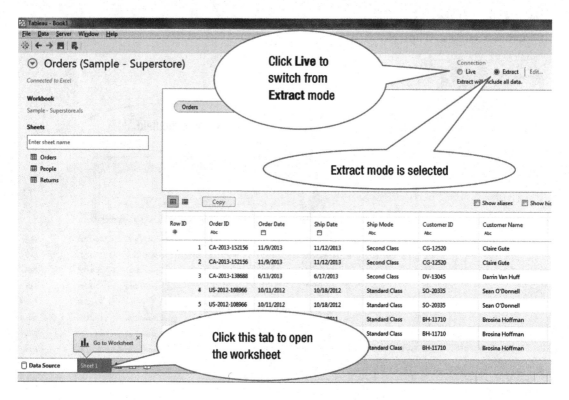

Figure 2-6. *Selecting Extract mode*

To switch to **Live** mode:

- Click the **Live** radio button, as shown in Figure 2-6

To access the worksheet:

- Click the **Worksheet** tab (Sheet 1), as shown in Figure 2-6, which leads to the worksheet displayed in Figure 2-7

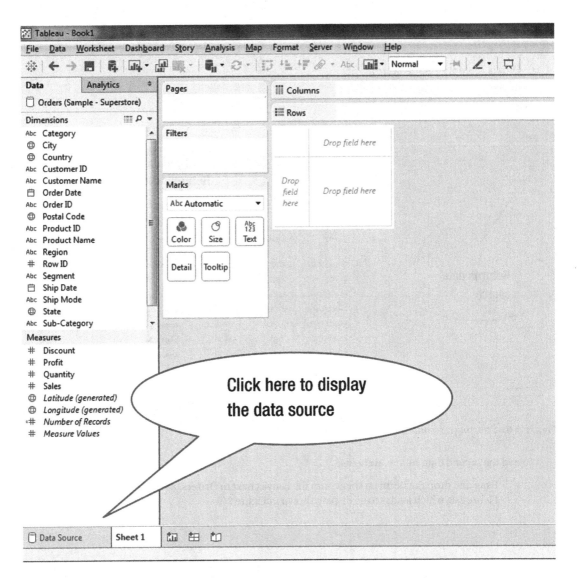

Figure 2-7. *Going back to the data source in data connection window*

If you are working with a worksheet and need to go back to the data source:

- Click the **Data Source** tab, as shown in Figure 2-7, which opens the data source window

Additional data sources can be added to an existing data source. Figure 2-8 shows three data sources: Orders, People, and Returns. **Orders** is already connected.

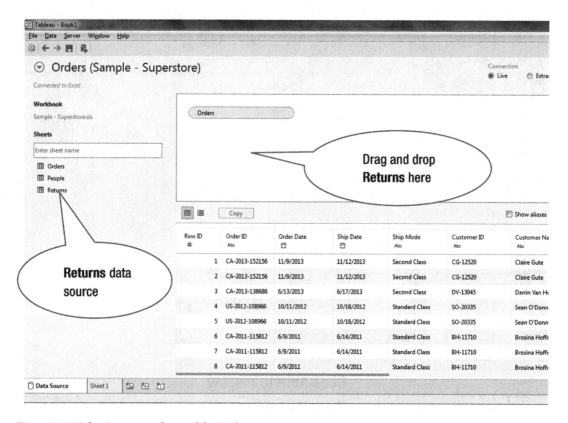

Figure 2-8. *Selecting a second spreadsheet tab*

To add the second data source, **Returns**:

- Drag and drop the **Returns** sheet onto the canvas next to **Orders**, as shown in Figure 2-8, which leads to the display shown in Figure 2-9

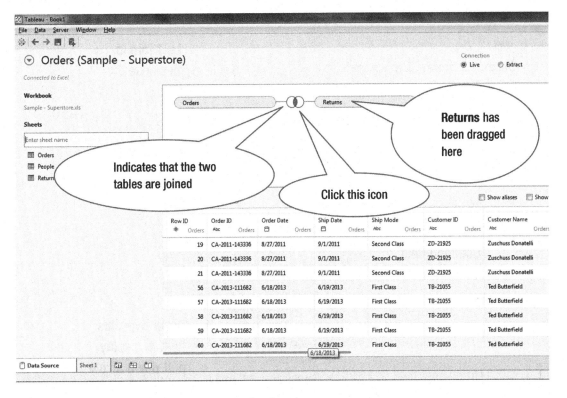

Figure 2-9. *Two selected data sources combined with a join*

Tableau automatically joined the two tables, **Orders** and **Returns**, as an inner join.

- Click the **Join** icon, as shown in Figure 2-9, which displays the join details, as shown in Figure 2-10

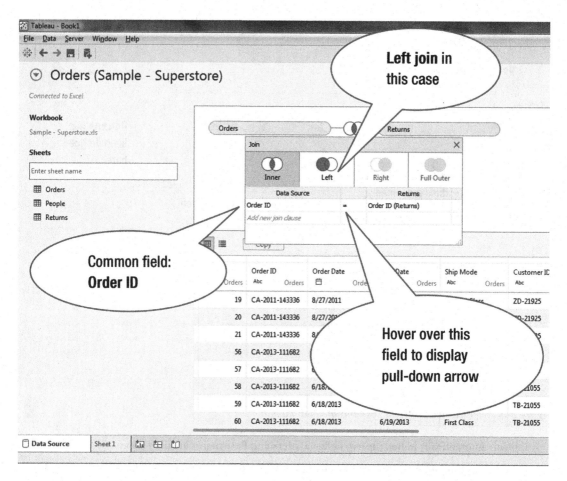

Figure 2-10. *Table joins*

Tableau automatically determined that **Order ID** is a common field in the two tables, **Orders** and **Returns**, as shown in Figure 2-10. It also provides the option to select a different field to join two tables. To use a different field for joining the two tables:

- Hover over the **Order ID** field, as shown in Figure 2-10, which displays its pull-down arrow, shown in Figure 2-11

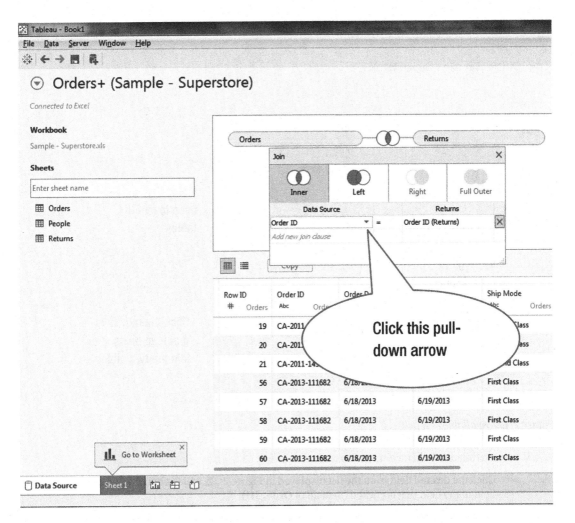

Figure 2-11. *Displaying the fields to change the join*

To use a different field for joining the two tables:

- Click the **Order ID** pull-down arrow shown in Figure 2-11, which leads to the display shown in Figure 2-12

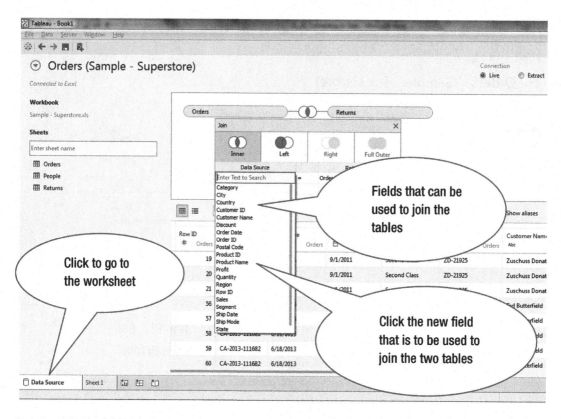

Figure 2-12. *Available join fields*

To select a different field to join the two tables:

- Click the desired field from the list displayed in Figure 2-12, which changes the join field to the field that is clicked (instead of **Order ID**)

This step was performed in the **Data Source** tab. To see how the worksheet was impacted due to the addition of the second data source:

- Click the **Sheet 1** tab, as shown in Figure 2-12, which leads to the display shown in Figure 2-13

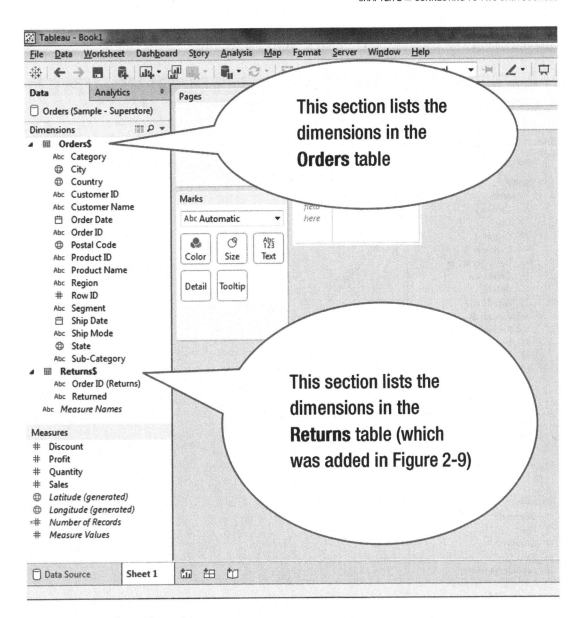

Figure 2-13. Display with two data sources

You can search for a field, which is a useful feature when a table has many dimensions or measures. Figure 2-14 shows a worksheet that has two sources: **Orders** and **Returns**.

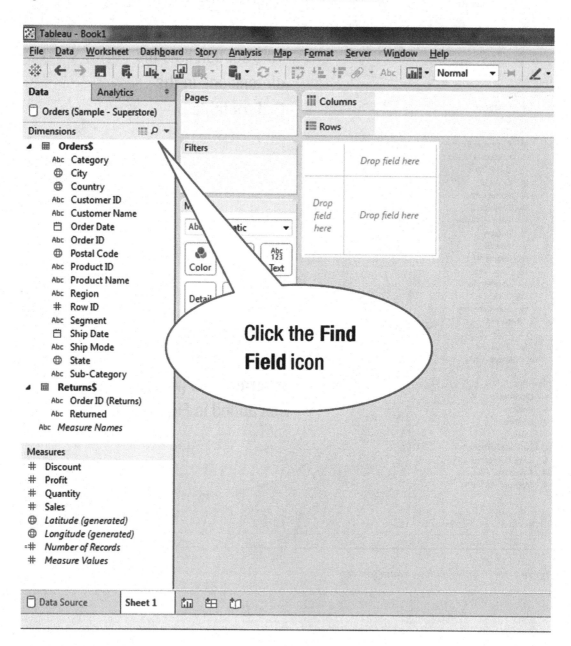

Figure 2-14. *Searching for a field*

To search for a dimension:

- Click the **Find Field** icon shown in Figure 2-14, which leads to Figure 2-15, where the search box is displayed (with the prompt **Enter Search Text**)

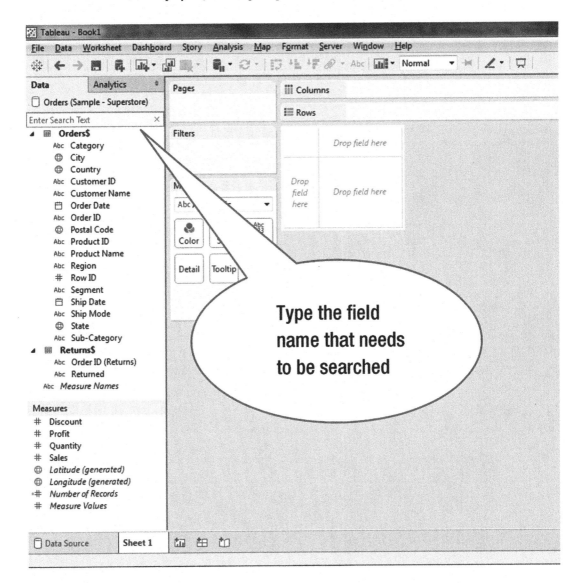

Figure 2-15. *Search box*

- Type the field name in the search box, which is highlighted in Figure 2-15
- Hit **Enter**, which highlights the field(s) matching the search criteria

CHAPTER 3

■ ■ ■

Exploring the Tableau Interface

Objective: This exercise provides an overview of the Tableau interface

After connecting to a data source, you see a blank sheet, as displayed in Figure 3-1, where data visualizations can be developed. Through the Tableau interface shown in Figure 3-1, many powerful and useful features can be accessed.

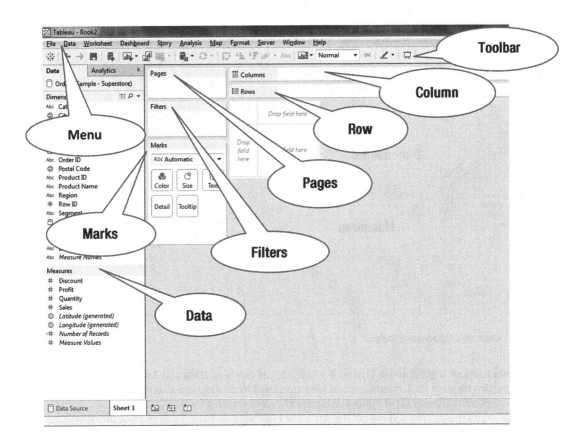

Figure 3-1. *Tableau interface*

© Arshad Khan 2016

A. Khan, *Jumpstart Tableau*, DOI 10.1007/978-1-4842-1934-8_3

The **menu bar** at the top of the window provides access to many powerful features. Below it is the **toolbar**, which contains many buttons, such as **Save**, **Undo**, **Redo**, **Add New Data Source**, and **Duplicate Sheet**. These buttons are contextual, therefore, only the relevant ones are highlighted—based on the current state of the worksheet.

The **Marks** card contains additional shelves on which fields can be placed directly (through drag and drop). **Shelves** include **Color**, **Size**, **Text**, **Detail**, and **Tooltip**. Clicking these shelves activate pop-up windows that enable their characteristics, such as labels to be edited. The default **Marks** type is **Automatic**, as shown in Figure 3-2. However, many Mark types can be used instead of the default (Automatic).

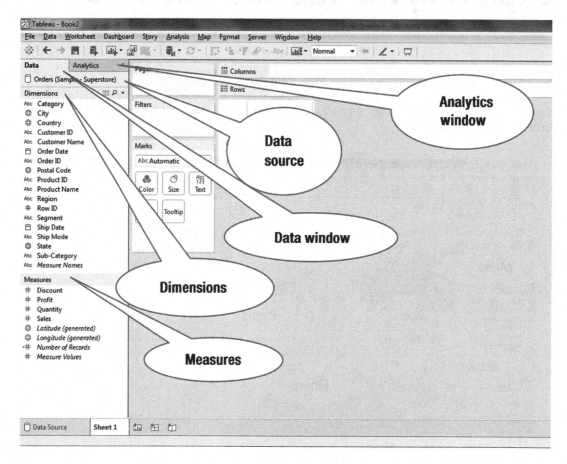

Figure 3-2. *Data and Analytics windows*

The **Data** window, highlighted in Figures 3-1 and 3-2, has two tabs: **Data** and **Analytics**. The default tab is **Data**, which displays the Dimensions and Measures used to develop visualizations. The **Analytics** tab displays a completely different set of options, which are focused on analysis.

The open data connection is shown at the top of the Data window pane. In Figure 3-2, the data connection displayed is **Orders (Sample – Superstore)**.

Views are built by dragging and dropping fields from the **Data** window onto the canvas or directly onto the shelves. The shelves, which are also sometimes referred to as *cards*, are as follows:

- Columns shelf
- Rows shelf
- Filter shelf
- Pages shelf
- Marks card

The layout that is displayed when a **Dashboard tab** is selected is somewhat different compared to the **Worksheet tab** layout. When a Dashboard window is active...

- The Data window (used in Worksheets) is replaced by the Dashboard Window
- It lists all the sheets available (in the left-hand window)
- It lists the Dashboard objects
- It displays the controls for the objects
- It displays the sizing options

Figure 3-3 displays the menu tree when the **File** option is selected on the menu bar when the Worksheet tab is active.

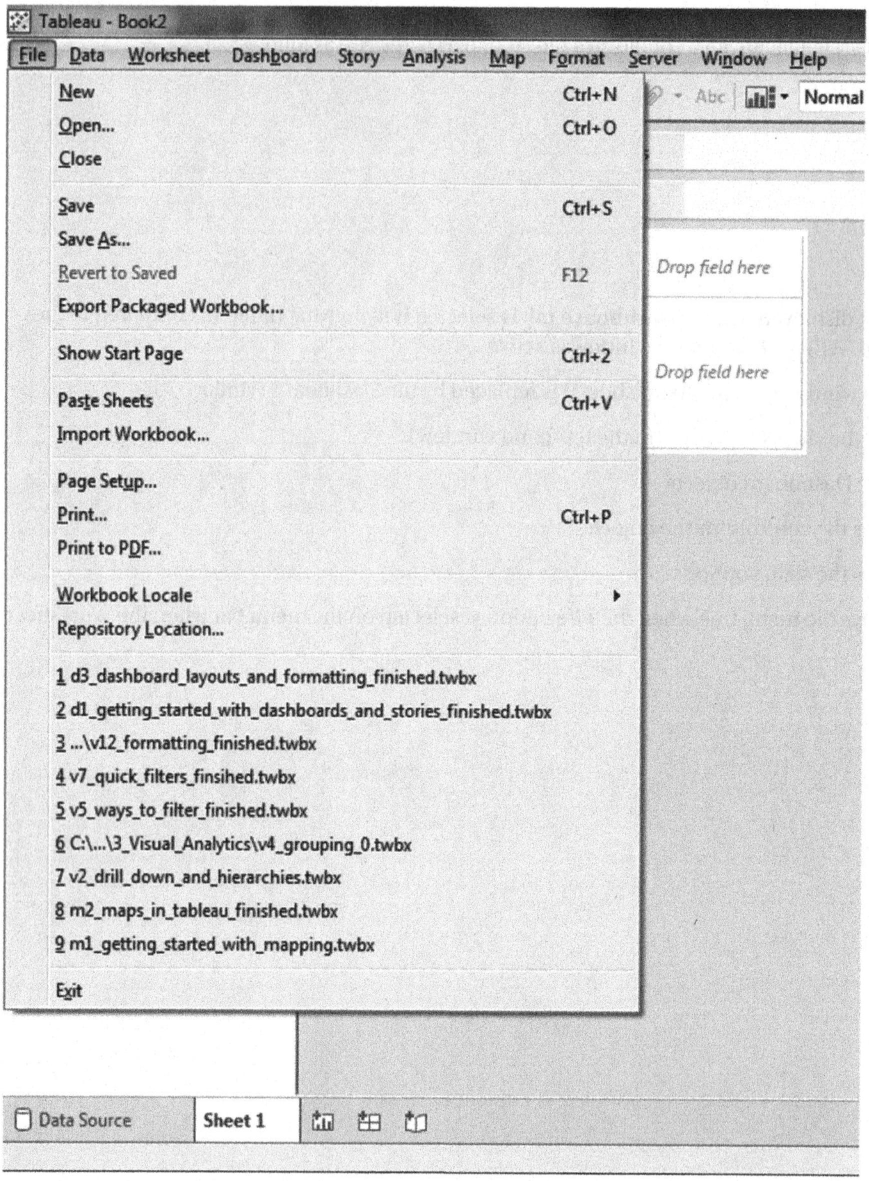

Figure 3-3. *File menu tree*

Figure 3-4 displays the menu tree when the **Data** option is selected on the menu bar.

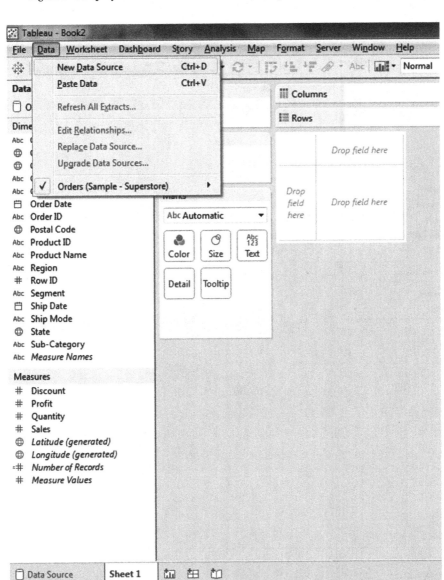

Figure 3-4. *Data menu tree*

Figure 3-5 displays the menu tree when the **Worksheet** option is selected on the menu bar.

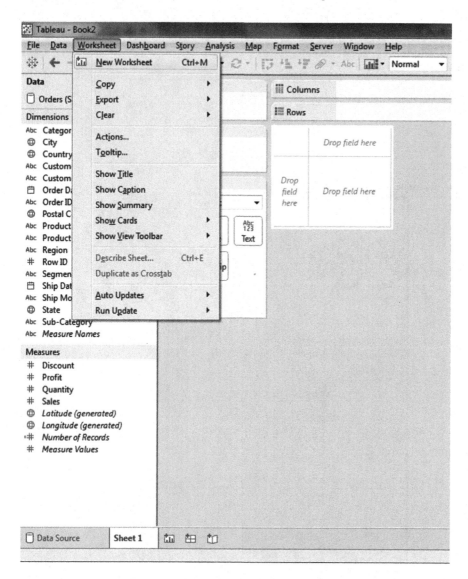

Figure 3-5. *Worksheet menu tree*

Figure 3-6 displays the menu tree when the **Dashboard** option is selected on the menu bar.

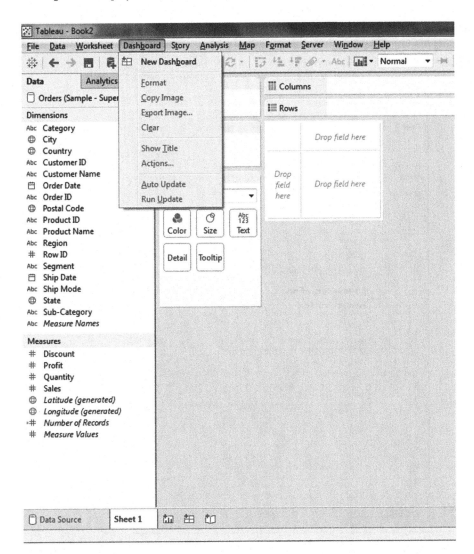

Figure 3-6. *Dashboard menu tree*

Figure 3-7 displays the menu tree when the **Analysis** option is selected on the menu bar.

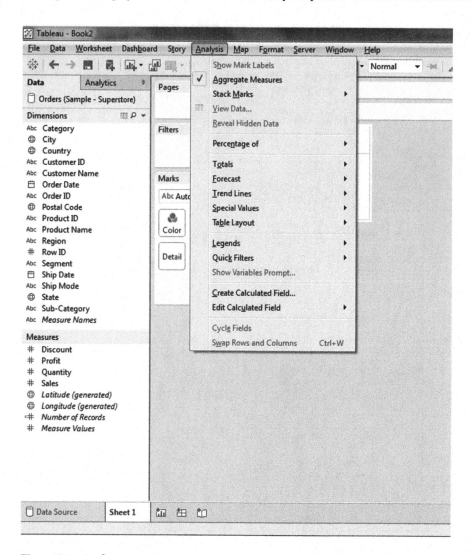

Figure 3-7. *Analysis menu tree*

Figure 3-8 displays the menu tree when the **Format** option is selected on the menu bar.

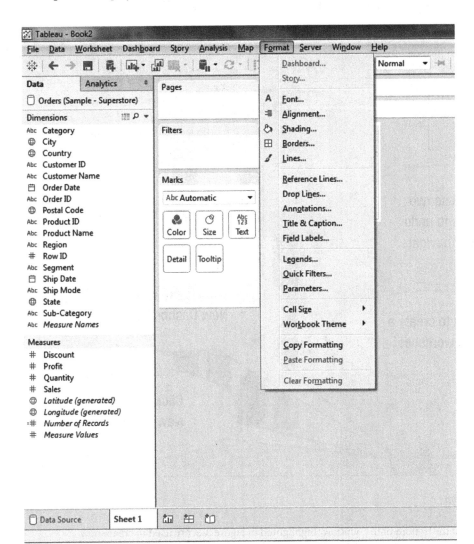

Figure 3-8. *Format menu tree*

The following should be noted:

- Tableau does not save a worksheet automatically; hence, you must save your work before exiting

- Buttons are contextual; hence, the functions available depend on what is going on in the sheet

To undo or reverse an action, use the **Back** arrow. The **Back** and **Forward** arrows, highlighted in Figure 3-9, can be used to navigate and go back/forward as visualizations are developed and/or modified.

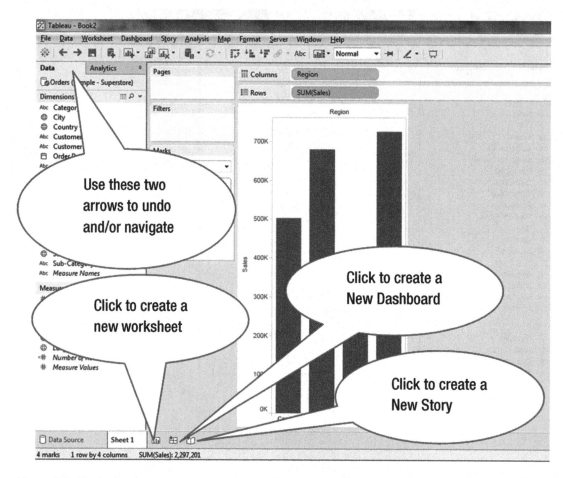

Figure 3-9. *Navigation*

The **Sheet** tabs at the bottom of the window, highlighted in Figure 3-9, are used to create new worksheets, dashboards, and stories. Sheets can be moved around (by dragging), renamed, and duplicated. By right-clicking the appropriate sheet, a menu tree pops up, which enables the following:

- Copying a sheet
- Renaming a sheet
- Deleting a sheet
- Exporting a sheet
- Creating a new worksheet, dashboard, or story

To create a new sheet, dashboard, or story:

- Click the **New Worksheet** icon, as shown in Figure 3-9

- Click the **New Dashboard** icon, as shown in Figure 3-9

- Click the **New Story** icon, as shown in Figure 3-9

If two data sources are used in a sheet, they are displayed in the **Data** window, as shown in Figure 3-10. The data sources are as follows:

- Country Codes

- Global Superstore

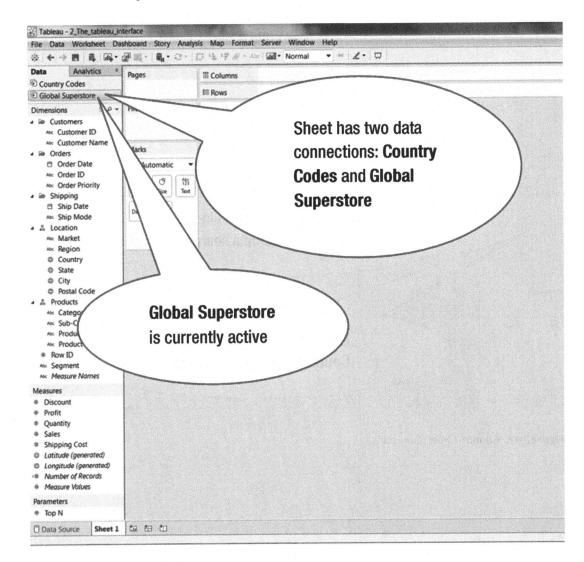

Figure 3-10. *Data connections*

The view that is displayed in the **Data** window—the list of dimensions and measures—depends on the data source that is selected. For example, if the **Global Superstore** is selected, then its dimensions and measures are displayed in the Data window. In Figure 3-10, the dimensions and measures displayed belong to the **Global Superstore** data source.

If **Country Codes** is clicked, it changes the view, as shown in Figure 3-11, where the list of dimensions and measures reflects the data contained in the **Country Codes** data source.

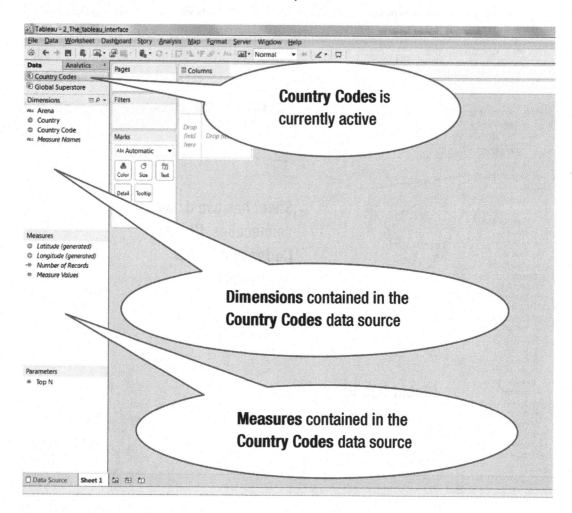

Figure 3-11. *Country Codes data source*

CHAPTER 4

Developing a Simple Visualization

Objective: This exercise demonstrates how a simple visualization can be developed

- Launch Tableau
- Connect to the **Sample - Superstore** Excel file using the procedure demonstrated in Chapter 1, which leads to the display shown in Figure 4-1

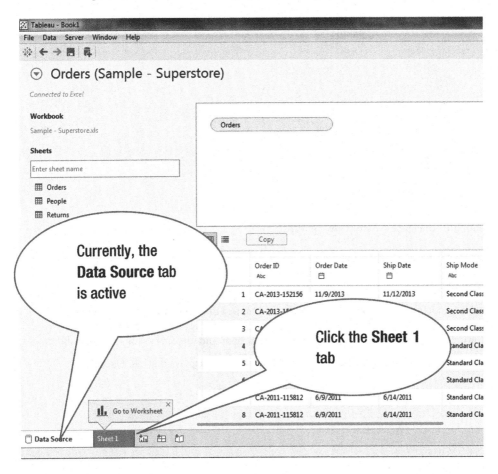

Figure 4-1. *Sample Superstore*

© Arshad Khan 2016
A. Khan, *Jumpstart Tableau*, DOI 10.1007/978-1-4842-1934-8_4

- Click the **Sheet 1** tab, as shown in Figure 4-1, which leads to Figure 4-2, where reports and visualizations can be developed

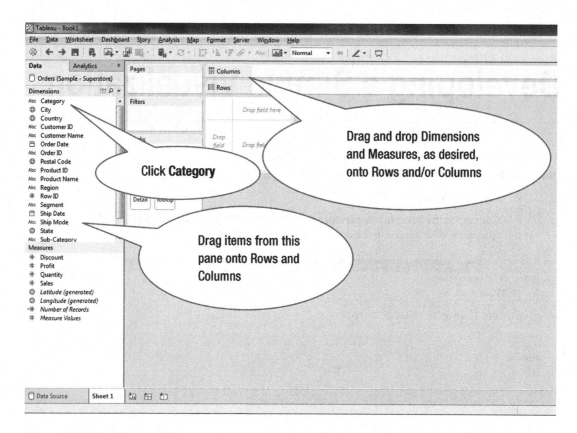

Figure 4-2. *Dimensions and Measures*

The left-hand side of Figure 4-2 shows two groups:

- Dimensions
- Measures

Dimensions are fields, such as product, region, and customer. They are used to slice and dice the data to provide different perspectives. Dimensions are color-coded blue in the data pane and in the view.

Measures are metrics—that is, the numbers—used for analysis. They are color-coded green.

In the following steps, we drag and drop the desired dimensions and measures onto Columns and Rows.

- Click **Category**, as shown in Figure 4-2, which leads to the display shown in Figure 4-3

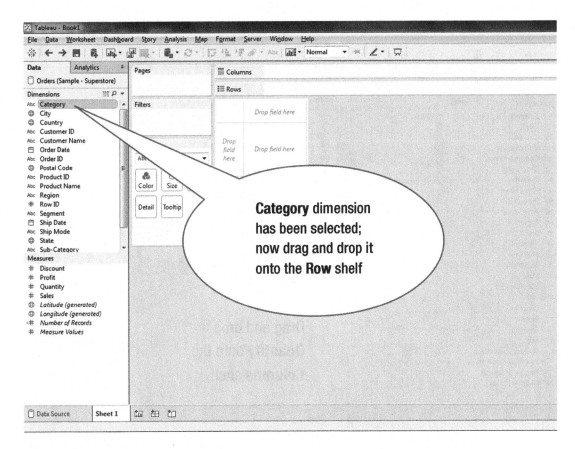

Figure 4-3. *Selecting a dimension*

- Drag and drop **Category** onto the **Rows** shelf, as shown in Figure 4-3, which leads to the display shown in Figure 4-4

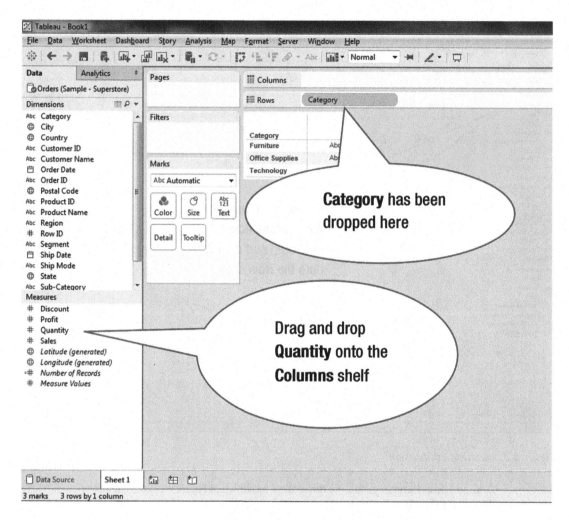

Figure 4-4. *Dropping a dimension onto the Rows shelf*

- Drag and drop **Quantity** onto the **Columns** shelf, as shown in Figure 4-4, which leads to the display shown in Figure 4-5

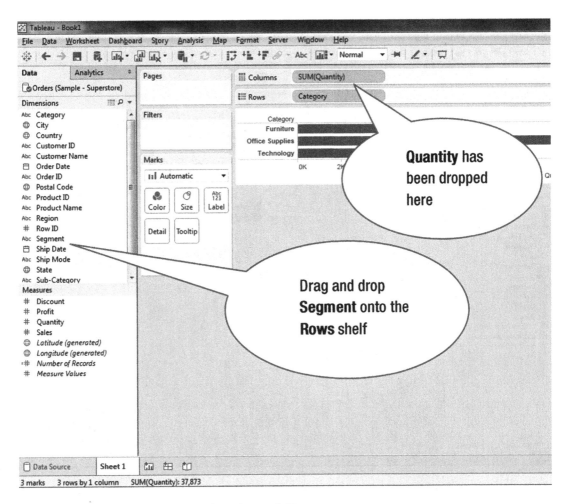

Figure 4-5. Dropping a measure onto the Columns shelf

- Drag and drop **Segment** onto the **Rows** shelf, as shown in Figure 4-5, which leads to the display shown in Figure 4-6

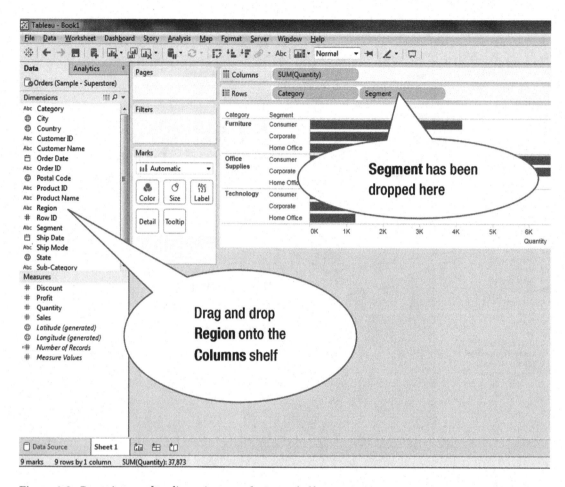

Figure 4-6. *Dropping another dimension onto the Rows shelf*

- Drag and drop **Region** onto the **Columns** shelf, as shown in Figure 4-6, which leads to the display shown in Figure 4-7

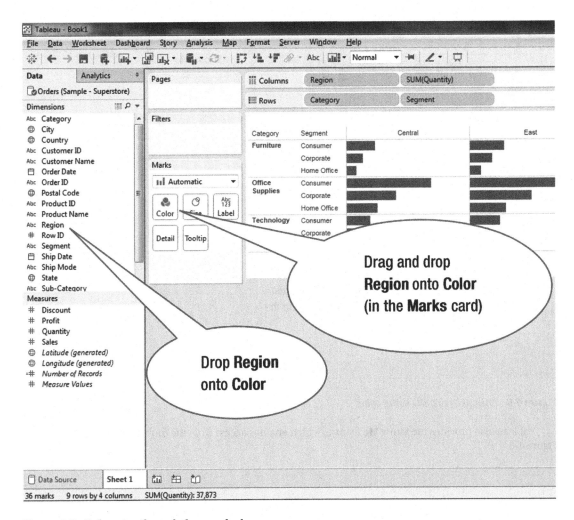

Figure 4-7. *Enhancing through the use of color*

To enhance the display by providing color:

- Drag and drop **Region** from the Dimensions pane onto the **Color** shelf (on the **Marks** card), as shown in Figure 4-7, which leads to the display shown in Figure 4-8

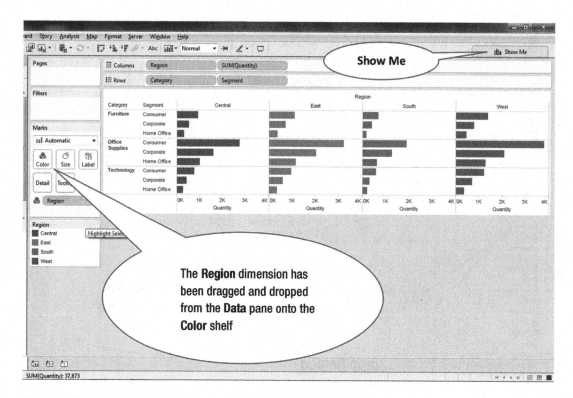

Figure 4-8. *Enhanced display using color*

Tableau also provides the **Show Me** feature, which enables access from the toolbar, as shown in Figure 4-8.

CHAPTER 5

Saving Tableau Workbook and Tableau Packaged Workbook

Objective: This exercise demonstrates how to save a Tableau Workbook (.twb) and a Tableau Packaged Workbook (.twbx)

Tableau provides two options to save a workbook. In the first option, only the workbook can be saved (as a .twb file). In the second option, the data associated with the workbook is packaged and saved (as a .twbx file).

Figure 5-1 displays a view based on category, region, and sales.

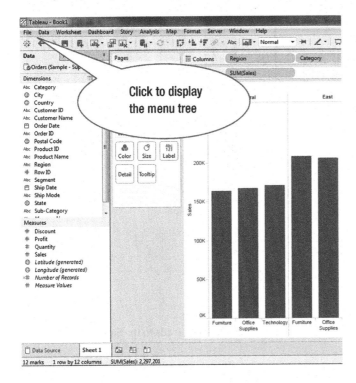

Figure 5-1. View based on two dimensions and one measure

- Click **File** on the menu bar, as shown in Figure 5-1, which pops up the menu tree displayed in Figure 5-2

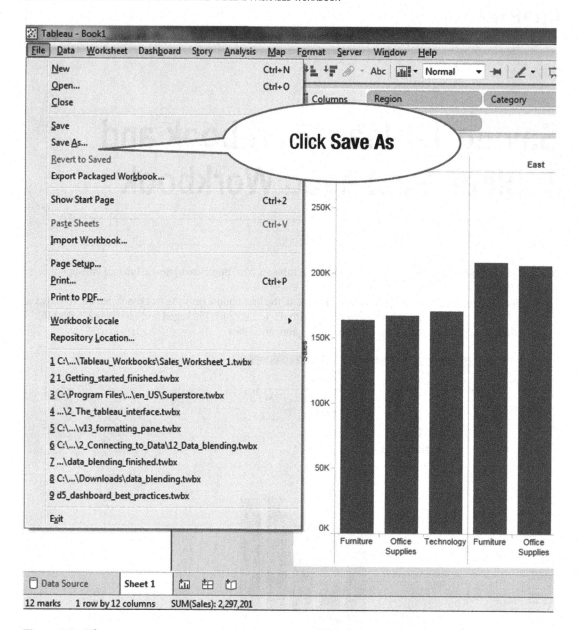

Figure 5-2. File menu tree

- Click the **Save As** menu tree item, as shown in Figure 5-2, which leads to the Save As window displayed in Figure 5-3

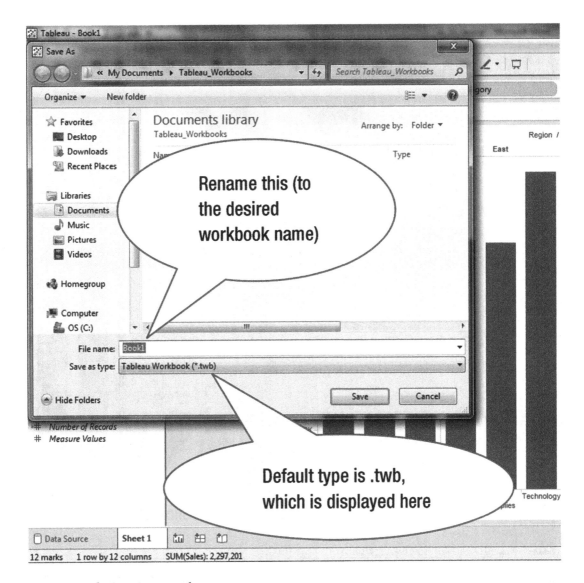

Figure 5-3. *The Save As pop-up box*

Selecting the **Save as** option enables you to rename the default file name, which is provided by the system. It also provides the option to select the file type.

- Rename the default File name (Book1), displayed in Figure 5-3, to **Sales_Analysis**, as shown in Figure 5-4

Figure 5-4. *Renaming the file*

- Click **Save**, as shown in Figure 5-4, which saves the workbook as **Sales_Analysis.twb**

The following procedure demonstrates how a workbook can be saved with its associated data as a .twbx file.

- Develop a worksheet with the following selections (which are shown in Figure 5-1):
  - Rows: Sales
  - Columns: Region and Category
- Click **File** on the menu bar, which leads to the menu tree displayed in Figure 5-5

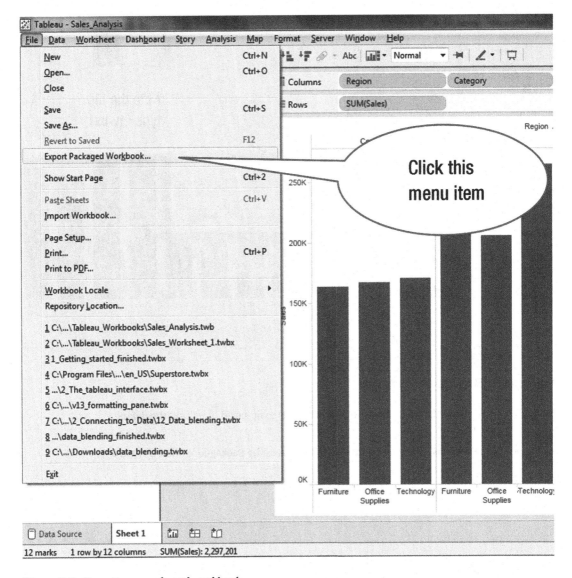

Figure 5-5. *Exporting a packaged workbook*

- Click the **Export Packaged Workbook** menu tree item, as shown in Figure 5-5, which pops up the Export Packaged Workbook window displayed in Figure 5-6

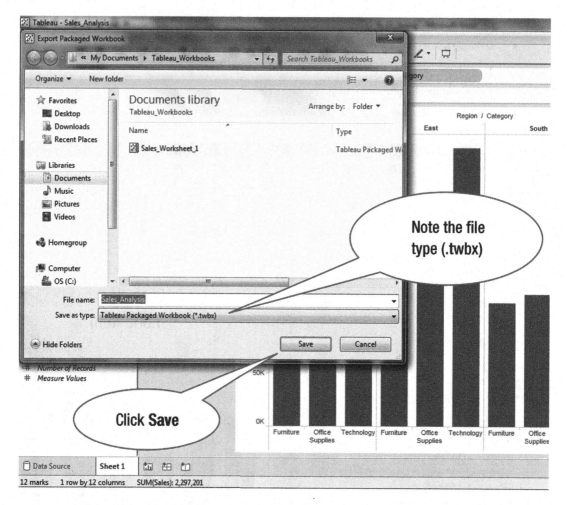

Figure 5-6. Packaged Workbook file type

- Navigate to the folder where the workbook is to be saved (or accept the default location)

- Click **Save as**, shown in Figure 5-6, which saves the Packaged Workbook (.twbx)

To display the saved files, navigate to the **Tableau_Workbooks** folder (where the two workbook files were saved in the previous two exercises). Figure 5-7 displays the folder that contains the two saved workbooks:

- Tableau Workbook (without the data)
- Tableau Packaged Workbook (with embedded data)

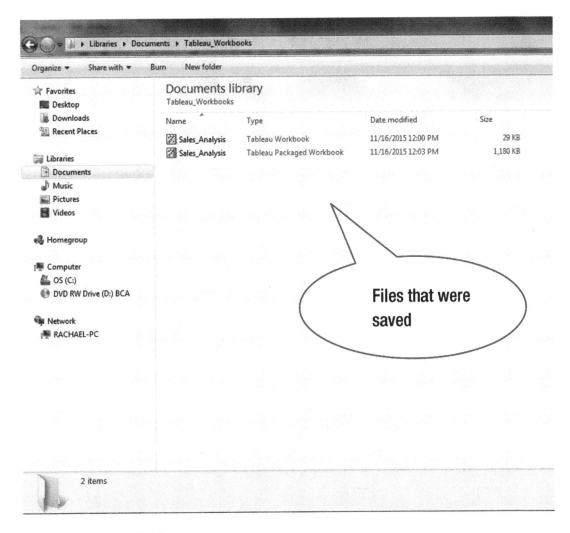

Figure 5-7. *Saved workbooks*

To open a workbook:

- Click **File** on the menu bar, which displays the menu tree shown in Figure 5-8

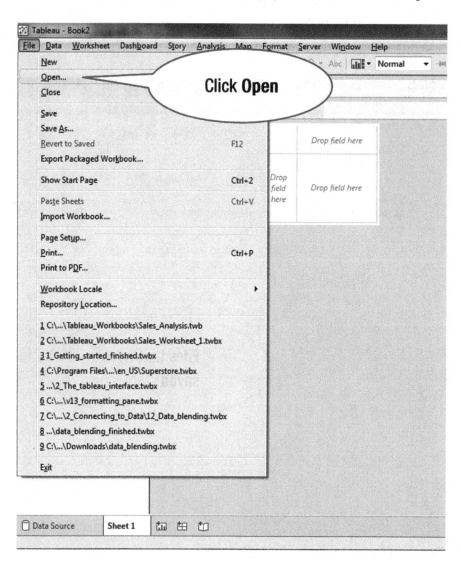

Figure 5-8. *File menu tree*

- Click **Open**, as shown in Figure 5-8, which pops up the **Open** window displayed in Figure 5-9

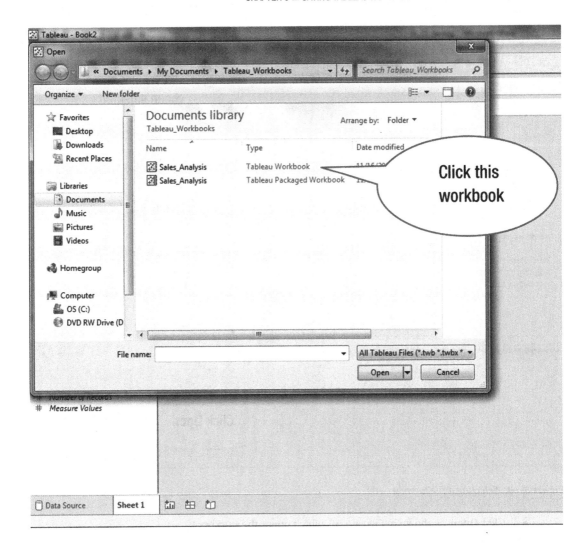

Figure 5-9. *Saved files that can be opened*

- Click the workbook to be opened, **Tableau Workbook** in this case, which highlights it, as shown in Figure 5-10

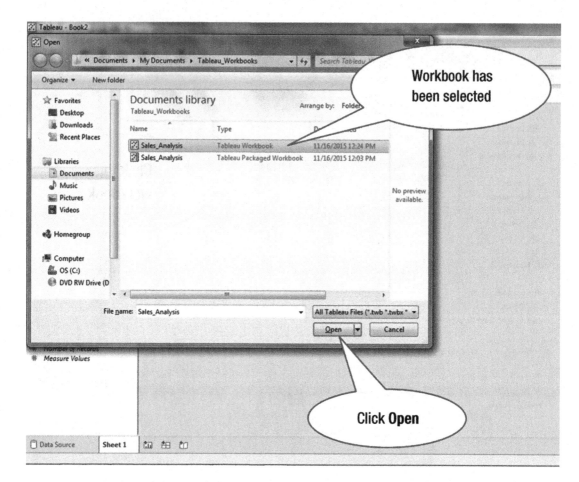

Figure 5-10. *Selecting a file to open*

- Click **Open**, as shown in Figure 5-10, which opens the workbook

CHAPTER 6

▪ ▪ ▪

Using Basic Analysis Functions

Objective: This exercise demonstrates some basic analysis functions in Tableau

- Launch Tableau
- Open a new worksheet and connect to the **Orders** sheet in the **Sample – Superstore** Excel file, as shown in Figure 6-1

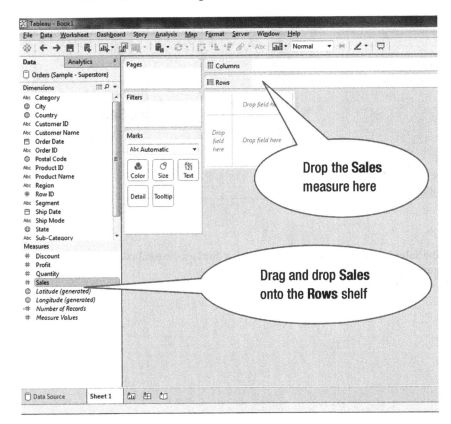

Figure 6-1. *Start analyzing data*

- Drag and drop the **Sales** measure onto the **Rows** shelf, as shown in Figure 6-1, which leads to the display shown in Figure 6-2

© Arshad Khan 2016
A. Khan, *Jumpstart Tableau*, DOI 10.1007/978-1-4842-1934-8_6

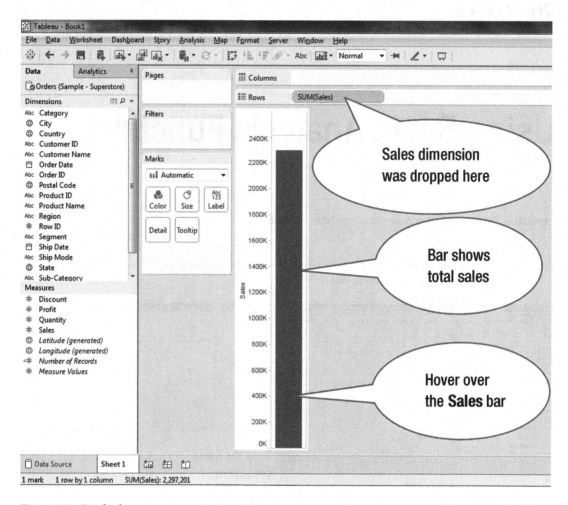

Figure 6-2. *Total sales*

- Hover over the **Sales** bar, as shown in Figure 6-2, which displays the total sales shown in Figure 6-3 ($2,297,201)

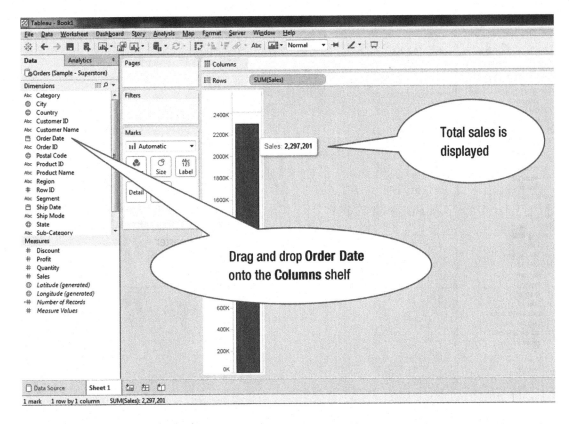

Figure 6-3. *Displaying total sales figure*

The Tooltip in the Marks card, which can be seen in Figure 6-2, allows you to customize the information displayed when you hover over the visualization.

To view results over time:

- Drag and drop **Order Date** onto the **Columns** shelf, as shown in Figure 6-3, which leads to the display shown in Figure 6-4

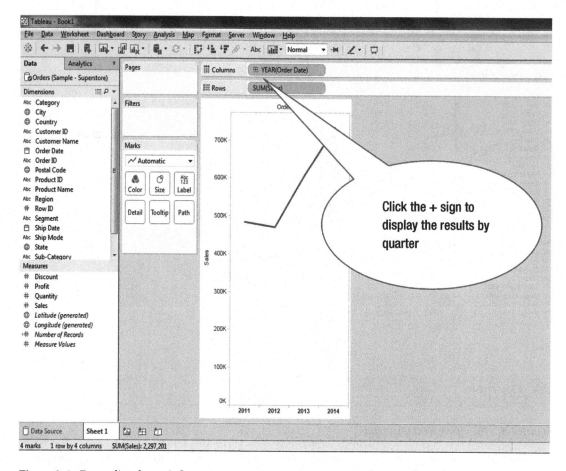

Figure 6-4. *Expanding the period*

Date fields in Tableau, depending on their level of granularity, are automatically brought into the view as hierarchies. For example, when you drag Order Date to the Column shelf, Tableau plots the data by Year and shows a + symbol next to it, which indicates that you can drill down.

- Expand the + sign, located just before the **Year (Order Date)** in the **Columns** shelf, as shown in Figure 6-4, which leads to the display shown in Figure 6-5

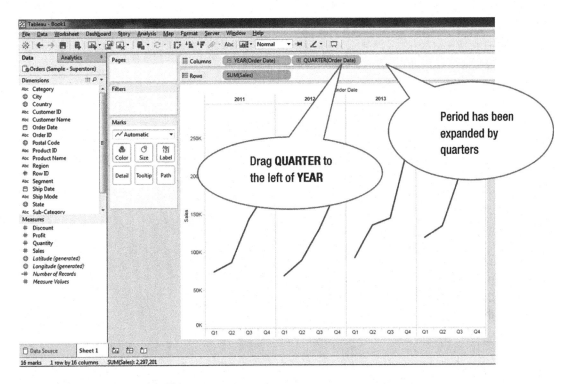

Figure 6-5. *Display expanded by quarter*

In Figure 6-5, both quarters and years are in the displayed view. To analyze the performance over various quarters, swap **Quarter** with **Year** by:

- Dragging and dropping **QUARTER** to the left of **YEAR** on the **Columns** shelf, as shown in Figure 6-5, which leads to the display shown in Figure 6-6

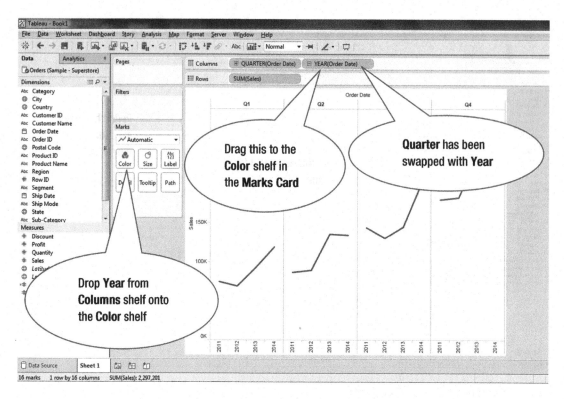

Figure 6-6. *Swapping position of items on the Columns shelf*

- Drag and drop **Year** from the **Columns** shelf onto the **Color** shelf in the **Marks** card, as shown in Figure 6-6, which leads to the display shown in Figure 6-7

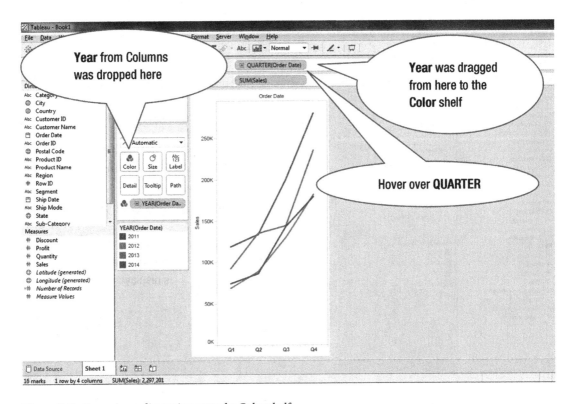

Figure 6-7. *Dropping a dimension onto the Color shelf*

To change the display from **Quarters** to **Months**:

- Hover over **Quarter** in the **Columns** shelf, as shown in Figure 6-7, which displays the pull-down arrow shown in Figure 6-8

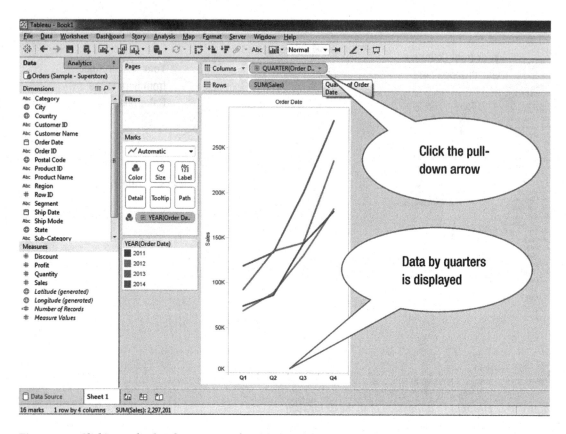

Figure 6-8. *Clicking to display the menu tree for a dimension*

- Click the pull-down arrow displayed in Figure 6-8, which leads to the menu tree displayed in Figure 6-9

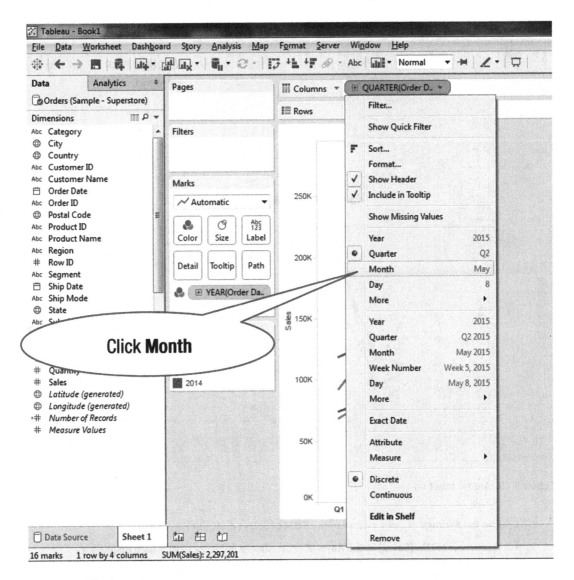

Figure 6-9. *Menu tree for selected dimension*

- Click the **Month** menu tree item, as shown in Figure 6-9, which leads to the display shown in Figure 6-10

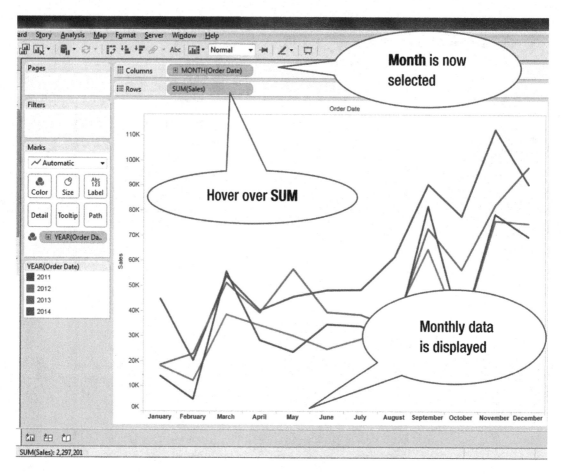

Figure 6-10. *Month selection*

To analyze the **Average** of Sales instead of the **SUM** of Sales (shown in Figure 6-10):

- Hover over **SUM (Sales)** in the **Rows** shelf, as shown in Figure 6-10, which displays a pull-down arrow

- Click the pull-down arrow when it is displayed, which leads to the menu tree displayed in Figure 6-11

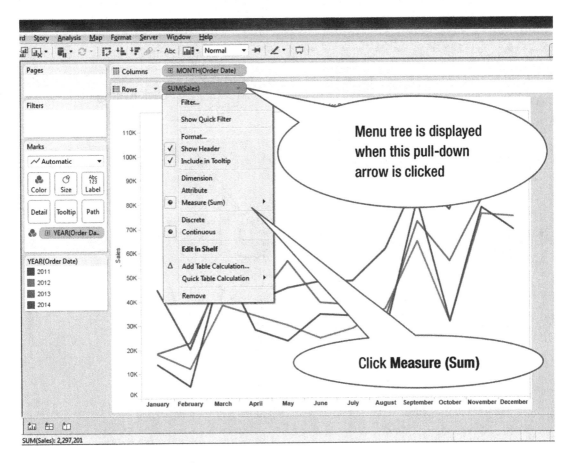

Figure 6-11. *Menu tree for selected measure*

- Click the menu tree item **Measure (Sum)**, as shown in Figure 6-11, which leads to the secondary menu tree displayed in Figure 6-12

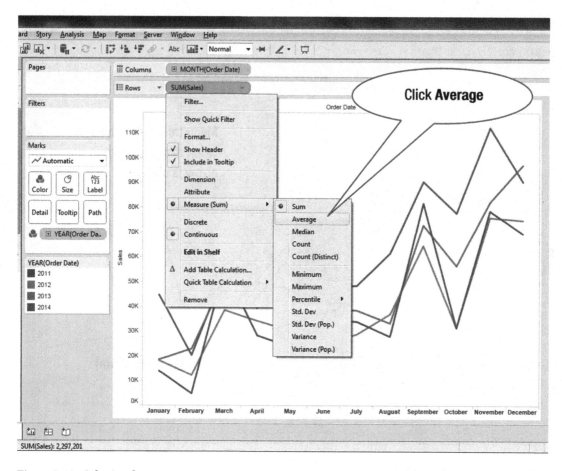

Figure 6-12. *Selecting the average*

- Click the menu tree item **Average**, as shown in Figure 6-12, which leads to the display shown in Figure 6-13

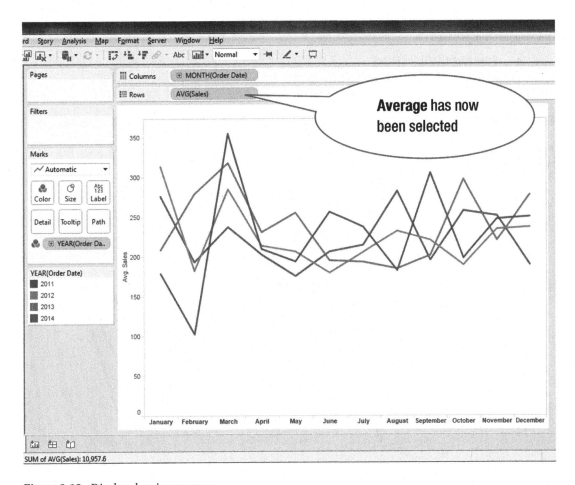

Figure 6-13. *Display showing average*

To analyze year-over-year growth, we start with Figure 6-14 (which is the same as Figure 6-10). This visualization is based on

- Row: Month (Order Date)
- Column: SUM(Sales)

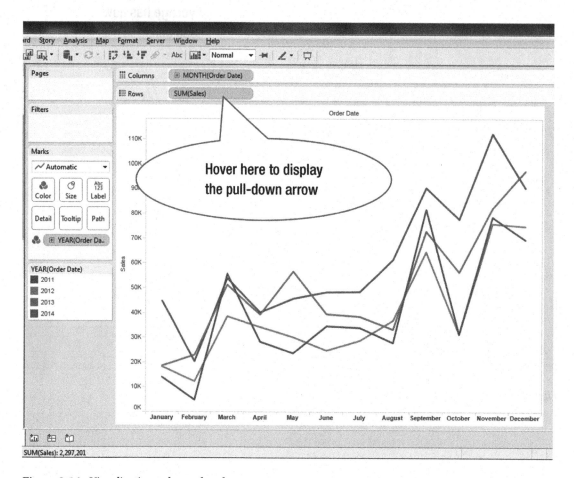

Figure 6-14. *Visualization to be analyzed*

- Hover over **SUM (Sales)** in the **Rows** shelf, as shown in Figure 6-14, which displays a pull-down arrow (shown in Figure 6-15)
- Click the pull-down arrow when it is displayed, which leads to the menu tree displayed in Figure 6-15

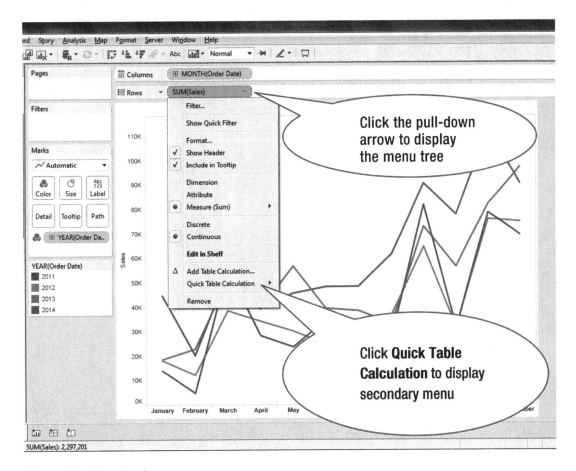

Figure 6-15. *Menu tree for measure*

- Click the menu tree item **Quick Table Calculation** as shown in Figure 6-15, which leads to the secondary menu tree displayed in Figure 6-16

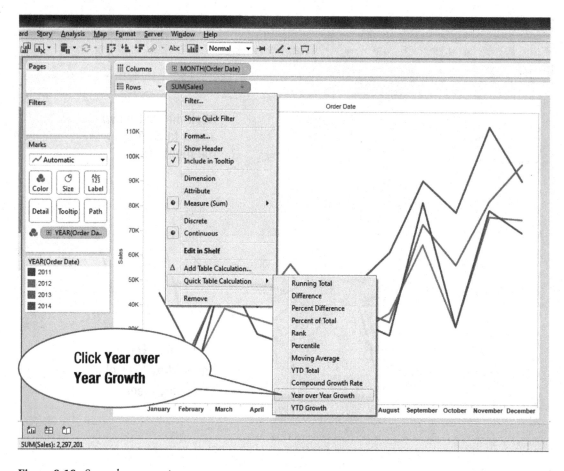

Figure 6-16. *Secondary menu tree*

- Click the menu tree item **Year over Year Growth**, as shown in Figure 6-16, which leads to the display shown in Figure 6-17

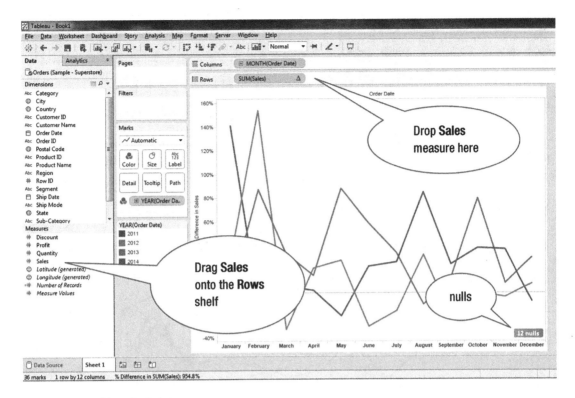

Figure 6-17. *Adding the Sales measure*

To display the original sales figures in the same chart:

- Drag and drop the **Sales** measure onto the **Rows** shelf, as shown in Figure 6-17, which leads to the display shown in Figure 6-18

When calculating comparisons such as year-over-year growth, the first year in the data table is empty. This causes it to show as null, because there is no existing data from the previous year that it can be compared to.

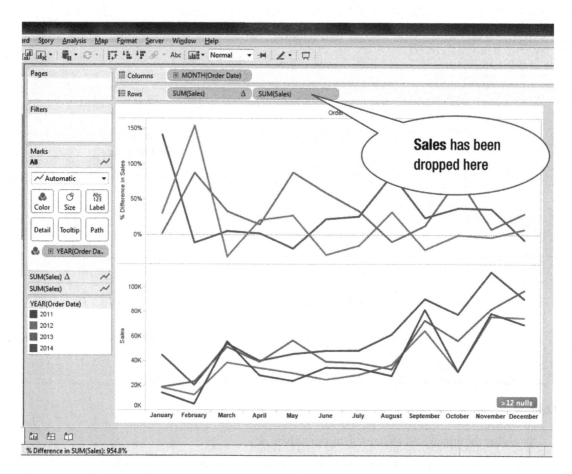

Figure 6-18. *Two charts displayed simultaneously*

This figure now enables analysis to be made from two different perspectives (Sales and % Difference in Sales).

To enable values to be displayed when the cursor is placed over an item, i.e., enable hovering:

- Drag **SUM (Sales)** from the **Rows** shelf onto the **Tooltip** shelf (in the **Marks** card area), as shown in Figure 6-19

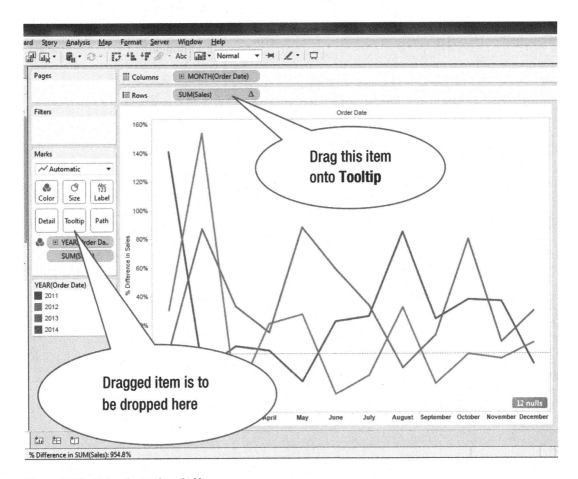

Figure 6-19. *Using the Tooltip shelf*

- Hover over a line in the chart, which causes its associated data to be displayed, as shown in Figure 6-20

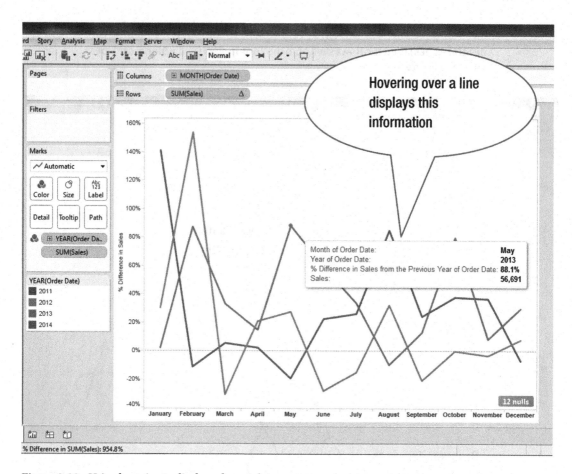

Figure 6-20. *Using hovering to display relevant date*

CHAPTER 7

■ ■ ■

Adding, Removing, and Renaming a Dimension

Objective: This exercise demonstrates how a dimension or measure is added or deleted from a visualization, and explains how to rename a dimension

We start with the visualization shown in Figure 7-1, which includes one dimension (**Region**) and one measure (**Sales**).

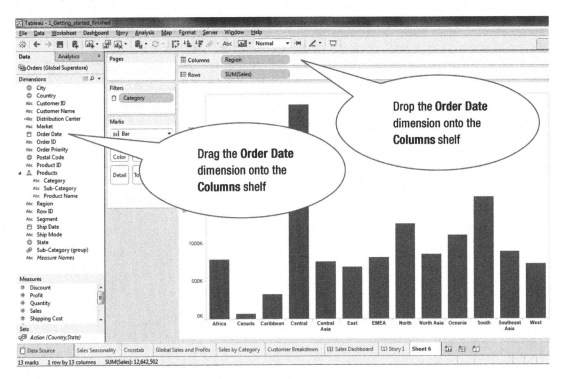

Figure 7-1. *Visualization to be modified*

To add the **Order Date** dimension:

- Drag and drop **Order Date** from the **Data** window onto the **Columns** shelf, as shown in Figure 7-1, which leads to the display shown in Figure 7-2

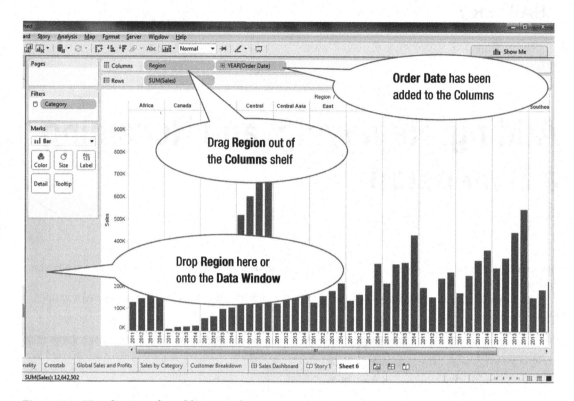

Figure 7-2. *Visualization after adding period*

To remove the **Region** dimension:

- Drag and drop **Region** from the **Columns** shelf onto the **Data** window or below the **Marks** card, as shown in Figure 7-2, which leads to the visualization displayed in Figure 7-3

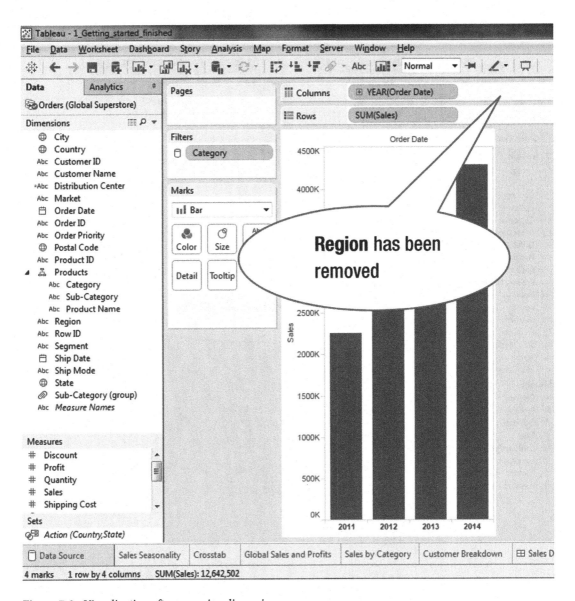

Figure 7-3. Visualization after removing dimension

The procedure to add and/or delete a measure is similar to the one used to add/delete a dimension, which was demonstrated earlier in this exercise.

Renaming is another useful feature. Sometimes, the dimensions and measures in the source files have names that are not clear to end users. Therefore, renaming them can make the system less confusing and more user-friendly. Tableau provides the ability to rename dimensions and measures in the Data window, where they are displayed.

We now rename the **Region** dimension, as shown in Figure 7-4.

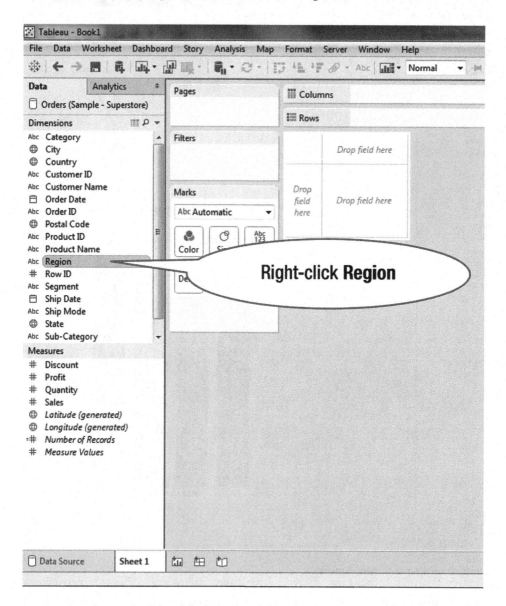

Figure 7-4. *Selecting the dimension to be renamed*

To rename the **Region** dimension:

- Right-click **Region**, as shown in Figure 7-4, which pops up the menu tree displayed in Figure 7-5

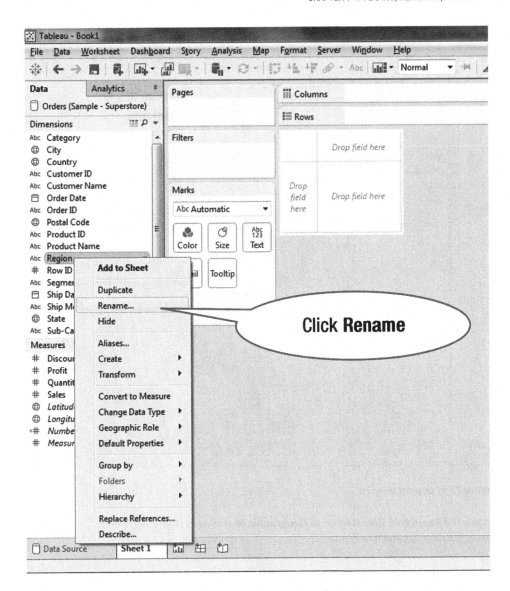

Figure 7-5. *Menu tree displaying the rename option*

- Click **Rename**, as shown in Figure 7-5, which pops up the **Rename Field** window shown in Figure 7-6

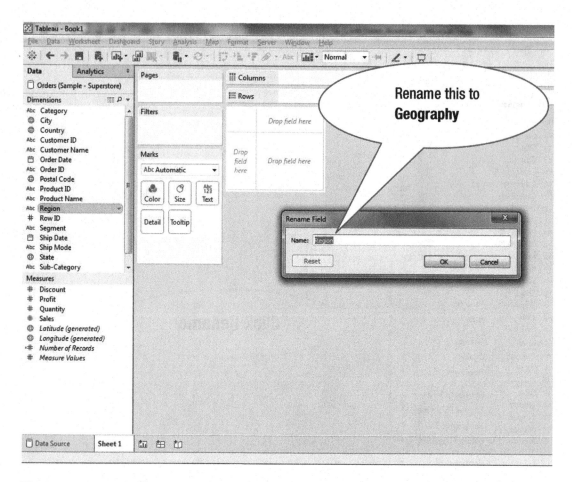

Figure 7-6. *Rename Field pop-up window*

- Rename the **Name** field from **Region** to **Geography**, as shown in Figure 7-6, which leads to the display shown in Figure 7-7

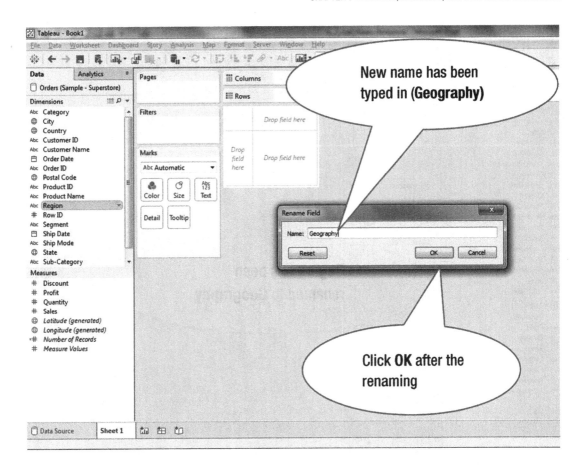

Figure 7-7. *Renamed dimension*

- Click **OK**, as shown in Figure 7-7, which leads to the display shown in Figure 7-8 where the dimension is displayed with the new name (**Geography**)

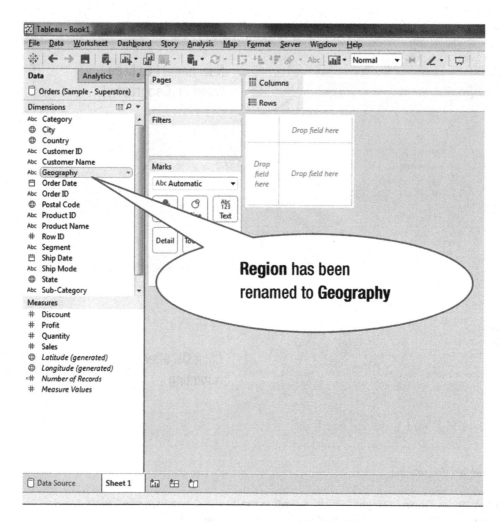

Figure 7-8. Renamed dimension displayed in Data window

CHAPTER 8

■ ■ ■

Copying or Deleting a Worksheet

Objective: This exercise demonstrates how to copy or delete a worksheet
We start with the **Sales by Region** worksheet displayed in Figure 8-1.

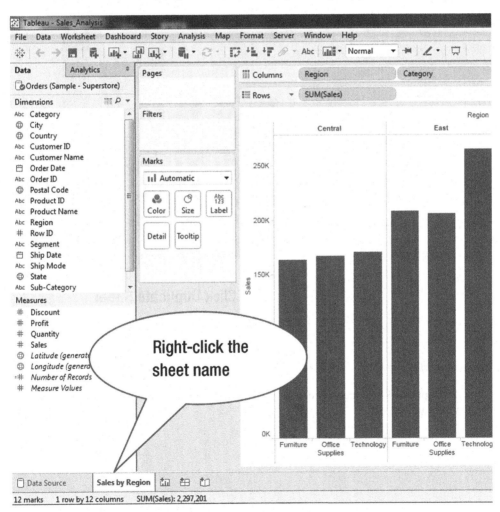

Figure 8-1. *Visualization to be duplicated*

© Arshad Khan 2016
A. Khan, *Jumpstart Tableau*, DOI 10.1007/978-1-4842-1934-8_8

To make a duplicate copy of the worksheet:

- Right-click the **Sales by Region** sheet, as shown in Figure 8-1, which pops up the menu tree displayed in Figure 8-2

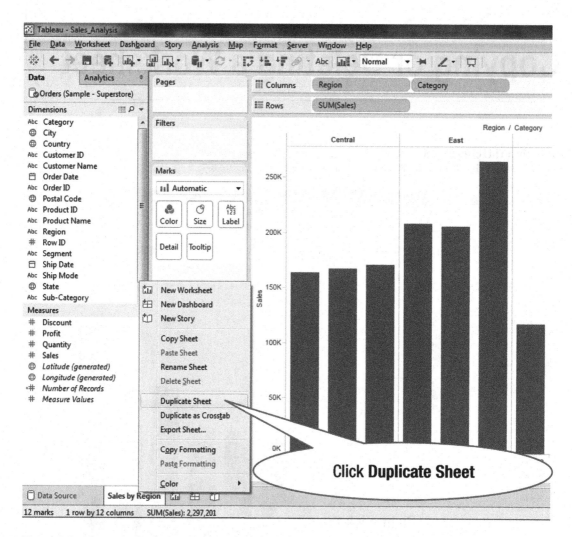

Figure 8-2. *Menu tree displaying option to duplicate sheet*

- Click the **Duplicate Sheet** menu tree item, as shown in Figure 8-2, which leads to the display in Figure 8-3

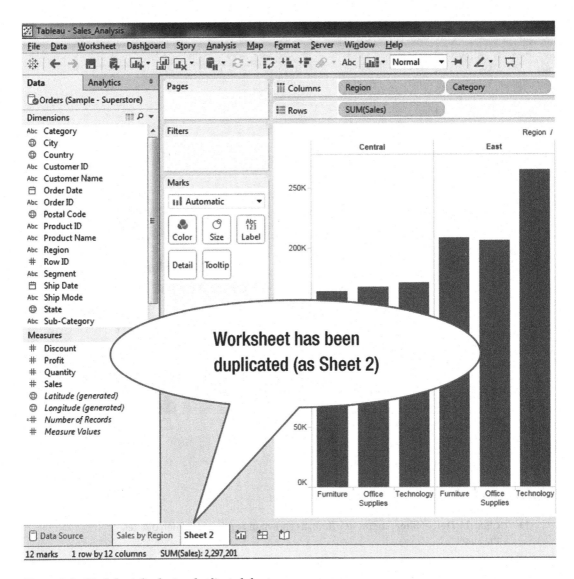

Figure 8-3. *Worksheet displaying duplicated sheet*

Figure 8-3 now shows two worksheets:

- Sales by Region (original)

- Sheet 2 (duplicate)

To delete a worksheet:

- Right-click the sheet to be deleted, which pops up the menu tree displayed in Figure 8-4

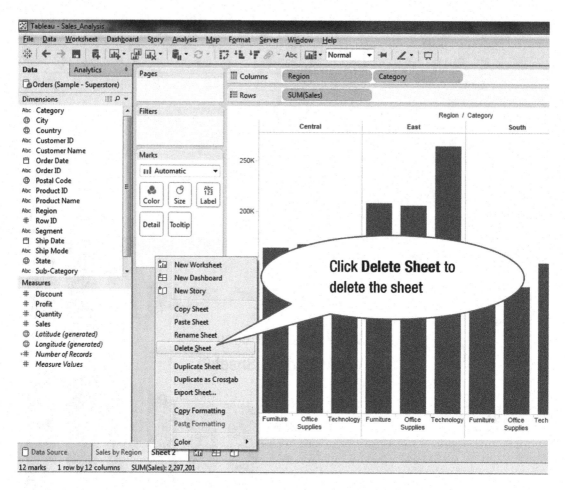

Figure 8-4. *Menu tree displaying the option to delete a sheet*

- Click the **Delete Sheet** menu tree item, as shown in Figure 8-4, which deletes
  the sheet

CHAPTER 9

Changing the Display from One Chart Type to Another

Objective: This exercise demonstrates how to change the display from one chart type to another Figure 9-1 shows a bar chart for the sum of Sales by Region and Category.

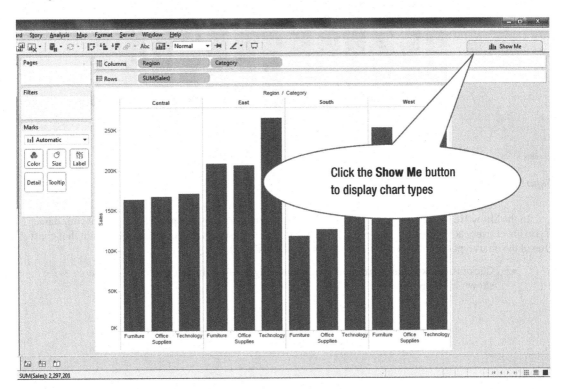

Figure 9-1. *Opening the Show Me window*

Figure 9-1 shows the **Show Me** button, which is used to suggest the appropriate chart based on the selected data or to change the type of chart that is displayed. While **Show Me** displays many chart types, it only highlights the ones that can be used with the underlying data. If a chart cannot be used, it is grayed out.

© Arshad Khan 2016
A. Khan, *Jumpstart Tableau*, DOI 10.1007/978-1-4842-1934-8_9

To change the displayed chart type:

- Click the **Show Me** button, as shown in Figure 9-1, which leads to Figure 9-2, where the various chart options are displayed

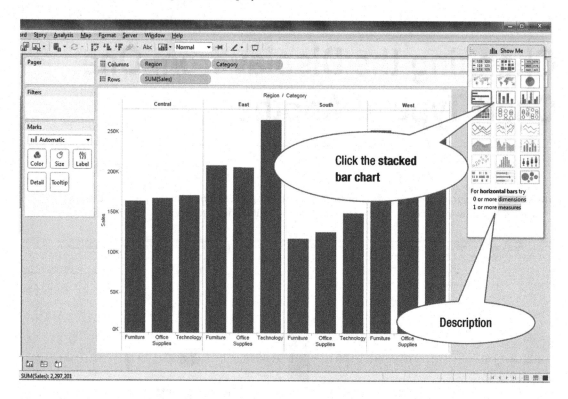

Figure 9-2. *Show Me window is displayed*

In the **Show Me** window in Figure 9-2, the chart type that is not gray can generate a view of your data. If you hover over each chart type, the description at the bottom displays the requirements to plot that chart. One of the chart types highlighted in Figure 9-2 is the stacked bar chart.

- Click the **stacked bar chart** icon, as shown in Figure 9-2, which leads to the display shown in Figure 9-3

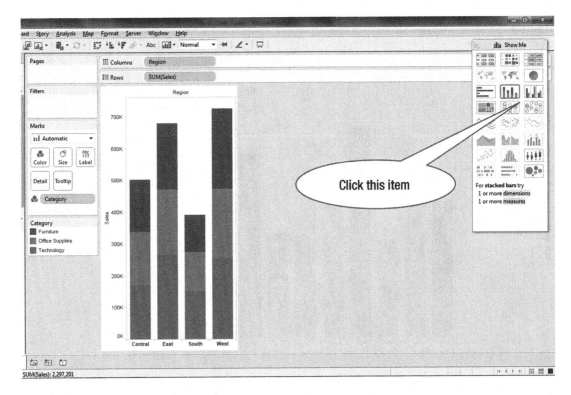

Figure 9-3. *Stacked bar chart*

To change the chart type, all you need to do is click the desired chart in the **Show Me** window.

- Click the **chart** icon, as shown in Figure 9-3, which leads to the chart displayed in Figure 9-4

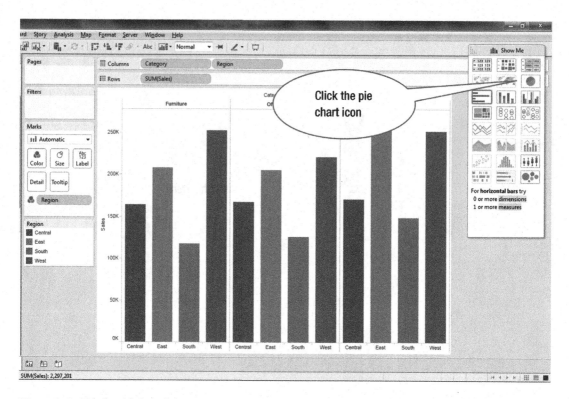

Figure 9-4. *Side-by-side bar chart*

To display the data as a pie chart:

- Click the **pie chart** icon, as shown in Figure 9-4, which leads to the display shown in Figure 9-5

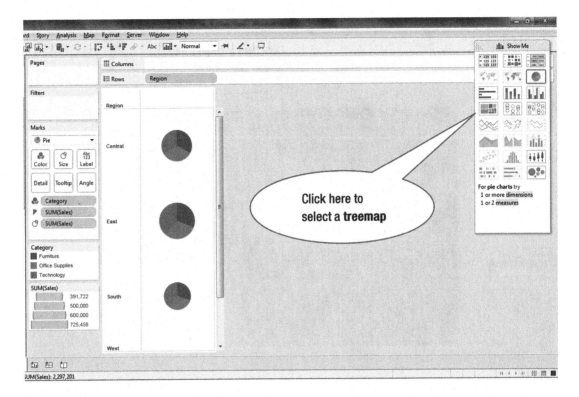

Figure 9-5. *Pie chart*

To display the data as a treemap:

- Click the **Treemap** icon, as shown in Figure 9-5, which leads to the display shown in Figure 9-6

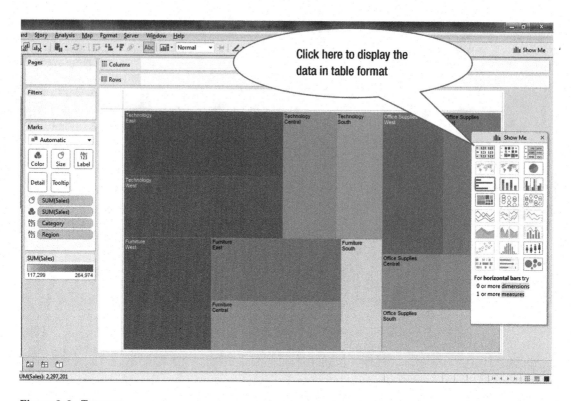

Figure 9-6. *Treemap*

To display the data in table format:

- Click the **Text Table** icon, as shown in Figure 9-6, which leads to Figure 9-7, where the data is displayed in a Text Table format

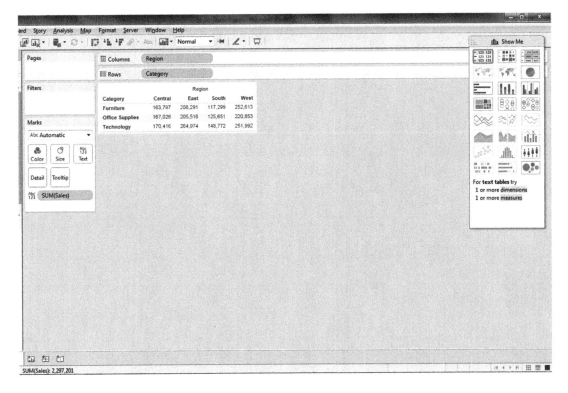

Figure 9-7. *Text table*

CHAPTER 10

■ ■ ■

Using the Show Me Tool for Selecting a Visualization

Objective: This exercise demonstrates how to use the **Show Me** tool to select the appropriate visualization for the data being analyzed

Show Me is a powerful tool that helps users pick the appropriate view for the data being analyzed. The **Show Me** window contains commonly used chart types, which can help a user to get started with visual analysis. Based on the data that is being analyzed, the **Show Me** tool highlights only the relevant views, while the others are grayed out.

Figure 10-1 shows a blank worksheet, where the **Show Me** window is minimized.

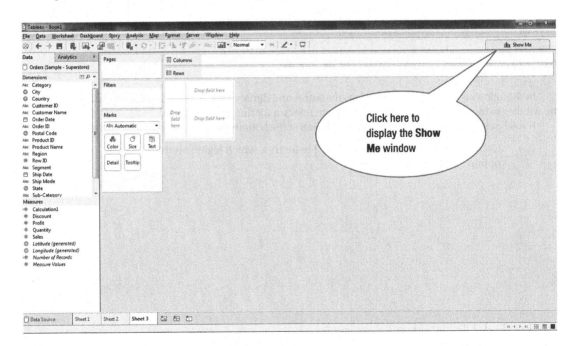

Figure 10-1. *Blank worksheet*

A. Khan, *Jumpstart Tableau*, DOI 10.1007/978-1-4842-1934-8_10

To display the **Show Me** window:

- Click the **Show Me** button, as shown in Figure 10-1, which leads to the display shown in Figure 10-2

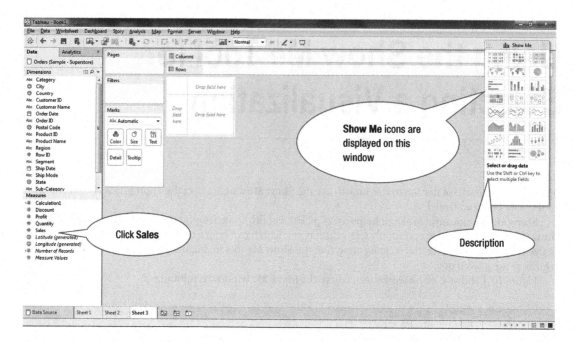

Figure 10-2. *Worksheet with displayed Show Me window*

In the following steps, we select various measures and dimensions, which immediately cause the **Show Me** window to highlight the visualizations that are relevant for the selected items.

If you hover over each chart type, the description at the bottom shows the requirements to plot the chart.

- Click the **Sales** measure, as shown in Figure 10-2, which highlights the bar chart option displayed in Figure 10-3

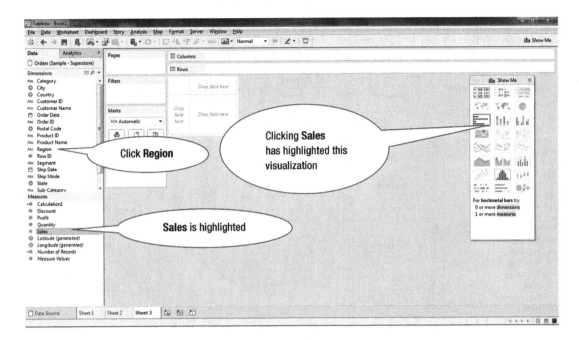

Figure 10-3. *Chart highlighted after a single measure is selected*

To add the **Region** dimension:

- Click the **Region** dimension, as shown in Figure 10-3, which highlights additional charts, besides the bar chart, as displayed in Figure 10-4

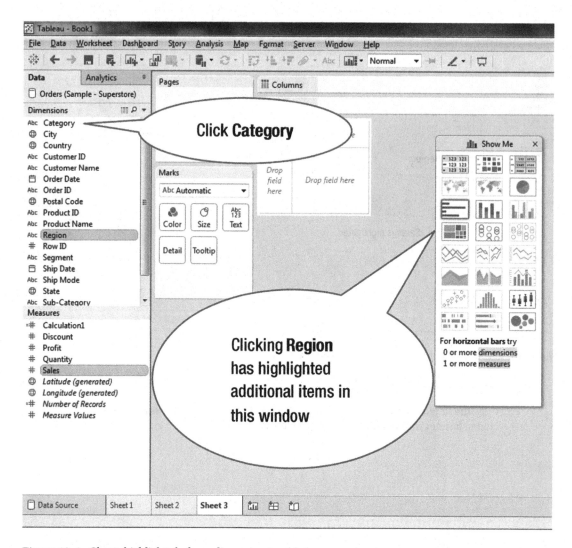

Figure 10-4. *Charts highlighted after a dimension is added*

To add an additional dimension, **Category**:

- Click the **Category** dimension, as shown in Figure 10-4, which leads to the display shown in Figure 10-5 (where more icons are highlighted)

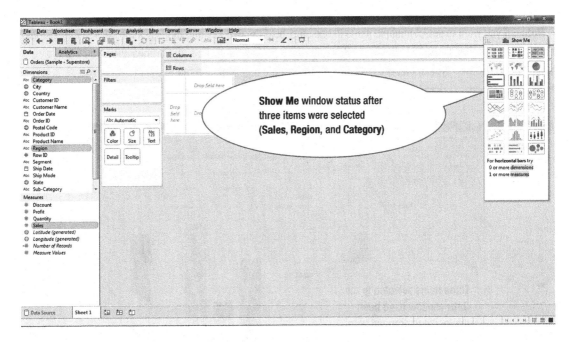

Figure 10-5. *Charts highlighted after three items being selected*

In Figure 10-5, three items have been highlighted in the **Data** window (**Category**, **Region**, and **Sales**).

- Drag and drop the **Category** and **Region** dimensions onto the **Columns** shelf

- Drag and drop the **Sales** measure onto the **Rows** shelf

This generates the visualization that is displayed in Figure 10-6.

▪ **Note** If you want to select multiple items in one step, hold the **Ctrl** key and then click the desired dimensions and/or measures. This is useful in the case where, for the selected dimensions and/or measures, you want to check the visualization type(s) that are relevant (which become highlighted in the **Show Me** window).

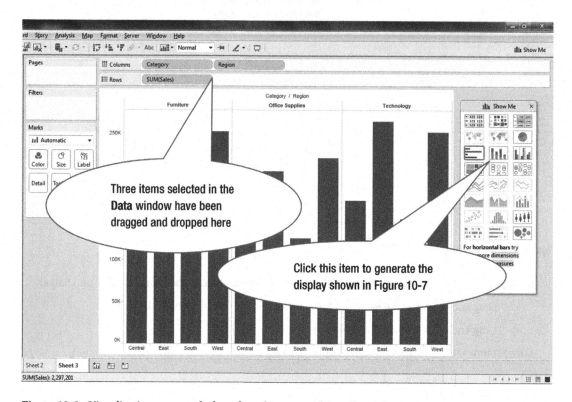

Figure 10-6. *Visualization generated after selected items are dragged and dropped*

Clicking any highlighted icon in the **Show Me** window displays the selected visualization. To select the stacked bar chart:

- Click the **stacked bar** icon in the **Show Me** window, as shown in Figure 10-6, which generate the visualization displayed in Figure 10-7

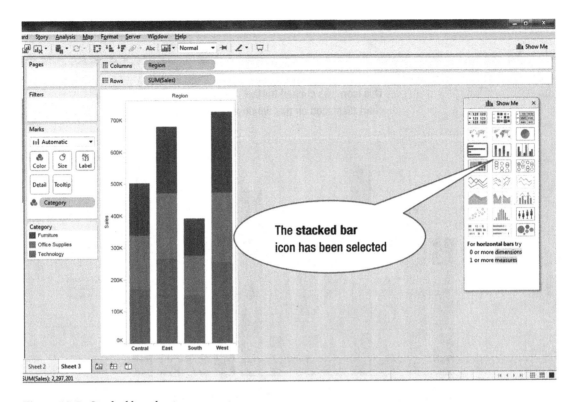

Figure 10-7. *Stacked bar chart*

Figure 10-8 displays the visualization generated when the side-by-side bars icon is selected.

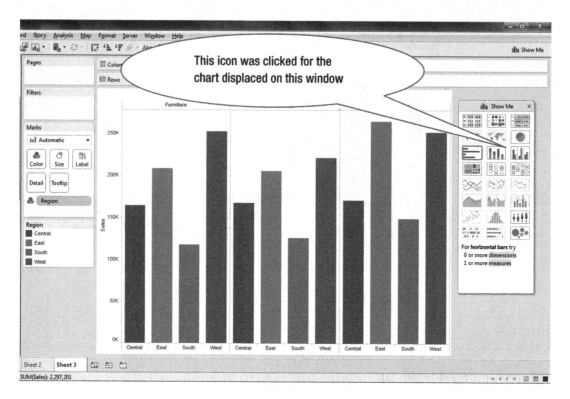

Figure 10-8. *Chart changed to side-by-side bar chart in the Show Me window*

CHAPTER 11

■ ■ ■

Crosstab Display and Swapping

Objective: This exercise demonstrates how to display visualization data in a crosstab format, how to swap axes so that data can be viewed from a different perspective, and how to resize a view

We start this exercise with Figure 11-1, which is based on two dimensions (**Category** and **Order Date**) and one measure (**Sales**).

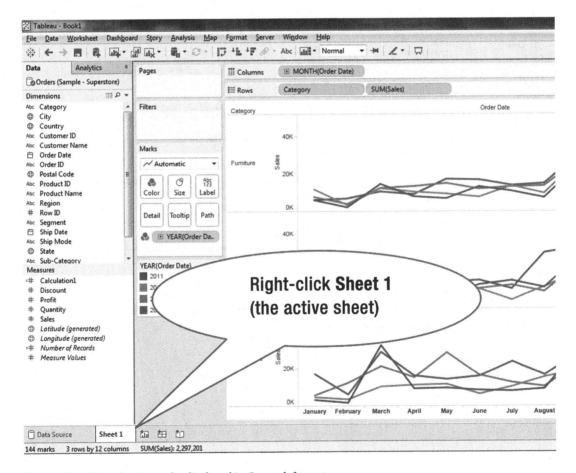

Figure 11-1. *Visualization to be displayed in Crosstab format*

© Arshad Khan 2016
A. Khan, *Jumpstart Tableau*, DOI 10.1007/978-1-4842-1934-8_11

- Right-click the **Sheet 1** tab, as shown in Figure 11-1, which pops up the menu tree displayed in Figure 11-2

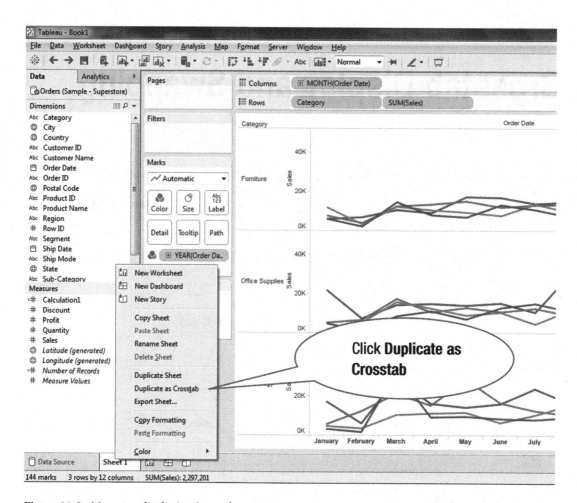

Figure 11-2. *Menu tree displaying Crosstab option*

- Click the **Duplicate as Crosstab** menu tree item, as shown in Figure 11-2, which leads to the display shown in Figure 11-3

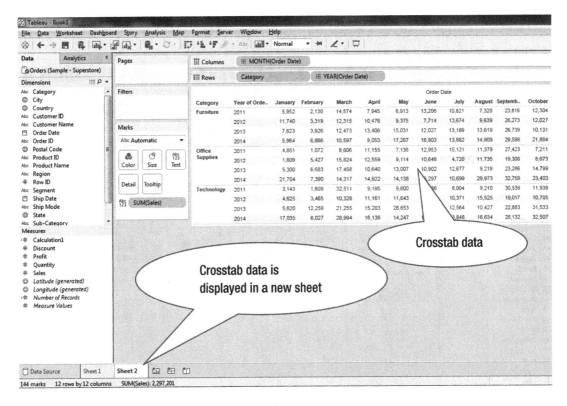

Figure 11-3. *Crosstab display*

Notice that a new worksheet has been created, **Sheet 2**, where the crosstab data is displayed.

The following steps demonstrate how to swap axes so that data can be viewed from a different perspective. We start this exercise with the data displayed in Figure 11-4.

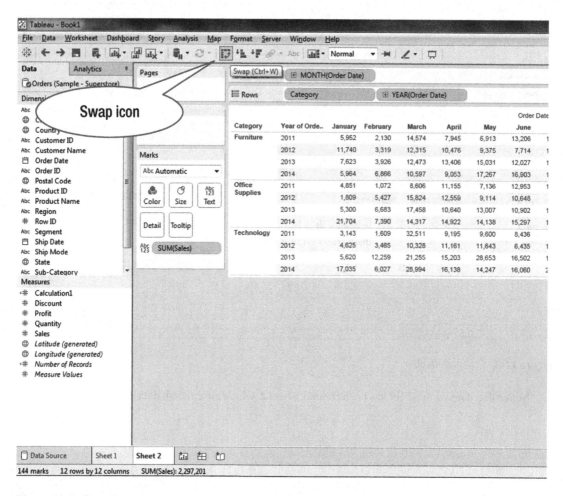

Figure 11-4. Swap icon

To perform the axis swap:

- Click the **Swap** icon, as shown in Figure 11-4, which leads to the display shown in Figure 11-5, where the rows have been swapped with the columns

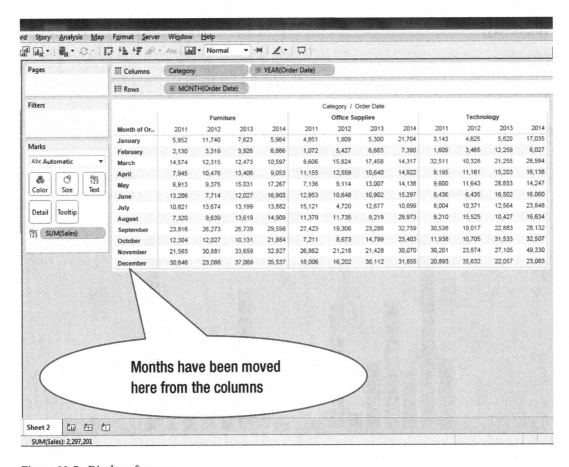

Figure 11-5. *Display after swap*

In Figure 11-5, due to the swap:

- Months are now displayed in the rows
- Categories are now displayed in the columns

Resizing

Sizing a view can be done quite easily in Tableau. The following steps demonstrate how to size a view. We start with Figure 11-6, which displays a visualization that covers only part of the available window. It does not cover the full screen, and therefore, valuable real estate is wasted. Hence, we resize the display so that it covers the width of the window.

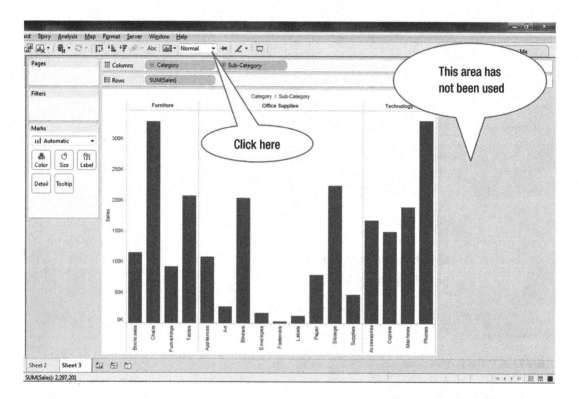

Figure 11-6. *Visualization with unused area*

To expand the visualization:

- Click the pull-down arrow, as shown in Figure 11-6, which displays the available screen size options shown in Figure 11-7

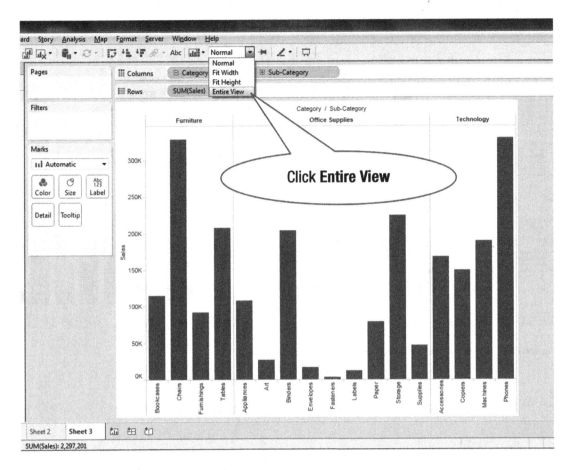

Figure 11-7. Sizing options

- Click the **Entire View** menu tree item, as shown in Figure 11-7, which leads to the display shown in Figure 11-8

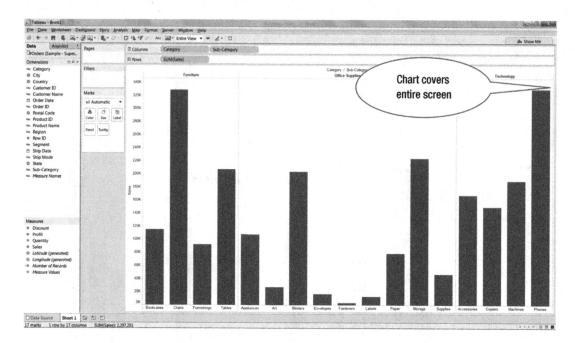

Figure 11-8. *Visualization covering available area*

CHAPTER 12

▪ ▪ ▪

Sorting

Objective: This exercise demonstrates how to perform the sort function

Figure 12-1 displays results that need to be sorted in descending order.

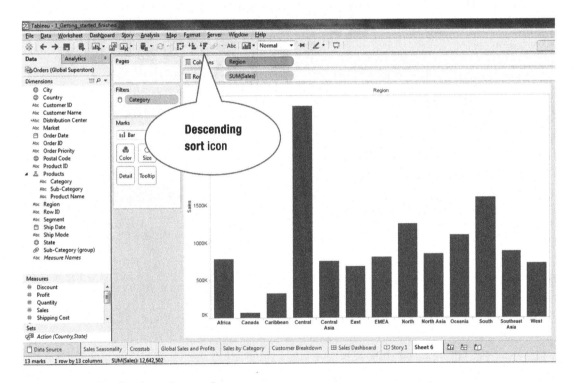

Figure 12-1. *Visualization to be sorted*

- Click the **descending sort** icon, highlighted in Figure 12-1, which leads to the display shown in Figure 12-2

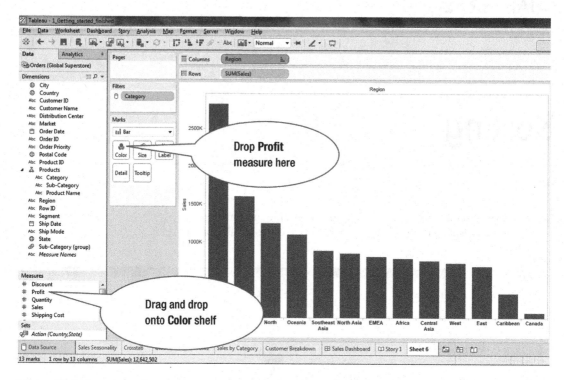

Figure 12-2. *Sorted visualization*

To analyze the results by profitability:

- Drag and drop the **Profit** measure onto the **Color** shelf in the **Marks** card, as shown in Figure 12-2, which leads to the display shown in Figure 12-3

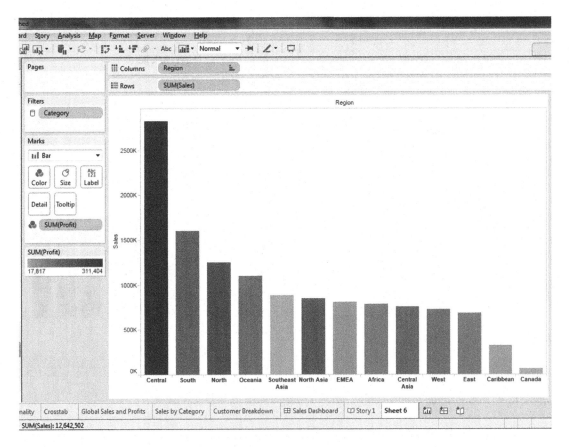

Figure 12-3. *Profitability indicated by color intensity*

The intensity of the color indicates the profitability. For example, while EMEA and Africa sales are nearly equal, Africa is far more profitable (as indicated by the intensity of the shade of green).

The following steps show how to sort within a sub-category. Figure 12-4 shows an initial view.

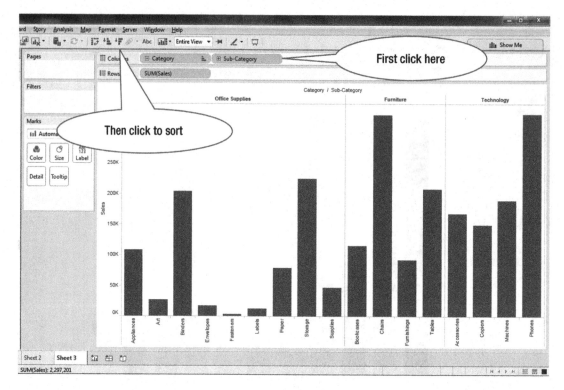

Figure 12-4. *Visualization to be sorted within Sub-Category*

- Click **Sub-Category** in Columns, as shown in Figure 12-4

- Click the **Descending sort** icon, also highlighted in Figure 12-4, which leads to the display shown in Figure 12-5

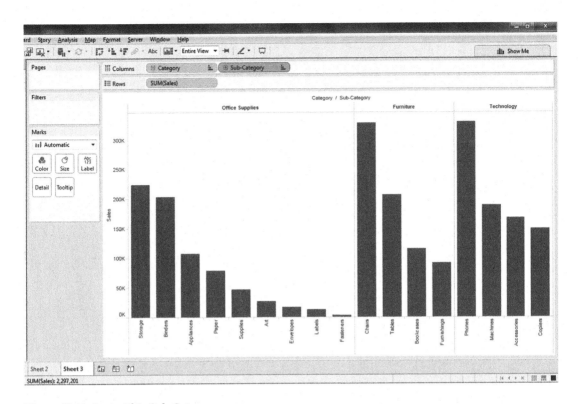

Figure 12-5. *Sort within Sub-Category*

CHAPTER 13

▆ ▆ ▆

More About Sorting

Objective: This exercise demonstrates the sort function in more detail

Figure 13-1 shows a chart that displays the sum of **Sales** by **Category** and **Sub-Category**.

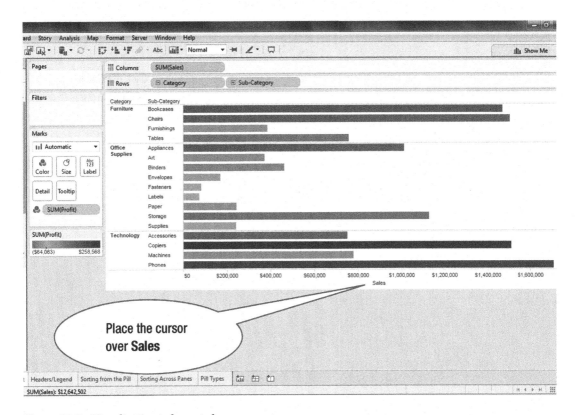

Figure 13-1. *Visualization to be sorted*

To sort the displayed data using the **Quick Sort** icon:

- Move the cursor over **Sales**, as shown in Figure 13-1, which displays the **Quick Sort** icon shown in Figure 13-2

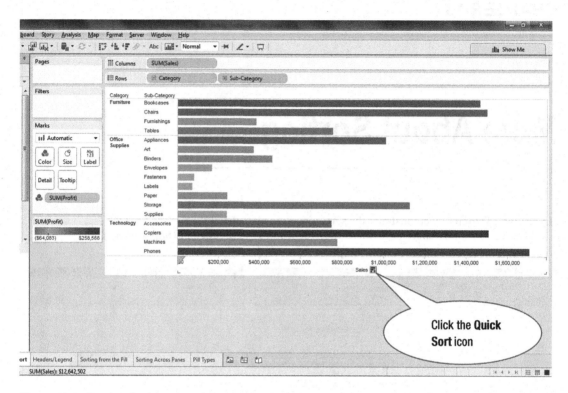

Figure 13-2. Sort icon location on axis

- Click the **Quick Sort** icon, as shown in Figure 13-2, which sorts the bars in each category in descending order, as shown in Figure 13-3

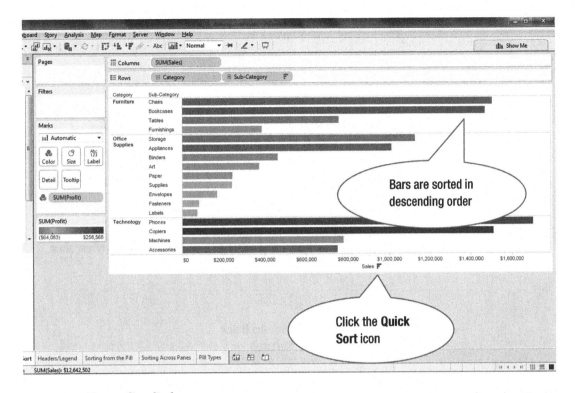

Figure 13-3. *Descending display*

- Click the **Quick Sort** icon again, as shown in Figure 13-3, which re-sort the bars in ascending order, as displayed in Figure 13-4

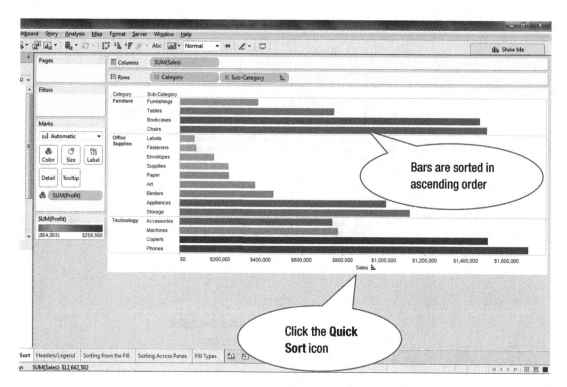

Figure 13-4. *Ascending display*

- Click the **Quick Sort** icon again, as shown in Figure 13-4, which removes the sort and the visualization reverts back to its original state (see Figure 13-2)

Advance sorting options are available via the sort option, as demonstrated in the following procedure, where we start from the visualization displayed in Figure 13-5.

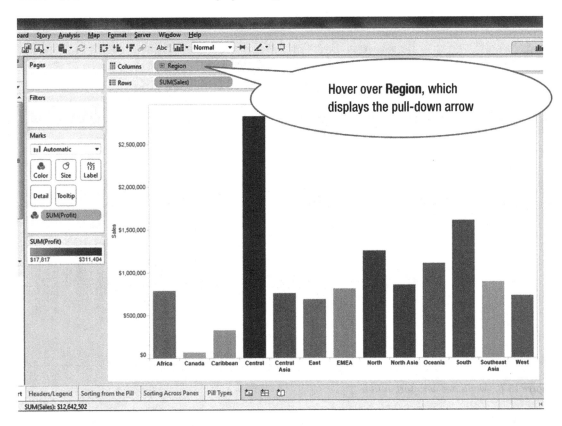

Figure 13-5. *Visualization to be sorted*

- Hover over **Region** (in the Columns shelf), as shown in Figure 13-5, which displays the pull-down arrow for the **Region** dimension

- Click the pull-down arrow when it is displayed, which leads to the menu tree shown in Figure 13-6

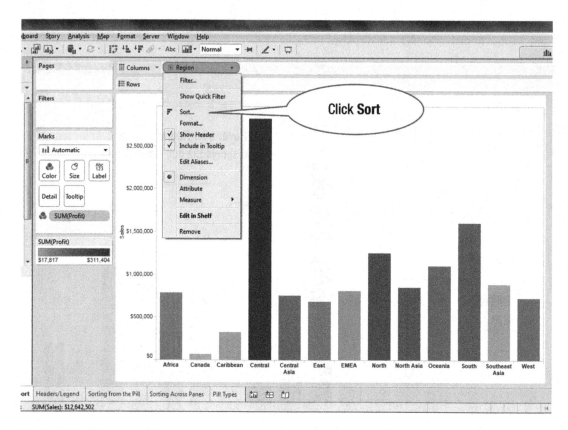

Figure 13-6. *Menu tree with sort option*

- Click the **Sort** menu tree item, as shown in Figure 13-6, which pops up the window displayed in Figure 13-7

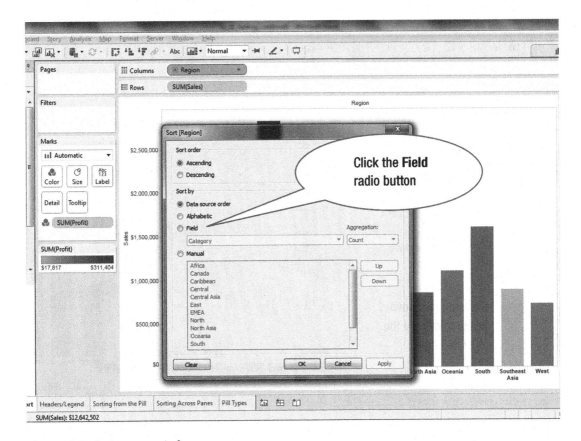

Figure 13-7. *Sort pop-up window*

In the pop-up window displayed in Figure 13-7, the ascending or descending sort order can be specified, as well as the field to be used for sorting.

To specify the field to be used for sorting:

- Click the **Field** radio button, as shown in Figure 13-7, which leads to the selection displayed in Figure 13-8

125

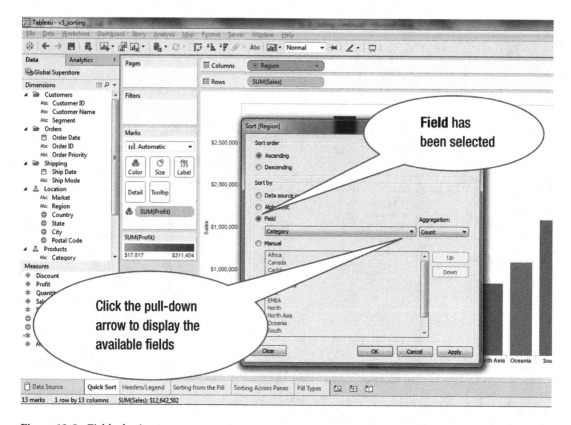

Figure 13-8. *Field selection*

- Click the pull-down arrow for **Category**, as shown in Figure 13-8, which displays the fields as shown in Figure 13-9

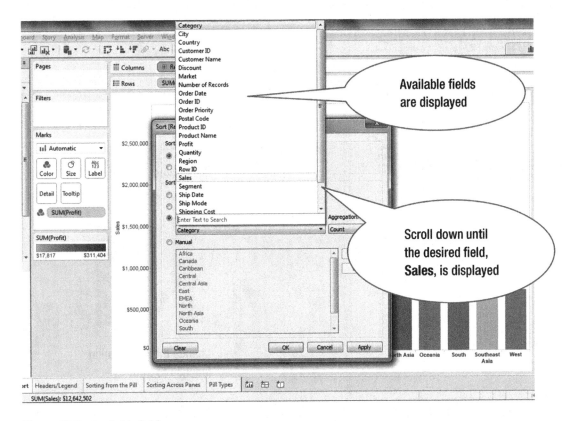

Figure 13-9. *Available fields*

- Scroll down the pop-up window until the **Sales** field is displayed, as shown in Figure 13-9

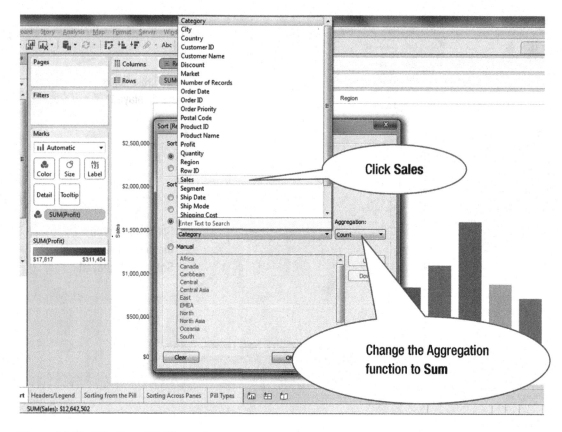

Figure 13-10. *Selecting a field for sorting*

- Click **Sales**, as shown in Figure 13-10

After selecting the field, the **Aggregation** function needs to be selected. In this case, **Count** is already selected. However, we will change that to **Sum**, using the pull-down arrow for **Aggregation**.

- Select **Sum**, as shown in Figure 13-10, which leads to the display shown in Figure 13-11

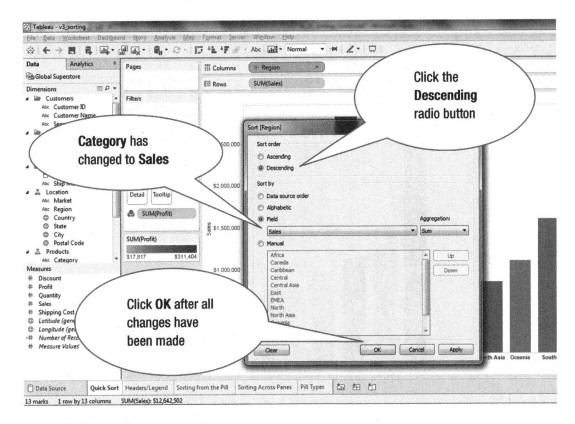

Figure 13-11. *Sort selections*

- Click the **Descending** radio button, as shown in Figure 13-11
- Click **OK** after all the changes have been made, which leads to the display shown in Figure 13-12 (which is in descending order)

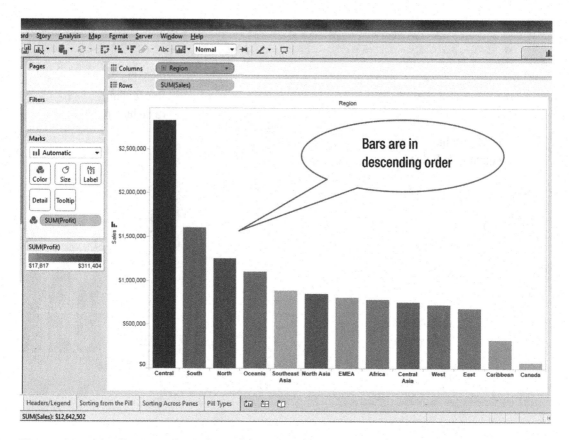

Figure 13-12. *Visualization in descending order*

■ ■ ■

CHAPTER 14

View Details/Underlying Data

Objective: This exercise demonstrates how to view the values for all the rows in the data source that make up the visualization

Figure 14-1 shows a chart with the sum of sales for various **Regions** by **Category** and **Sub-Category**.

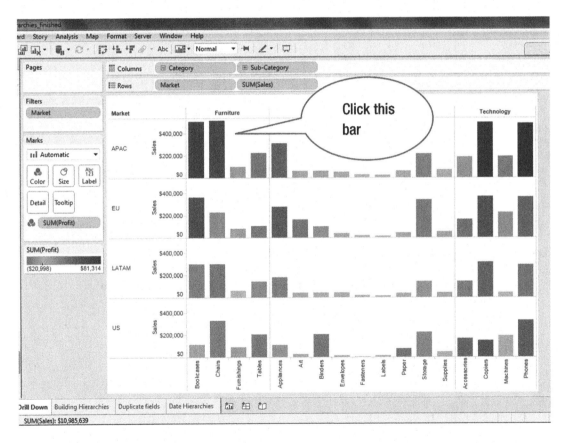

Figure 14-1. *Chart with sum of sales*

- Click the **Furniture** bar for APAC, as shown in Figure 14-1, which leads to Figure 14-2, where a pop-up box is displayed

© Arshad Khan 2016
A. Khan, *Jumpstart Tableau* DOI 10.1007/978-1-4842-1934-8_14

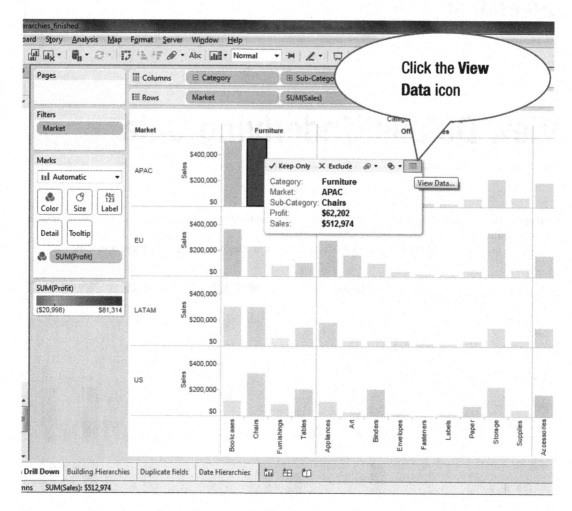

Figure 14-2. *Popup box with view data option highlighted*

- Click the **View Data** icon, as shown in Figure 14-2, which pops up the **View Data** window shown in Figure 14-3

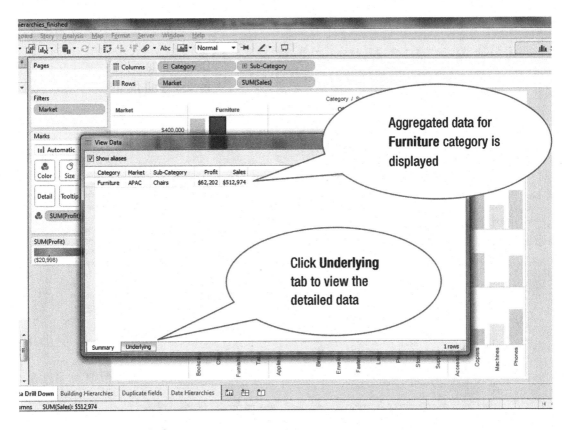

Figure 14-3. *View Data window*

The **Summary** tab displays the aggregated data for the fields used in the report.

- Click the **Underlying** tab, as shown in Figure 14-3, which leads to the display in Figure 14-4, where the detailed data is displayed

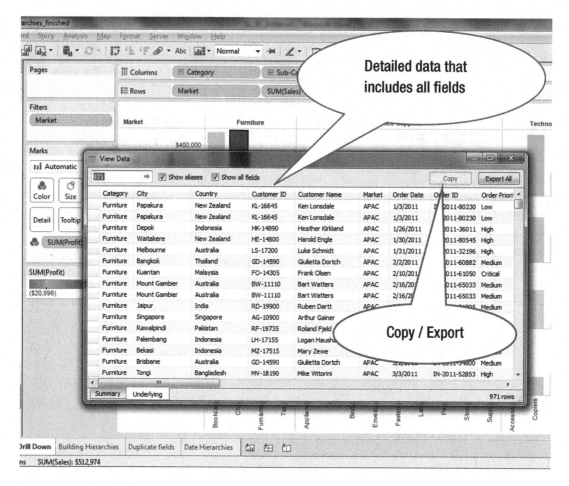

Figure 14-4. *Detailed data window*

By default, the **Show all fields** option is selected, as shown in Figure 14-4. This ensures that all the fields in the dataset are displayed. If you uncheck this option, you will be able to view only the fields used in your visualization.

This window also offers the option to copy and paste or export data in .csv format (as indicated in Figure 14-4).

CHAPTER 15

▪▪▪ ▪

Grouping

Objective: This exercise demonstrates how grouping is performed

Figure 15-1 shows a chart with the sum of Sales for various Sub-Categories.

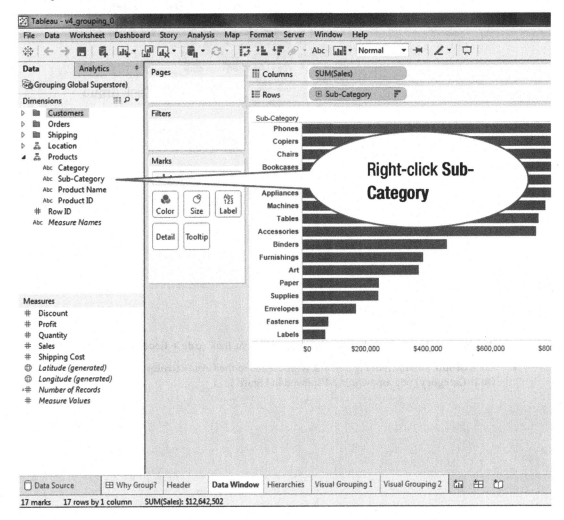

Figure 15-1. Dimensions to be grouped

- Right-click **Sub-Category**, as shown in Figure 15-1, which pops up the menu tree displayed in Figure 15-2

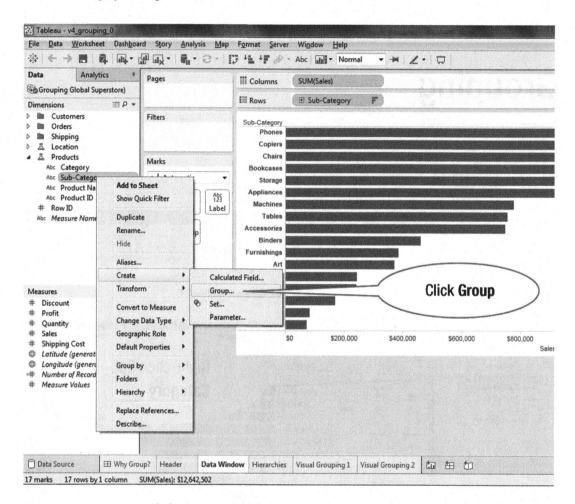

Figure 15-2. *Menu tree with the group option*

- Navigate to the secondary menu shown in Figure 15-2 via the **Create ➤ Group** menu path
- Click **Group**, as shown in Figure 15-2, which leads to the **Create Group (Sub-Category)** pop-up window displayed in Figure 15-3

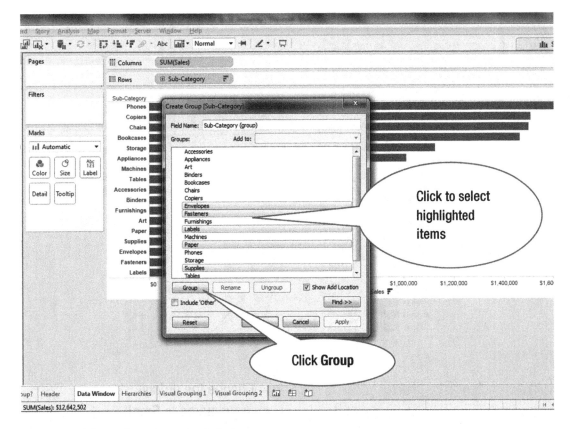

Figure 15-3. *Create Group pop-up window*

Select the items displayed in the **Create Group (Sub-Category)** window in Figure 15-3.
To select multiple items:

- Hold down the **Ctrl** key and then click the desired items

After the items highlighted in Figure 15-3 have been selected:

- Click the **Group** button, as shown in Figure 15-3, which leads to the display shown in
  Figure 15-4

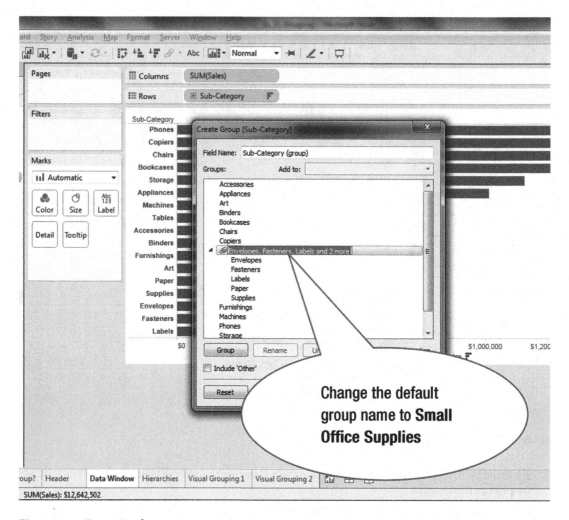

Figure 15-4. *Renaming the group*

To make the title more meaningful, we will change the default group name to **Small Office Supplies**. To change the name:

- Overwrite the default name shown in Figure 15-4 by typing **Small Office Supplies**, which leads to the display shown in Figure 15-5

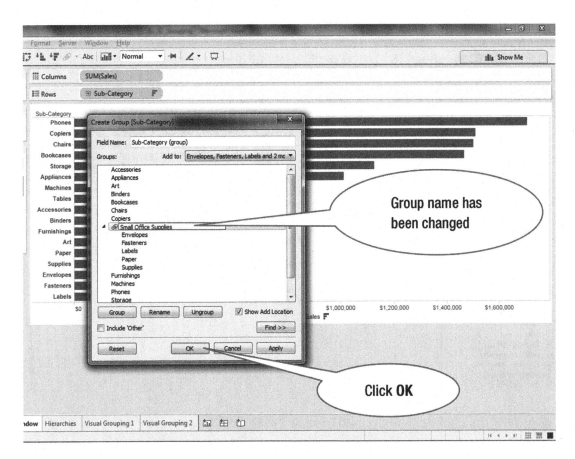

Figure 15-5. *Renamed group*

After the group name has been changed:

- Click **OK**, which saves the group and places it in the list of dimensions in the **Data** window, as shown in Figure 15-6

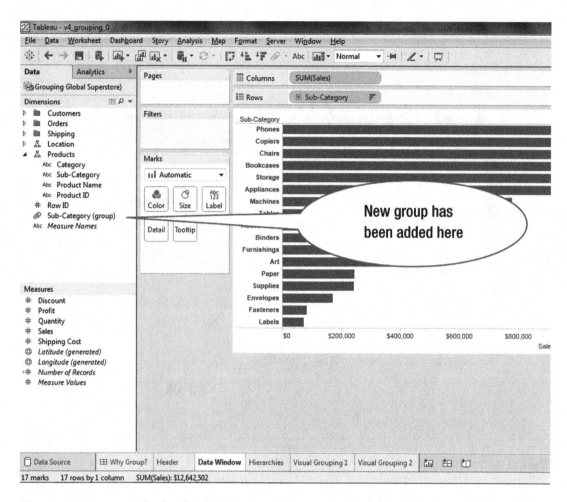

Figure 15-6. *New group displayed in the Dimensions pane*

A group can be edited, and, as needed, items can be added to it or deleted from it. In Figure 15-7, the **Sub-Category** group is modified.

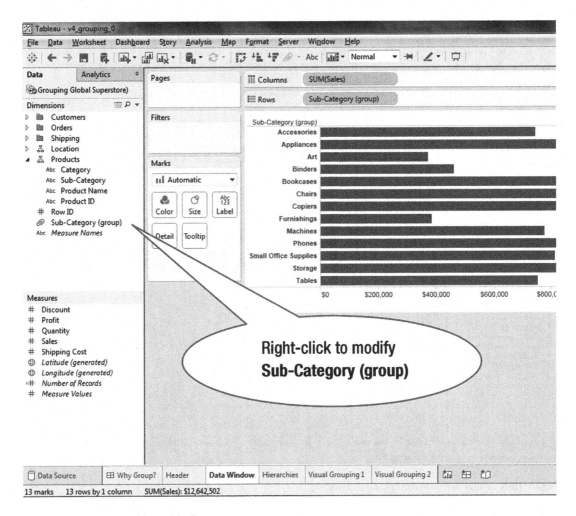

Figure 15-7. *Group to be modified*

To modify the Sub-Category (group):

- Right-click **Sub-Category (group)**, as shown in Figure 15-7, which pops up the menu tree displayed in Figure 15-8

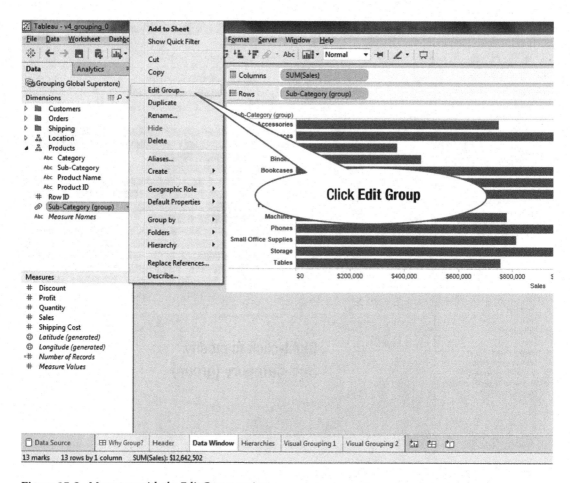

Figure 15-8. *Menu tree with the Edit Group option*

- Click the menu tree item **Edit Group**, as shown in Figure 15-8, which pops up the **Edit Group (Sub-Category (group))** window displayed in Figure 15-9

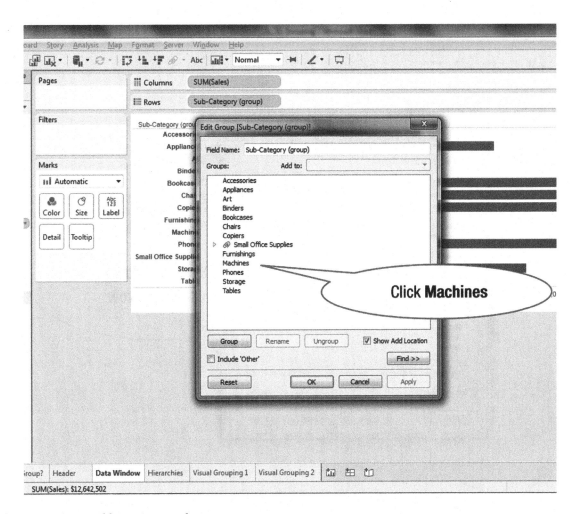

Figure 15-9. *Adding an item to the group*

To add the item **Machines** to the group:

- Click **Machines**, as shown in Figure 15-9, which leads to the display shown in Figure 15-10

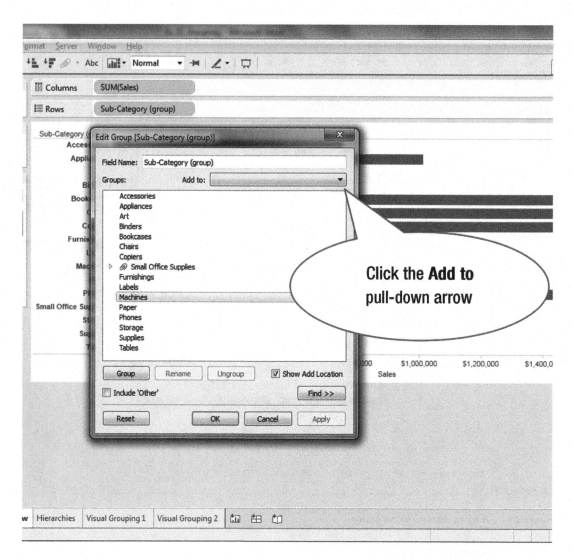

Figure 15-10. *Selecting the group*

To select the group to which the highlighted item, **Machines**, is to be added:

- Click the pull-down arrow for **Add to**, as shown in Figure 15-10, which leads to the display shown in Figure 15-11

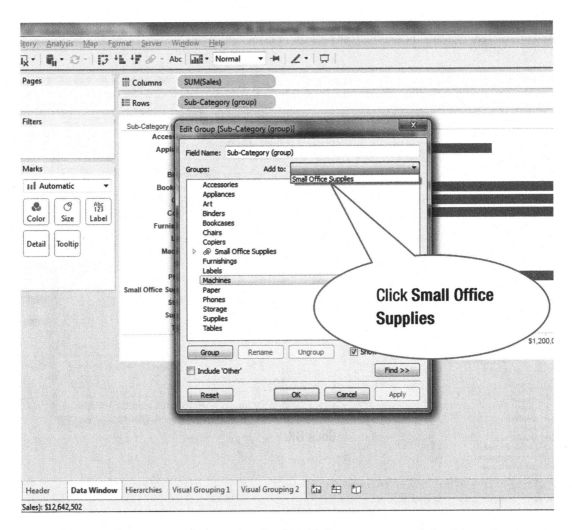

Figure 15-11. Displays group to which new item is to be added

- Click **Small Office Supplies**, as shown in Figure 15-11, which leads to the display shown in Figure 15-12

Note that in this case, only one item (**Small Office Supplies**) is displayed when the pull-down arrow for **Add to** is clicked. Typically, the selection can be made from multiple groups.

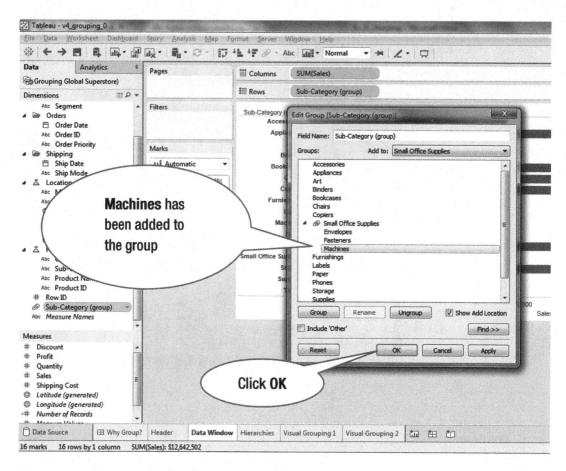

Figure 15-12. *New item added to group*

- Click **OK**, as shown in Figure 15-12, which saves the changes and adds the selected item (**Machines**) to the group

Another method of creating a group is to press and hold the **Command** key, multiselect headers in the view, and then click the **Group** icon.

CHAPTER 16

■ ■ ■

Building a Hierarchy

Objective: This exercise demonstrates how to build a hierarchy

Create the report shown in Figure 16-1, which is based on the following selections:

- Columns: Sales

- Rows: Category and Sub-Category

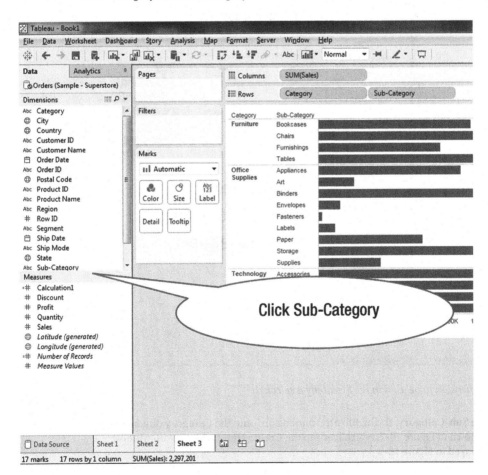

Figure 16-1. *Data pane displaying dimensions to be used*

© Arshad Khan 2016

A. Khan, *Jumpstart Tableau*, DOI 10.1007/978-1-4842-1934-8_16

To create a **Product** hierarchy:

- Click **Sub-Category** in the **Data** window, as shown in Figure 16-1, which leads to the display shown in Figure 16-2 (where the **Sub-Category** dimension is highlighted)

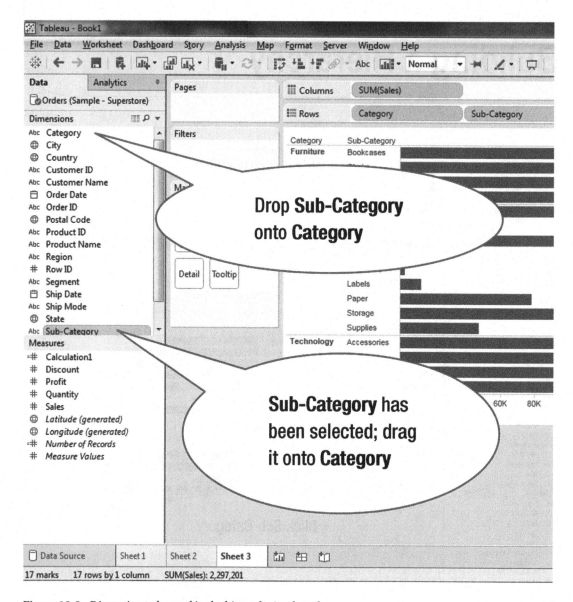

Figure 16-2. *Dimension to be used in the hierarchy is selected*

- Drag **Sub-Category**, the highlighted dimension, onto the **Category** dimension, as shown in Figure 16-2, which leads to the **Create Hierarchy** pop-up window displayed in Figure 16-3

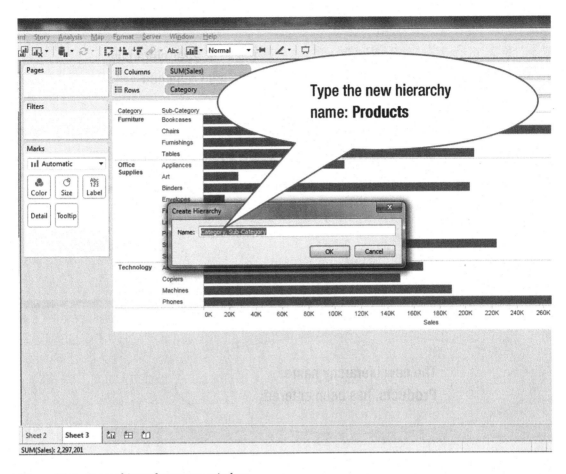

Figure 16-3. *Create hierarchy pop-up window*

We now rename the default hierarchy name that is provided by Tableau. In the **Name** field shown in the pop-up window displayed in Figure 16-3:

- Type **Products**, which leads to the display shown in Figure 16-4

149

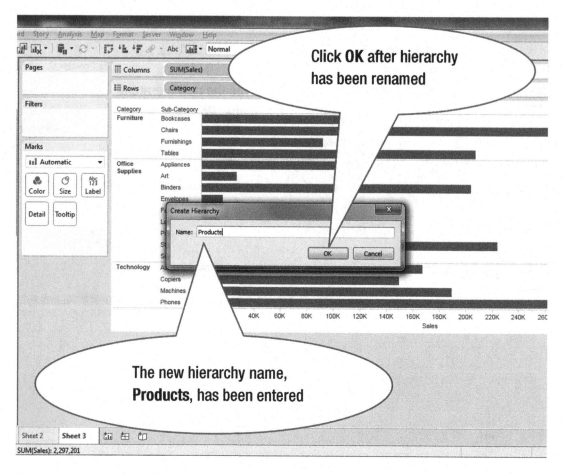

Figure 16-4. Renaming the hierarchy

- Click **OK** to save the hierarchy

The hierarchy can now be viewed in the **Data** window, as shown in Figure 16-5.

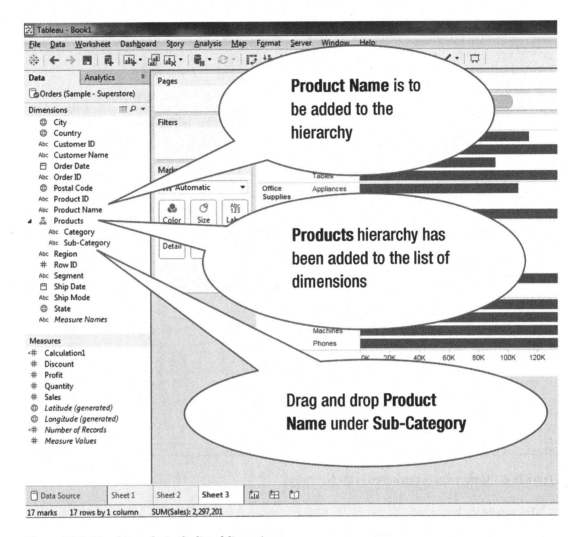

Figure 16-5. *New hierarchy in the list of dimensions*

To add an additional item, **Product Name**, to the hierarchy:

- Drag and drop **Product Name** under the **Sub-Category** dimension, as shown in Figure 16-5, which leads to the display shown in Figure 16-6

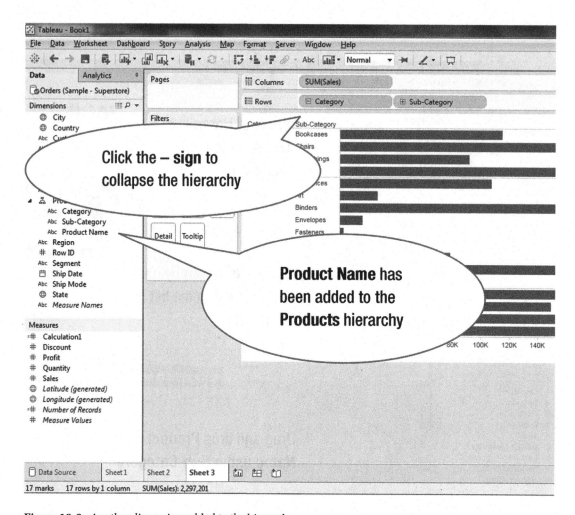

Figure 16-6. *Another dimension added to the hierarchy*

To collapse the hierarchy:

- Click the **– sign** next to **Category** (in Rows), as shown in Figure 16-6, which collapses the hierarchy and leads to the display shown in Figure 16-7

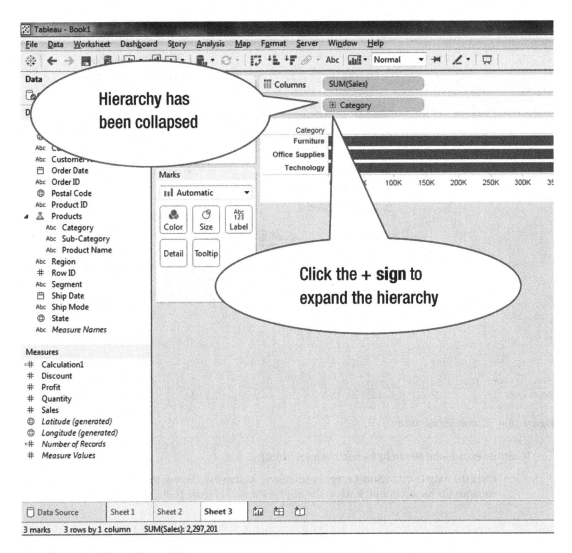

Figure 16-7. *Collapsed hierarchy*

To expand the hierarchy:

- Click the **+sign** next to **Category** (in Rows), as shown in Figure 16-7, which expands the hierarchy and leads to the display shown in Figure 16-8

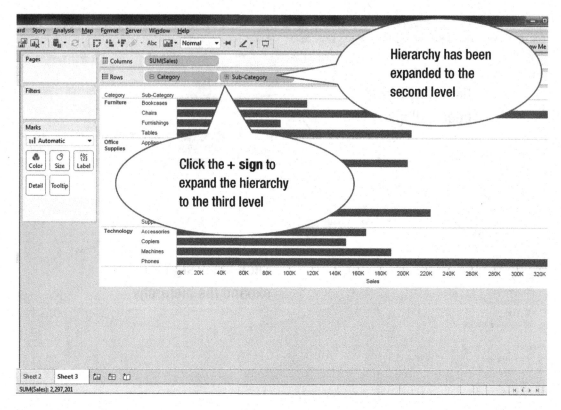

Figure 16-8. *Expanded hierarchy*

To further expand the hierarchy by another level (third):

- Click the **+sign** next to **Sub-Category** (in Rows), as shown in Figure 16-8, which expands the hierarchy and leads to the display shown in Figure 16-9

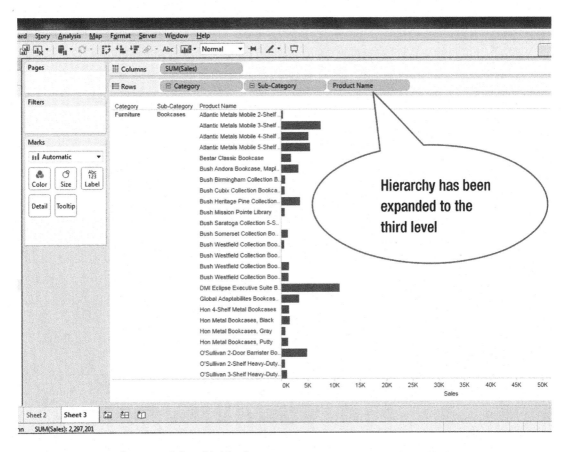

Figure 16-9. *Hierarchy expanded to third level*

CHAPTER 17

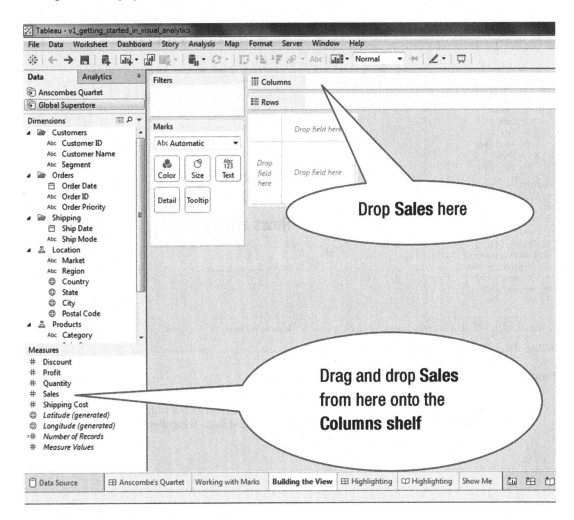

Aggregate Measures

Objective: This exercise demonstrates how to work with aggregates
Figure 17-1 displays a blank worksheet.

Figure 17-1. Blank worksheet

© Arshad Khan 2016
A. Khan, *Jumpstart Tableau*, DOI 10.1007/978-1-4842-1934-8_17

- Drag and drop **Sales** onto the **Columns** shelf, as shown in Figure 17-1, which leads to the display shown in Figure 17-2

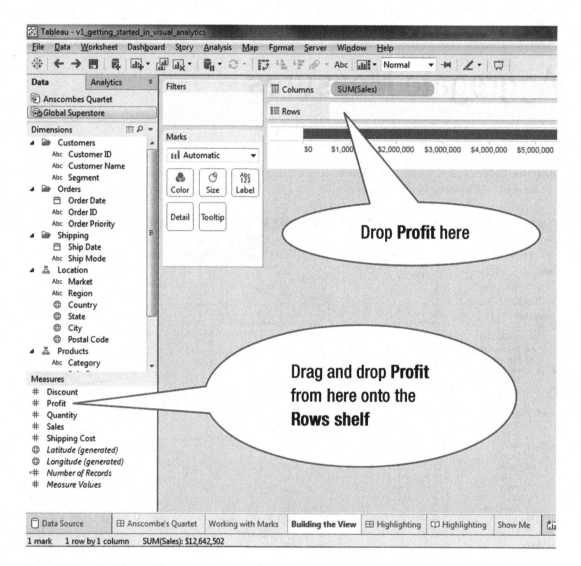

Figure 17-2. *Worksheet with one measure*

- Drag and drop **Profit** onto the **Rows** shelf, as shown in Figure 17-2, which leads to the display shown in Figure 17-3, where the aggregated value is highlighted

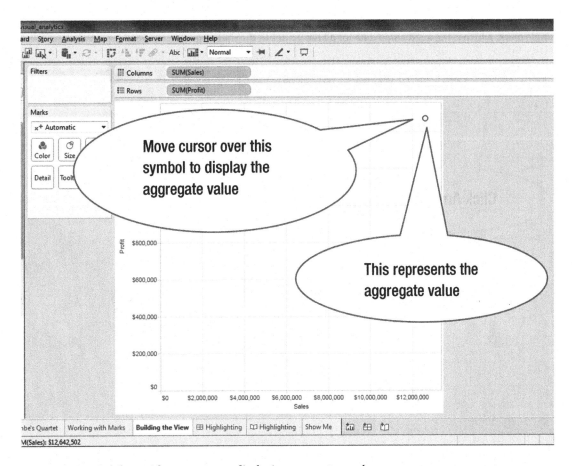

Figure 17-3. Worksheet with two measures displaying aggregate numbers

To display the aggregate value:

- Move the cursor over the aggregate symbol, as shown in Figure 17-3, which leads to Figure 17-4, where the exact value for the total sales and total profit is displayed

When two measures to be visualized are selected, Tableau chooses a scatterplot by default. It displays a single mark, which is the aggregated data for all the values in the database.

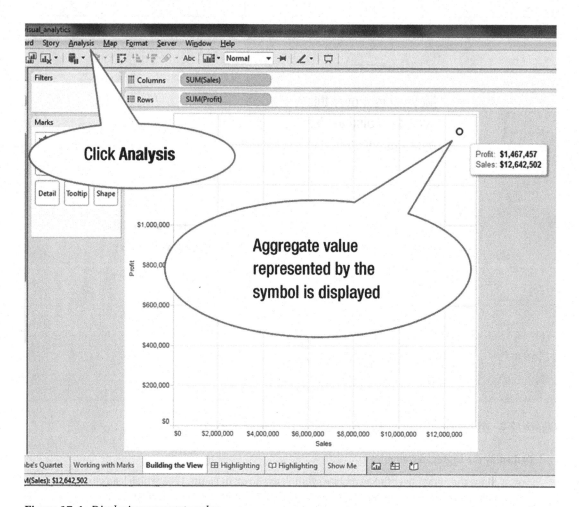

Figure 17-4. Displaying aggregate value

To deaggregate and display individual values:

- Click **Analysis** on the **menu bar**, as shown in Figure 17-4, which pops up the menu tree displayed in Figure 17-5

Note that when you deaggregate measures, the view shows a mark for every row in the data.

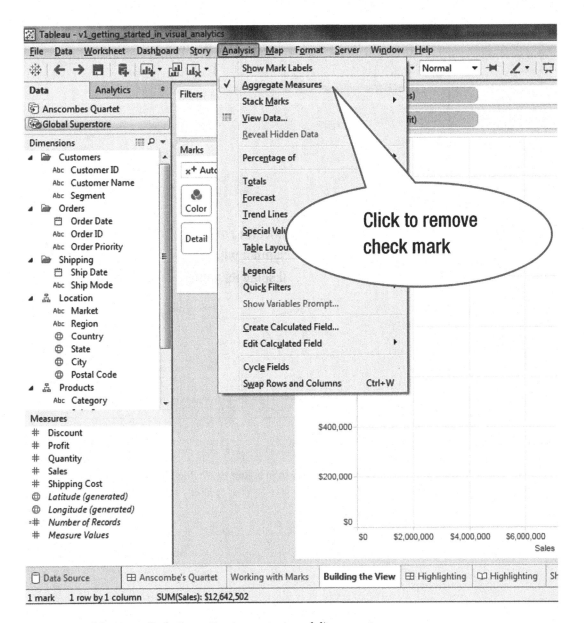

Figure 17-5. *Menu tree displaying option to aggregate and disaggregate measures*

To remove the check mark for **Aggregate Measures**:

- Click the **Aggregate Measures** menu tree item, as shown in Figure 17-5, which leads to the display shown in Figure 17-6

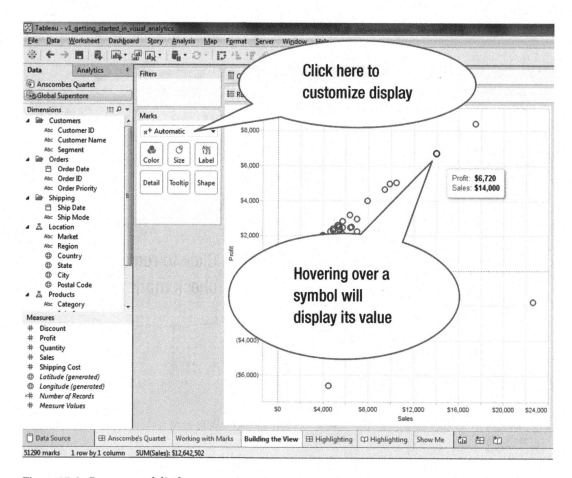

Figure 17-6. *Deaggregated display*

- Click **Automatic** in the **Marks** card, as shown in Figure 17-6, which pops up the menu tree displayed in Figure 17-7

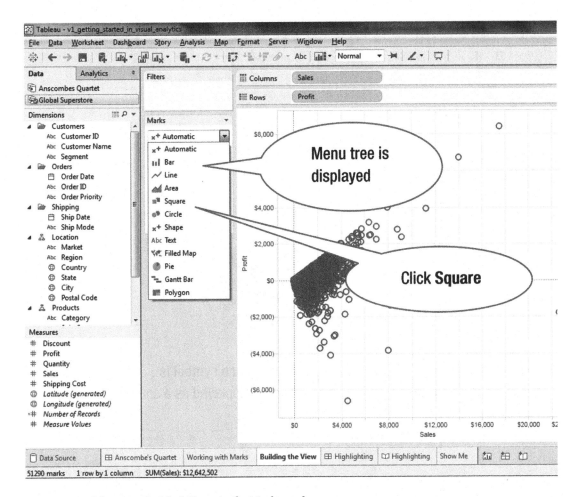

Figure 17-7. *Menu tree for Mark Types in the Marks card*

- Click the **Square** option from the menu tree item, as shown in Figure 17-7, which leads to the display shown in Figure 17-8

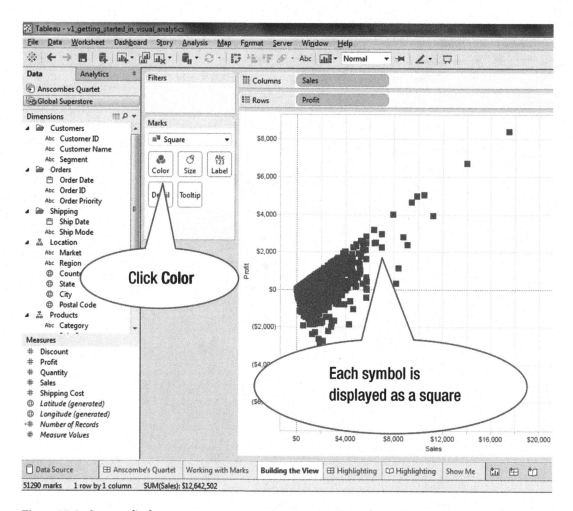

Figure 17-8. *Squares display*

- Click **Color** on the **Marks** card, as shown in Figure 17-8, which leads to the display shown in Figure 17-9

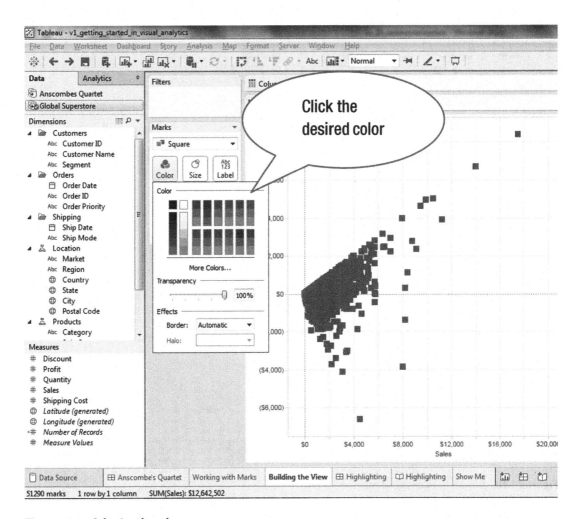

Figure 17-9. *Selecting the color*

- Click the desired color (green), as shown in Figure 17-9, which leads to the display shown in Figure 17-10, where the color has changed (from blue to green)

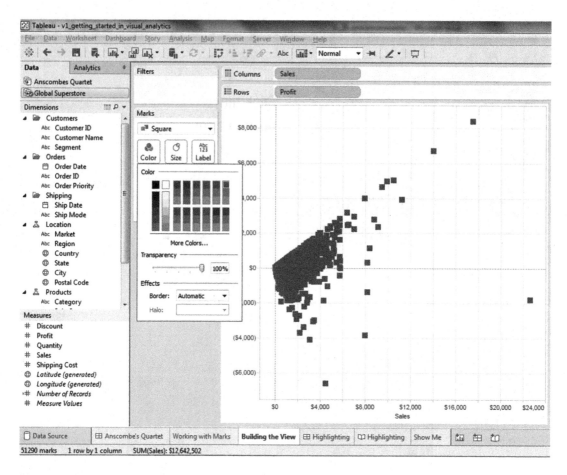

Figure 17-10. *Display with changed color*

In the printed book, which is in black and white, the changed color display can be observed in the relative darkness (intensity) of the symbols.

CHAPTER 18

■■■

Exclude and Keep

Objective: This exercise demonstrates how the Exclude and Keep functions are used
Figure 18-1 shows a chart with the sum of sales for four regions.

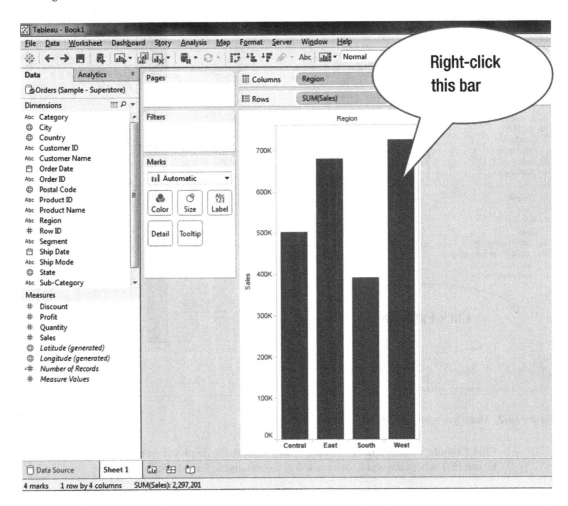

Figure 18-1. Visualization to be modified

© Arshad Khan 2016
A. Khan, *Jumpstart Tableau*, DOI 10.1007/978-1-4842-1934-8_18

Suppose we want to exclude the sales for a specific region and only focus on the sales for the remaining three regions. In other words, we want to "exclude" one region from the analysis. The following steps show how this is done.

To exclude the **West** region:

- Right-click the fourth bar (i.e., for the West region, which needs to be excluded), as shown in Figure 18-1, which pops up the menu tree displayed in Figure 18-2

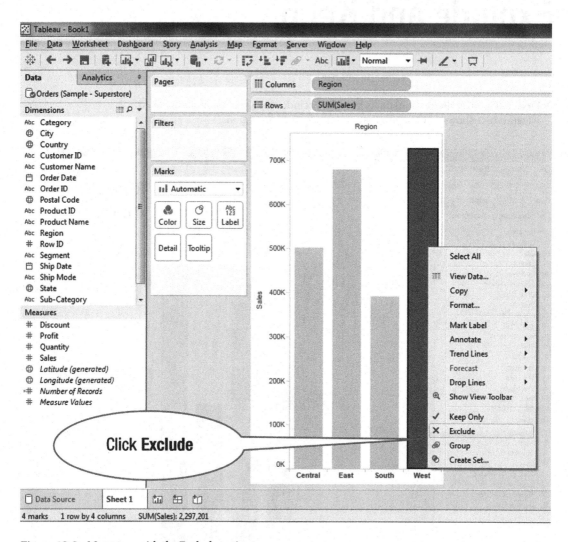

Figure 18-2. *Menu tree with the Exclude option*

- Click **Exclude**, as shown in Figure 18-2, which leads to the display shown in Figure 18-3, where the results are limited to the remaining three regions

When the **Exclude** or **Keep** option is used, Tableau creates a filter for the selected dimension. This is shown in Figure 18-3, where the **Region** filter has been created. What this does is exclude/filter out all the data for the West region from the view.

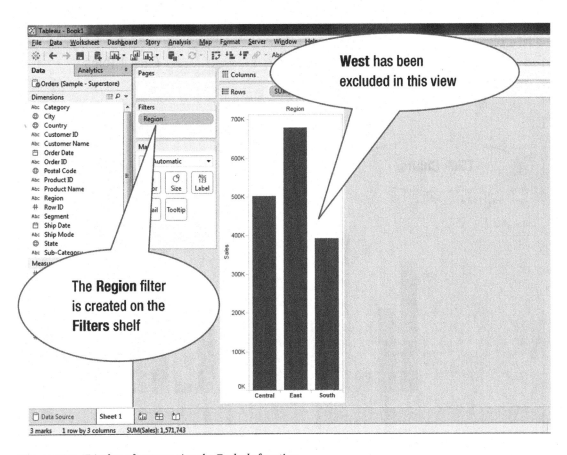

Figure 18-3. *Display after executing the Exclude function*

Another useful Tableau function is **Keep**. It retains selected items while excluding all the other displayed items. The following steps show how this is done.

Figure 18-4 displays the sum of sales for various sub-categories.

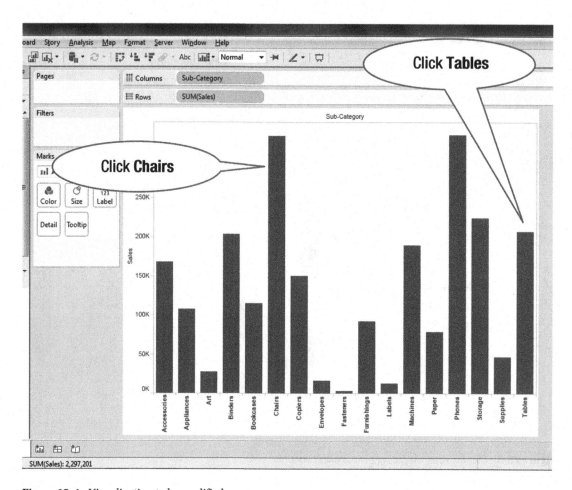

***Figure 18-4.** Visualization to be modified*

Suppose that you want to analyze the sales for only two items: chairs and tables.

- Hold down the **Ctrl** key on the keyboard and then:

  - Click the **Chairs** bar

  - Click the **Tables** bar

This leads to the display shown in Figure 18-5, where two bars are selected and highlighted. Notice the small pop-up window that displays the **Keep Only** and **Exclude** options.

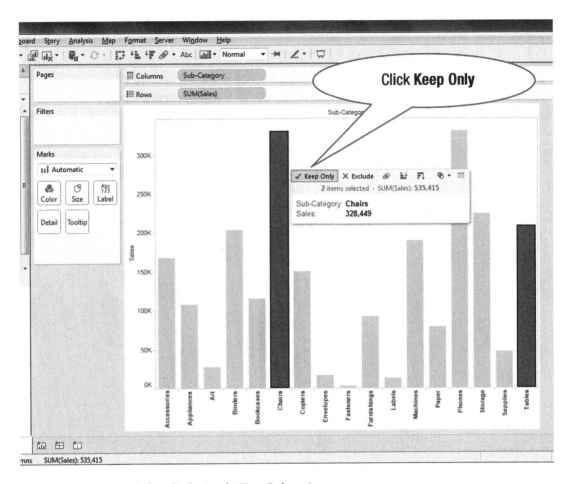

Figure 18-5. *Pop-up window displaying the Keep Only option*

- Click **Keep Only** in the pop-up window, as shown in Figure 18-5, which leads to the display shown in Figure 18-6

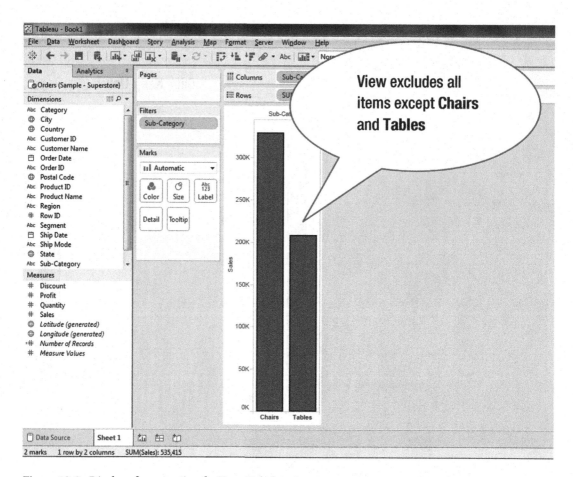

Figure 18-6. *Display after executing the Keep Only function*

■ ■ ■

CHAPTER 19

Filtering on the Filter Shelf

Objective: This exercise demonstrates how to filter using the Filter shelf

Figure 19-1 shows a chart that plots the sum of sales against the sum of profits.

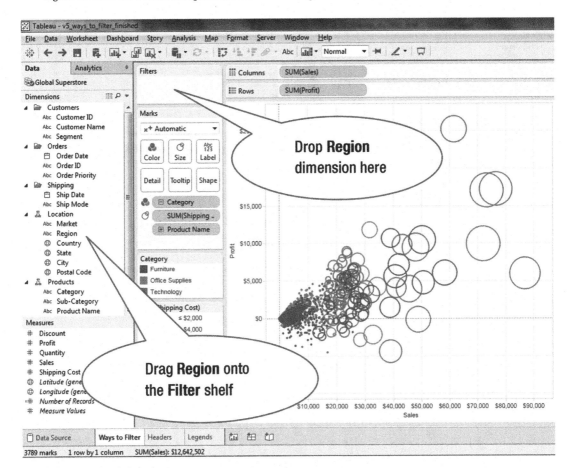

Figure 19-1. *Scatter plot view on which filtering is to be applied*

- Drag and drop **Region** from the **Data** window onto the **Filters** shelf, as shown in Figure 19-1, which pops up the **Filter (Region)** window displayed in Figure 19-2

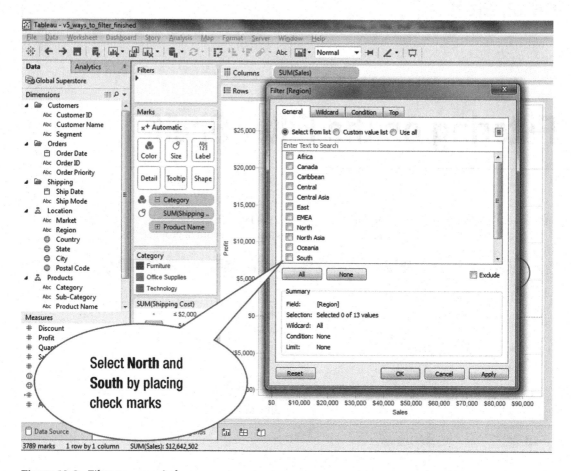

Figure 19-2. *Filter pop-up window*

- Place check marks for **North** and **South**, as shown in Figure 19-2, which leads to the display shown in Figure 19-3

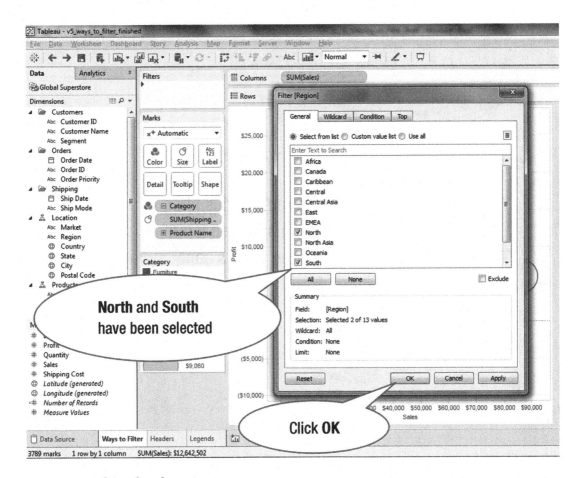

Figure 19-3. *Filters selected*

- Click **OK**, as shown in Figure 19-3, which leads to the display shown in Figure 19-4, where the filtered data is displayed

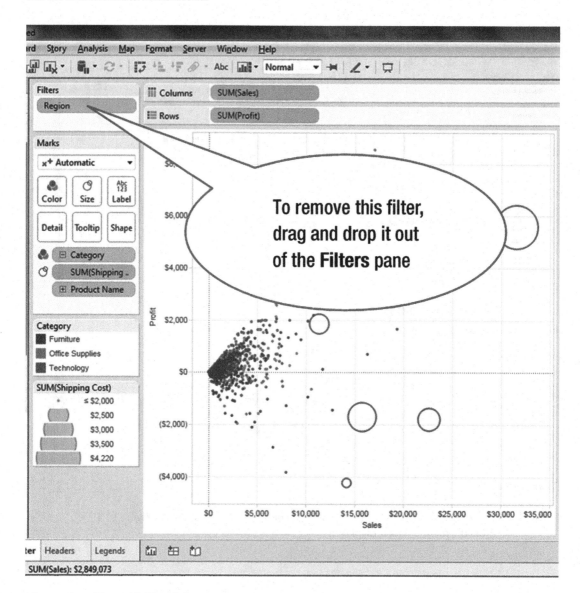

Figure 19-4. *View with filtered data*

To remove a filter:

- Drag and drop the filter out of the **Filters** shelf, as shown in Figure 19-4

The following steps can also be used to remove a filter:

- Click the pull-down arrow for the **Region** filter, as shown in Figure 19-5, which pops up the menu tree displayed in Figure 19-5

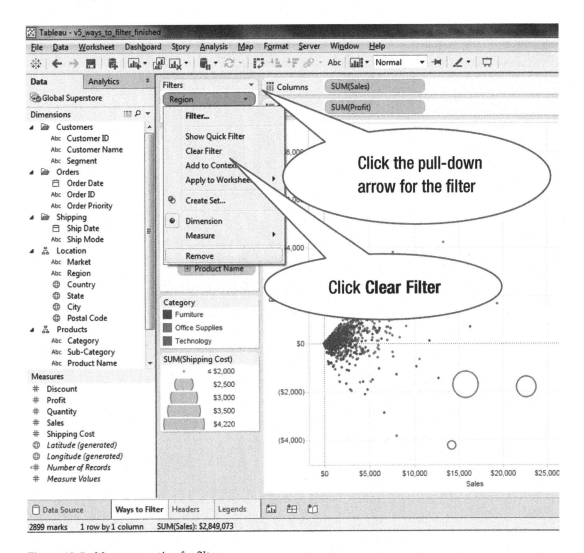

Figure 19-5. *Menu tree option for filters*

- Click **Clear Filter**, as shown in Figure 19-5, which removes the filter

CHAPTER 20

■ ■ ■

Quick Filters

Objective: This exercise demonstrates how a Quick Filter is created, used, and removed

Figure 20-1 displays a view based on Category, Region, and Sales.

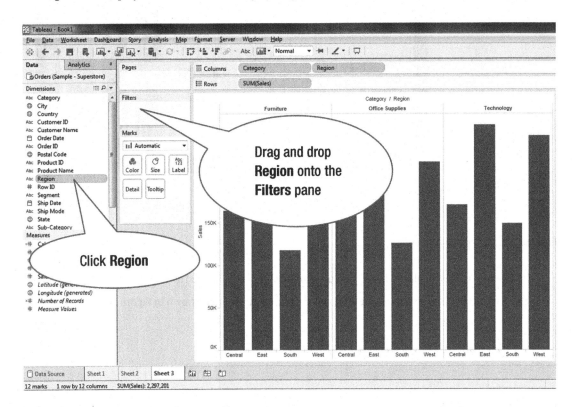

Figure 20-1. *Visualization without any filter*

Quick Filters enable users to focus on smaller datasets so that they can perform analysis from different perspectives. The following steps show how a Quick Filter is added.

- Click **Region**, as shown in Figure 20-1

- Drag and drop **Region** onto the **Filter** shelf, as shown in Figure 20-1, which pops up the **Filter (Region)** window displayed in Figure 20-2

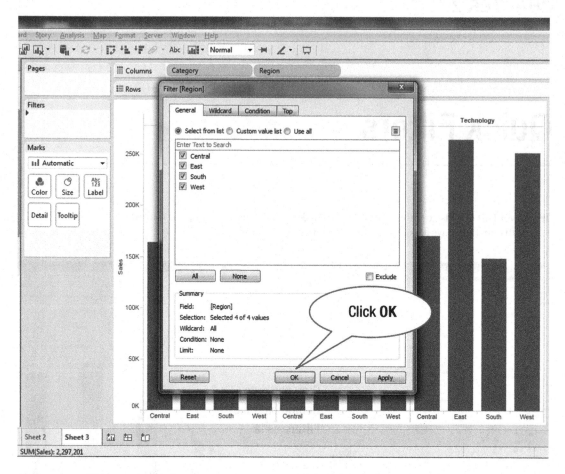

Figure 20-2. *Filter pop-up window*

If the default values displayed in the pop-up window are to be accepted as-is:

- Click **OK**, as shown in Figure 20-2, which leads to the display shown in Figure 20-3

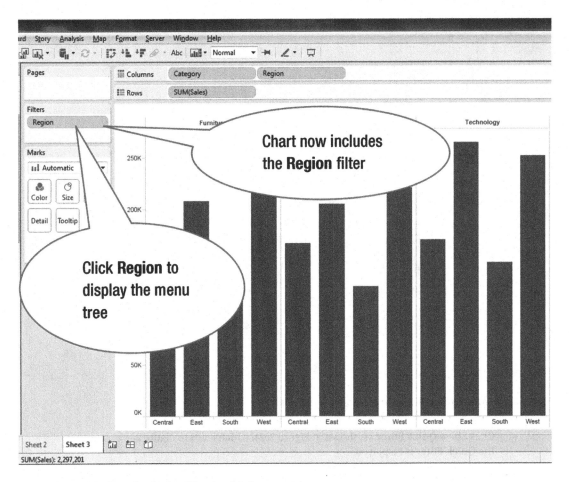

Figure 20-3. *Display after Region filter is added*

The Quick Filter is not displayed in Figure 20-3. To display it so that it is available for easy access:

- Click **Region** in the **Filter** shelf, as shown in Figure 20-3, which leads to the menu tree displayed in Figure 20-4

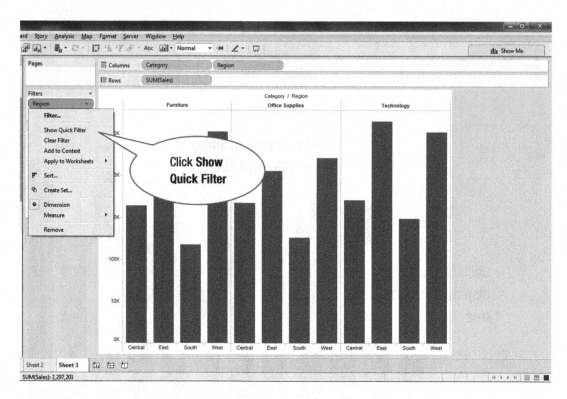

Figure 20-4. *Menu tree with option to display Quick Filter*

- Click **Show Quick Filter**, as shown in Figure 20-4, which leads to Figure 20-5, where the **Quick Filter** is displayed

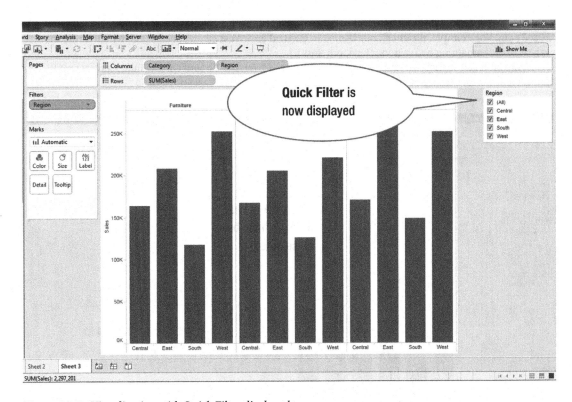

Figure 20-5. *Visualization with Quick Filter displayed*

Items in the Quick Filter can be selected or deselected by adding or removing a check mark next to the desired item. For example, the check marks next to **Central** and **West** can be deselected, which limits the analysis to the remaining two regions (**East** and **South**).

Figure 20-6 shows that two items have been deselected from the **Region** Quick Filter: Central and West. Hence, the displayed results are limited to the remaining two regions: East and South.

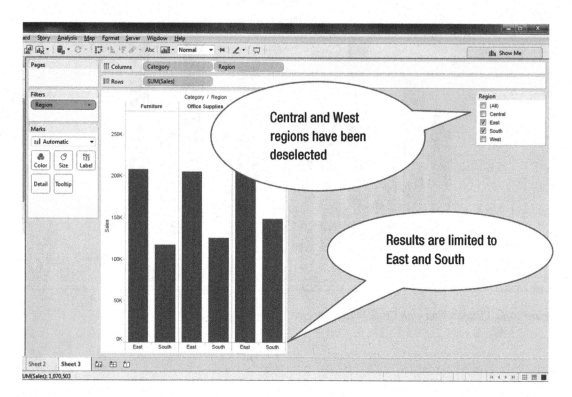

Figure 20-6. *Deselecting two regions*

A Quick Filter can be added for any dimension contained in the Data window. We will now add a Quick Filter for **Category** to the visualization displayed in Figure 20-7.

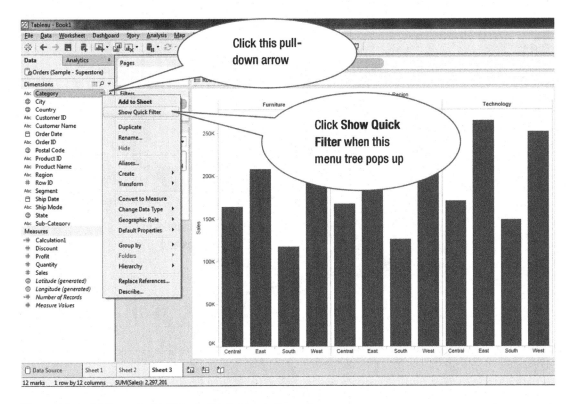

Figure 20-7. *Adding a Quick Filter to the Category dimension*

- Click the pull-down arrow next to **Category** in the **Data** window, as shown in Figure 20-7, which pops up the menu tree (**Add to Sheet)**

- Click **Show Quick Filter**, as shown in Figure 20-7, which leads to Figure 20-8, where the **Category** Quick Filter has been added

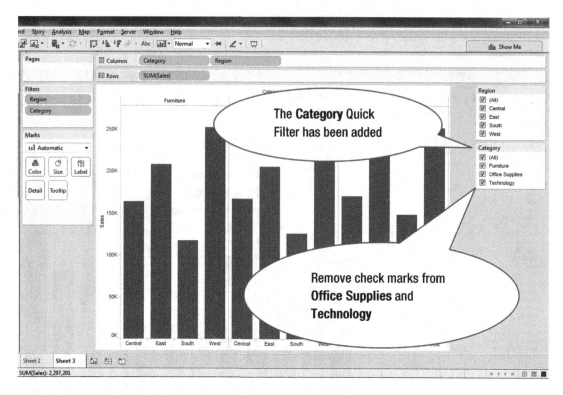

Figure 20-8. *The Category Quick Filter has been added*

Suppose that we want to display the results only for the **Furniture** category (i.e., filter out the data for **Office Supplies** and **Technology**):

- Deselect **Office Supplies** and **Technology** by removing their associated check marks from the **Category** Quick Filter, as shown in Figure 20-8, which leads to the visualization displayed in Figure 20-9

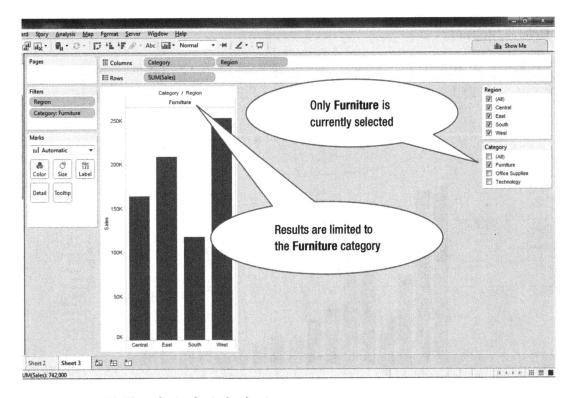

Figure 20-9. *Quick Filter selection limited to furniture*

Quick Filters can be removed when they are not needed. Figure 20-10 shows two Quick Filters in place: **Market** and **Region**.

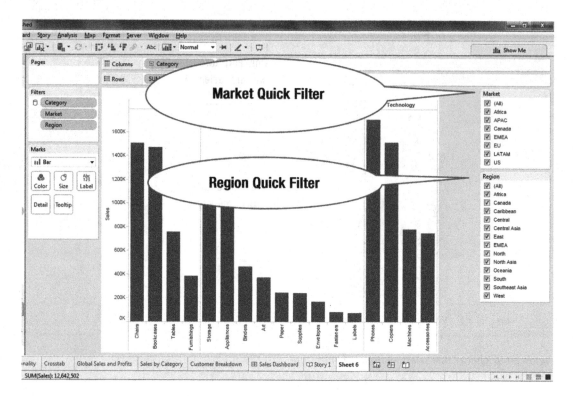

Figure 20-10. *View with two Quick Filters*

To remove the **Region** Quick Filter:

- Place cursor within the **Region** Quick Filter box, which causes a pull-down arrow to be displayed, as shown in Figure 20-11

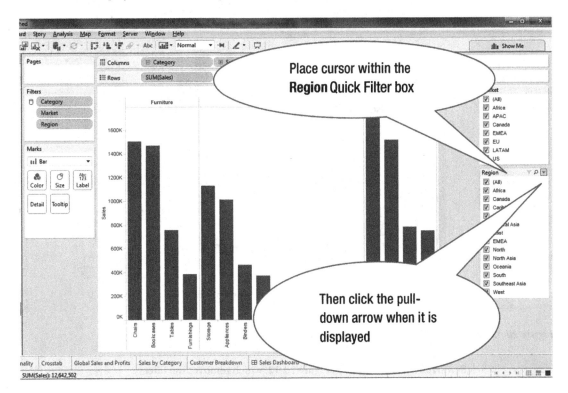

Figure 20-11. *Removing a Quick Filter*

When the pull-down arrow is displayed in the Quick Filter box:

- Click the **pull-down arrow**, as shown in Figure 20-11, which pops up the menu tree displayed in Figure 20-12

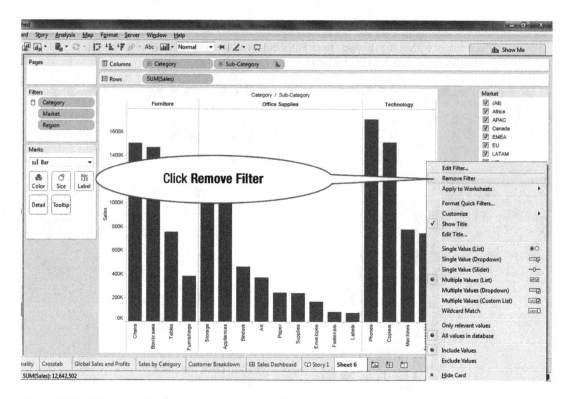

Figure 20-12. *Menu tree displaying option to remove filter*

- Click **Remove Filter**, as shown in Figure 20-12, which removes the filter

CHAPTER 21

■■■

Customization for Quick Filters

Objective: This exercise demonstrates Quick Filter customization

Figure 21-1 displays a visualization with the **Sub-Category** Quick Filter, which can be customized using options that can be accessed via its menu tree.

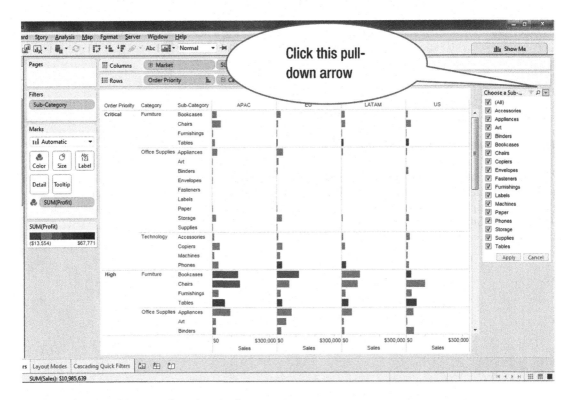

Figure 21-1. Visualization to be customized

- Click the **Quick Filter** pull-down arrow, as shown in Figure 21-1, which pops up the menu tree displayed in Figure 21-2

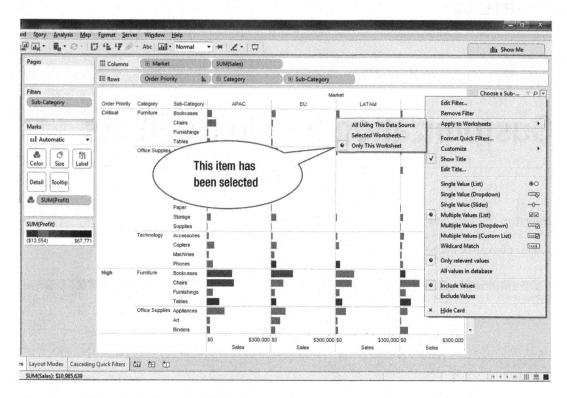

Figure 21-2. *Menu tree displaying Quick Filter options*

The menu highlighted in Figure 21-2 displays three options for applying the Quick Filter. Depending on which sub-menu tree item is selected, the Quick Filter can be applied to the selected worksheet or the currently displayed worksheet. In Figure 21-2, the **Only This Worksheet** menu tree item is selected. Therefore, the Quick Filter only applies to the currently displayed worksheet.

We will now navigate through some of the commonly used items displayed in the Quick Filter menu tree. Figure 21-3 displays various options for the **Customize** menu item:

- Click **Customize**, which pops up the sub-menu tree shown in Figure 21-3, where five out of the seven displayed items are currently check marked, and hence, selected

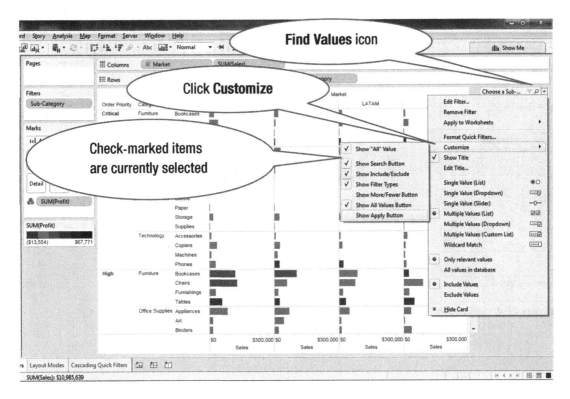

Figure 21-3. *Customize options*

Each of these sub-menu tree items enables useful functionality. For example, if a list is very long, the search box can be used to narrow the search.

To access the search box:

- Click the **Find Values** icon, as shown in Figure 21-3, which opens a small box, displayed in Figure 21-4, where the name to be searched can be typed

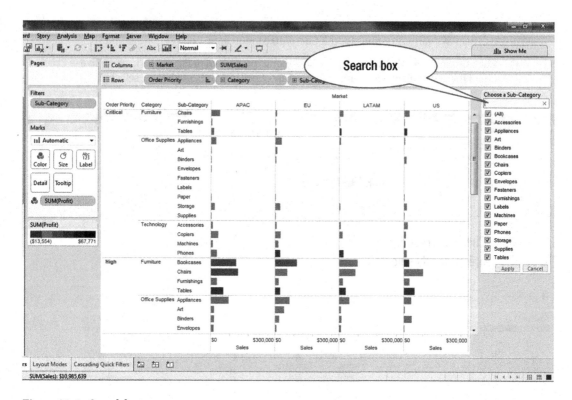

Figure 21-4. *Search box*

In Figure 21-5, the seventh item in the **Customize** sub-menu tree, **Show Apply Button**, is unchecked. This item is used to display or hide the **Apply** button.

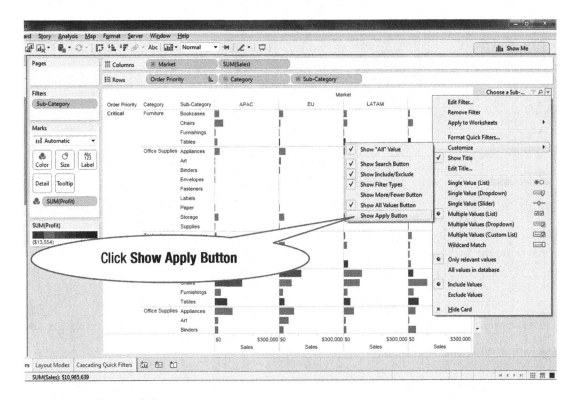

Figure 21-5. *Show Apply Button*

To display the **Apply** button:

- Click **Show Apply Button**, as shown in Figure 21-5, which leads to the display shown in Figure 21-6

Figure 21-6. *View with Apply button*

The Quick Filter title can be edited to make the title more meaningful or to provide a prompt to the users.

To edit the Quick Filter title:

- Click the Quick Filter's pull-down arrow, as shown in Figure 21-7, which pops up the menu tree

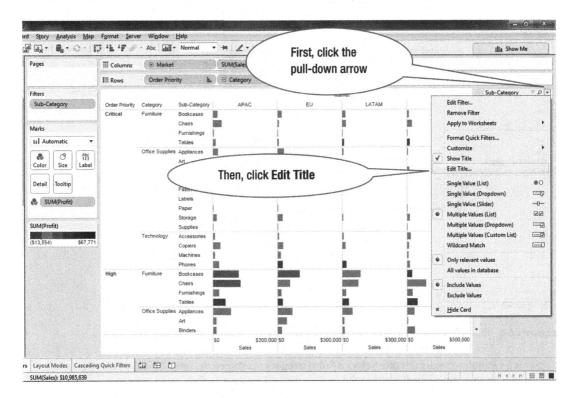

Figure 21-7. *Editing the Quick Filter title*

- Click **Edit Title**, as shown in Figure 21-7, which pops up the **Edit Quick Filter Title** window displayed in Figure 21-8

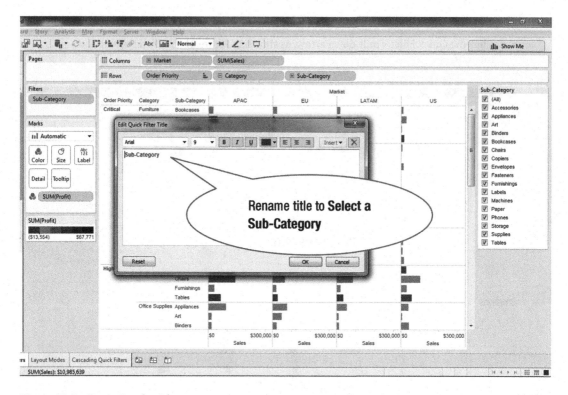

Figure 21-8. *Renaming the title*

- Rename the default title **Select a Sub-Category**, as shown in Figure 21-8, by entering the new title, which leads to the display shown in Figure 21-9

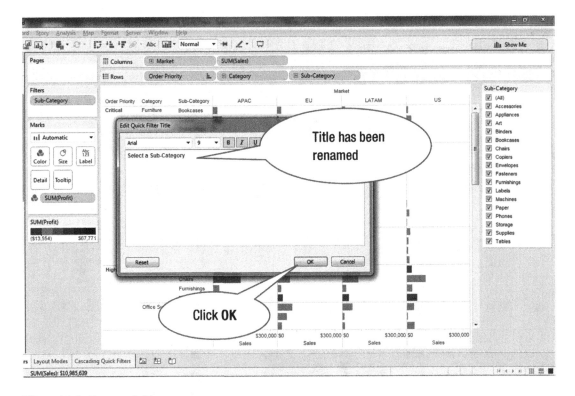

Figure 21-9. *Renamed title*

- Click **OK** after the title has been renamed, as shown in Figure 21-9, which leads to the display shown in Figure 21-10

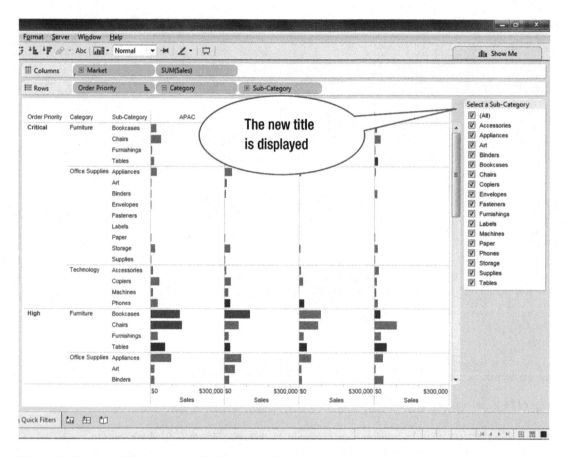

Figure 21-10. *Quick Filter prompt with title renamed*

Renaming the filter title provides the **Select a Sub-Category** prompt to the users, as shown in Figure 21-10, which makes the visualization more user-friendly.

CHAPTER 22

■ ■ ■

Quick Filters Single and Multiple Value Lists

Objective: This exercise demonstrates how single and multiple value lists can be used in Quick Filters

Tableau provides many categorical filter options—single or multiple—for displaying the values in a Quick Filter. These are displayed in Figure 22-1.

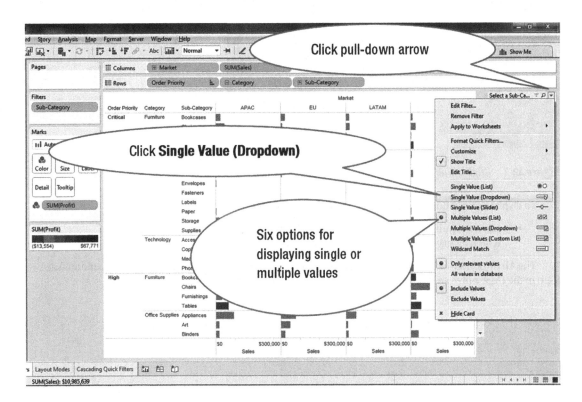

Figure 22-1. *Quick Filter options menu tree*

- Click the pull-down arrow for **Select a Sub-Category**, as shown in Figure 22-1, which pops up the menu tree displayed in Figure 22-1

© Arshad Khan 2016

A. Khan, *Jumpstart Tableau*, DOI 10.1007/978-1-4842-1934-8_22

To provide the Single Value (Dropdown):

- Click the **Single Value (Dropdown)** menu tree item, as shown in Figure 22-1, which leads to the display shown in Figure 22-2

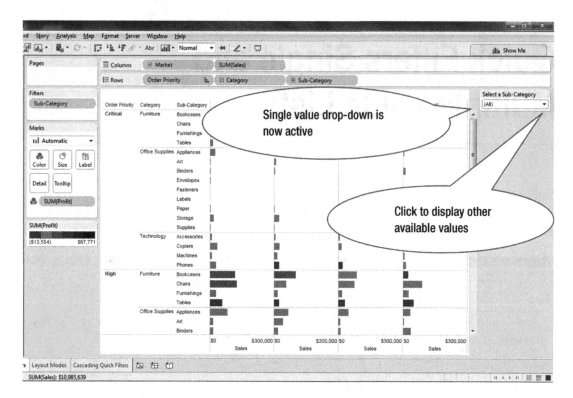

Figure 22-2. *Single value drop-down*

To display other values, besides **All** (which is currently displayed):

- Click the pull-down arrow under **Select a Sub-Category**, as shown in Figure 22-2, which displays other possible values, as shown in Figure 22-3

The **All** option shown in Figure 22-2 can be removed by unchecking the **Show "All" Value** menu tree item in the **Customize** secondary menu (which is displayed in Figure 21-3).

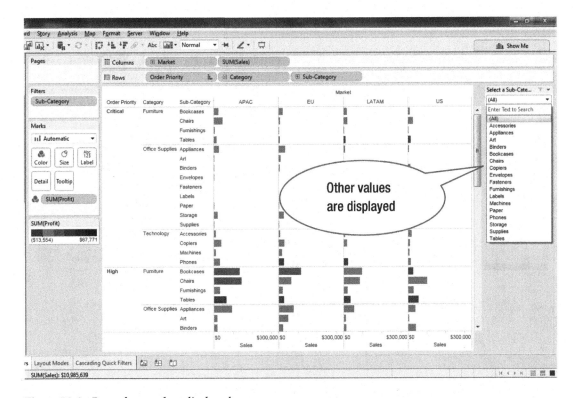

Figure 22-3. Drop-down values displayed

The next step demonstrates how to select the **Single Value (List)**, commonly known as *radio buttons.*

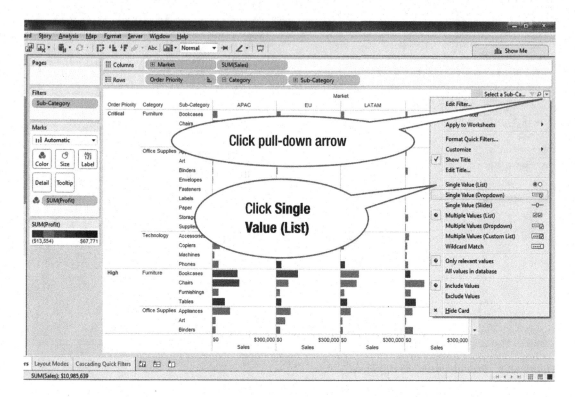

Figure 22-4. *Selecting Single value (List)*

- Click the pull-down arrow for **Select a Sub-Category**, as shown in Figure 22-4, which pops up the menu tree displayed in Figure 22-4

To provide the Single Value (List):

- Click the **Single Value (List)** menu tree item, as shown in Figure 22-4, which leads to the display shown in Figure 22-5

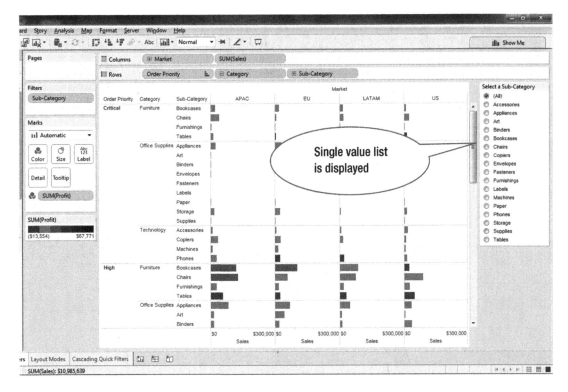

Figure 22-5. *Single Value (List) displayed*

In this case, only a single value can be selected, because the system only allows one radio button to be checked at any time. If multiple selections need to be made, then the **Multiple Values (List)** option can be used, as shown in the next step.

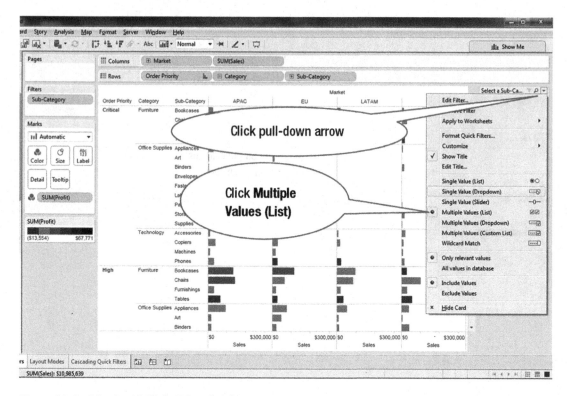

Figure 22-6. *Selecting Multiple Values (List)*

- Click the pull-down arrow for **Select a Sub-Category**, as shown in Figure 22-6, which pops up the menu tree displayed in Figure 22-6

To provide the Multiple Values (List):

- Click the **Multiple Values (List)** menu tree item, as shown in Figure 22-6, which leads to the display shown in Figure 22-7

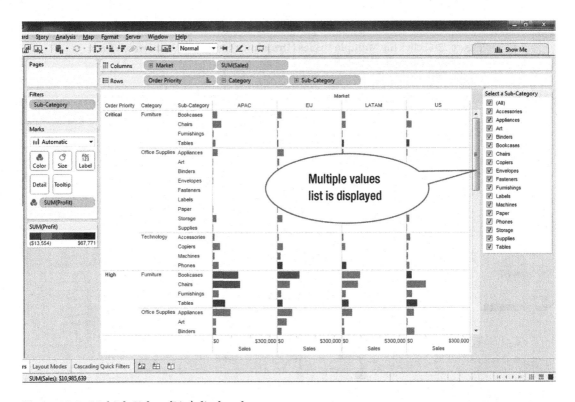

Figure 22-7. *Multiple Values (List) displayed*

If multiple values need to be selected using a drop-down:

- In Figure 22-6, click the **Multiple Values (Dropdown)** menu tree item, which leads to the display shown in Figure 22-8

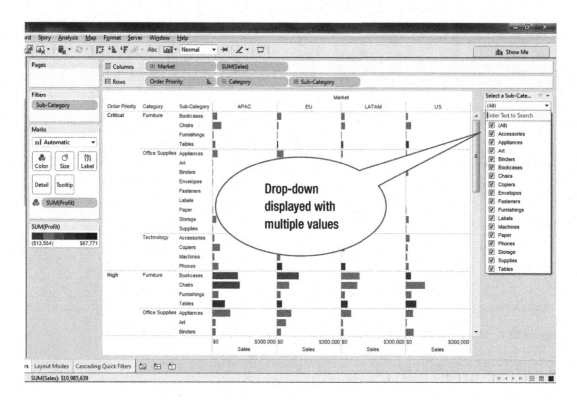

Figure 22-8. *Drop-down with multiple values*

Figure 22-8 displays a drop-down with multiple items. Using check marks, individual items can selected or deselected.

CHAPTER 23

■ ■ ■

Quick Filter Sliders

Objective: This exercise demonstrates how sliders are set up and used

A slider is quite useful when working on filtering quantitative data, since this type of filtering generally involves a range that needs to be specified dynamically.

To set up a Single Value slider:

- Click the **Quick Filter** pull-down arrow, as shown in Figure 23-1, which pops up the menu tree displayed in Figure 23-1

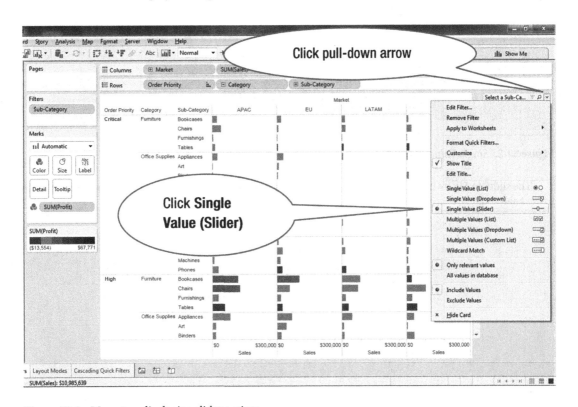

Figure 23-1. *Menu tree displaying slider options*

- Click the **Single Value (Slider)** menu tree item, as shown in Figure 23-1, which leads to the display shown in Figure 23-2

© Arshad Khan 2016

A. Khan, *Jumpstart Tableau*, DOI 10.1007/978-1-4842-1934-8_23

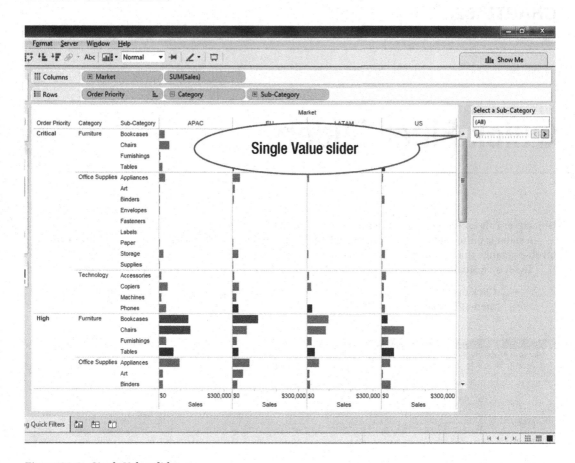

Figure 23-2. *Single Value slider*

The slider in Figure 23-2 can be moved to the left or right, as needed, to dynamically change the range being analyzed.

A Multiple Value slider contains two sliders that can dynamically specify the low and high range values. To set up a Multiple Value slider:

- Populate the Rows and Columns, as shown in Figure 23-3

Figure 23-3. *View needing a Multiple Value slider*

- Drag and drop the **Shipping Cost** measure onto the **Filters** pane, as shown in Figure 23-3, which causes the **Filter Field (Shipping Cost)** window to pop up, as displayed in Figure 23-4

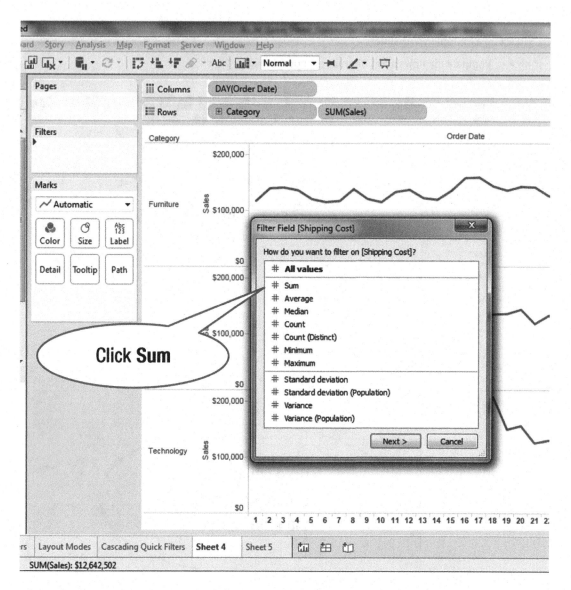

Figure 23-4. *Filter field pop-up menu*

- Click **Sum**, as shown in Figure 23-4, which leads to Figure 23-5, where the **Sum** measure is selected and highlighted

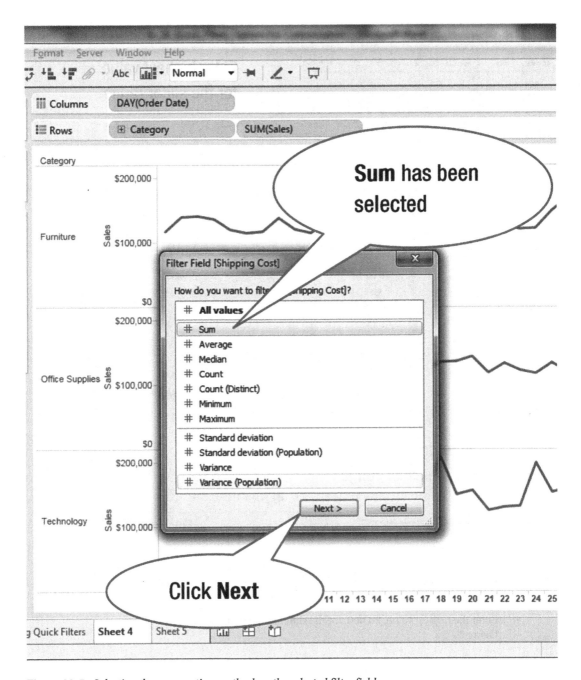

Figure 23-5. *Selecting the aggregation method on the selected filter field*

- Click **Next**, as shown in Figure 23-5, which pops up the **Filter (Shipping Cost)** window displayed in Figure 23-6

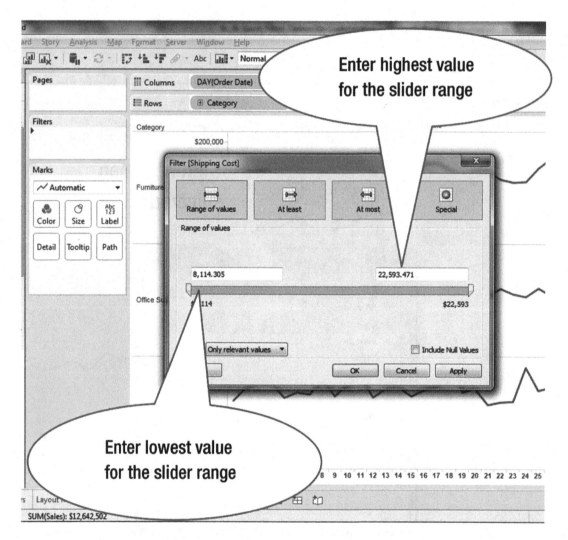

Figure 23-6. *Entering values for slider range*

- Enter the lowest value, **12,000**, for the slider range in the field highlighted in Figure 23-6

- Enter the highest value, **20,000**, for the slider range in the field highlighted in Figure 23-6

Figure 23-7 shows that the lowest and the highest values have been entered.

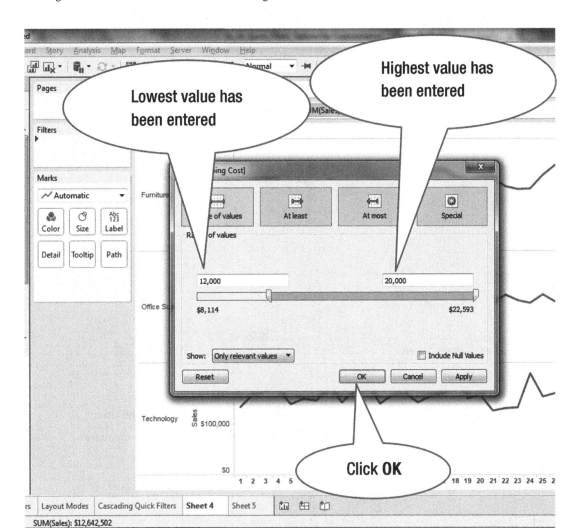

Figure 23-7. *Values specified for slider range*

- Click **OK**, as shown in Figure 23-7, which leads to the display shown in Figure 23-8

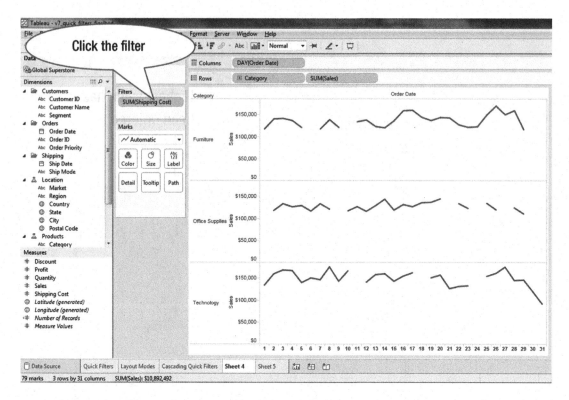

Figure 23-8. *View with active shipping cost filter*

The Quick Filter slider is not currently displayed, although it is active. To display the filter:

- Click **SUM** in the **Filters** pane, as shown in Figure 23-8, which pops up the menu tree displayed in Figure 23-9

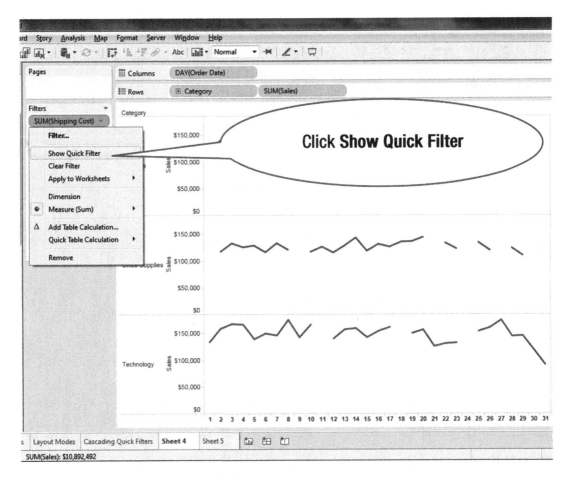

Figure 23-9. *Menu tree with Show Quick Filter option*

- Click **Show Quick Filter**, as shown in Figure 23-9, which leads to Figure 23-10, where the slider is displayed

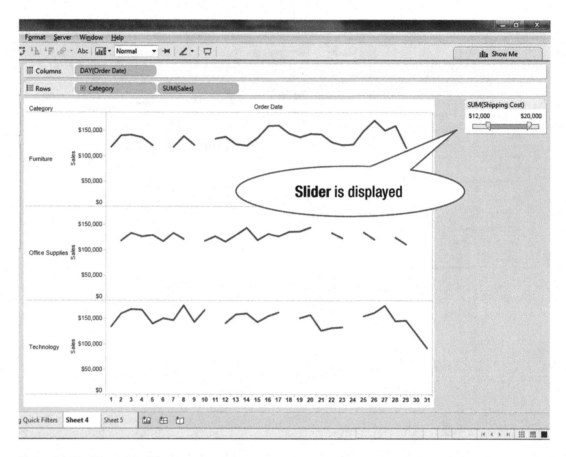

Figure 23-10. *View with slider*

There are three options available in a slider, which are displayed in Figure 23-6:

- **At Least**: Includes all values that are greater than or equal to a specified value

- **At Most**: Includes all values that are less than or equal to a specified value

- **Special**: Allows you to specify whether only null values, non-null values, or all values are to be included

CHAPTER 24

Dependency in Quick Filters

Objective: This exercise demonstrates how two filters can be made dependent, which is also known as cascading filters

If there are two Quick Filters on a worksheet, the items displayed in the second filter can be made dependent on the item selected in the first filter. The filters can be set up so that, for example, if Africa is selected as the **Region** in the first filter, only the countries in Africa will be displayed in the **Countries** Quick Filter—instead of every country in every region.

Figure 24-1 displays a visualization based on **Sales** by **Region**.

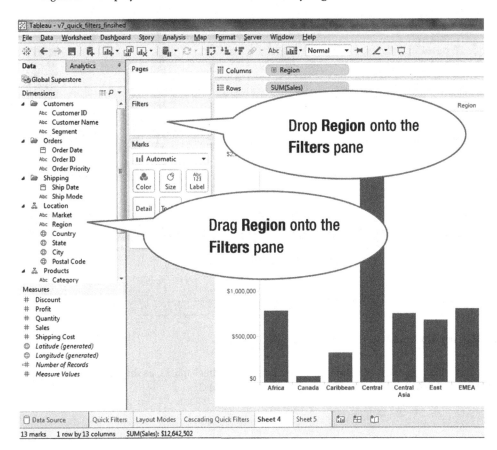

Figure 24-1. *Visualization where two filters will be added*

- Drag and drop **Region** onto the **Filters** pane, as shown in Figure 24-1, which pops up the window displayed in Figure 24-2

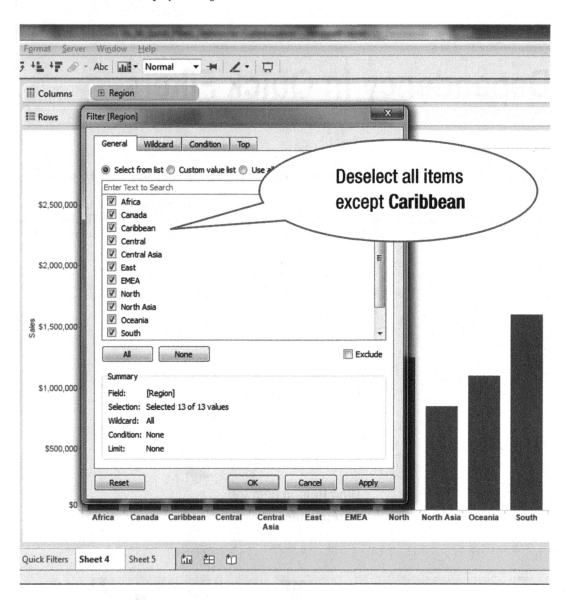

Figure 24-2. *Filter pop-up window*

- Deselect all items except **Caribbean** by removing their check marks, as shown in Figure 24-2, which leads to the display shown in Figure 24-3

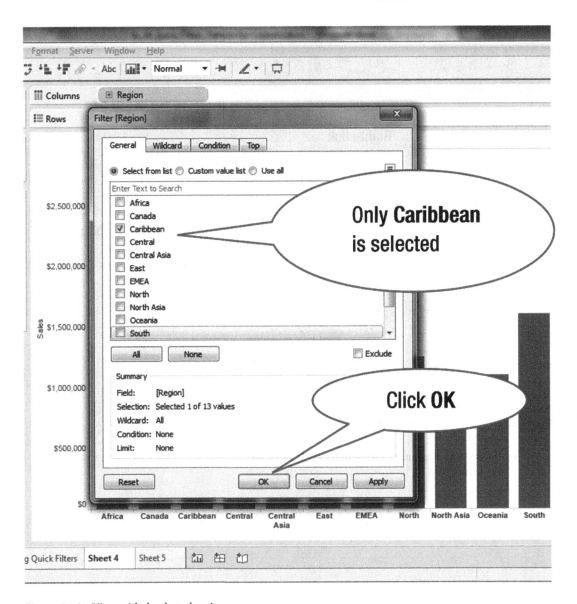

Figure 24-3. *View with deselected regions*

- Click **OK**, as shown in Figure 24-3, which leads to Figure 24-4, where the results displayed are limited to the Caribbean region

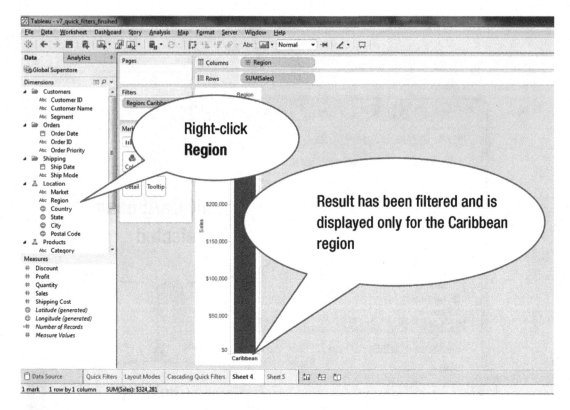

Figure 24-4. *View with single region (Caribbean)*

- Right-click **Region**, as shown in Figure 24-4, which pops up the menu tree displayed in Figure 24-5

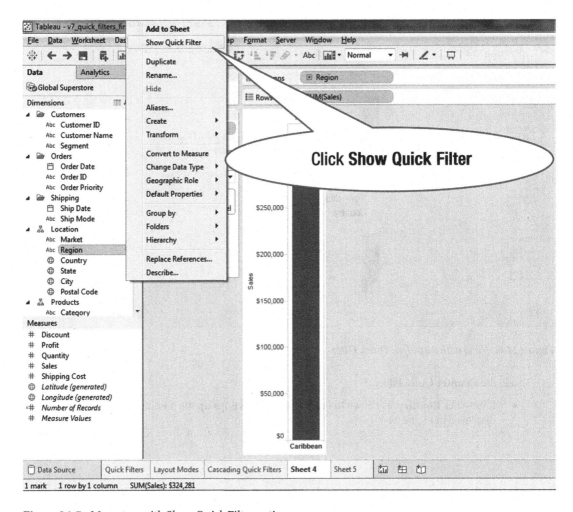

Figure 24-5. *Menu tree with Show Quick Filter option*

- Click **Show Quick Filter**, as shown in Figure 24-5, which leads to the **Region** Quick
  Filter being displayed, as shown in Figure 24-6

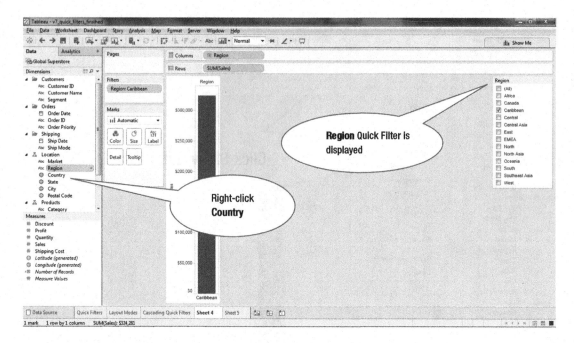

Figure 24-6. *View with displayed Quick Filter*

To add the **Country** Quick Filter:

- Right-click **Country**, as shown in Figure 24-6, which pops up the menu tree displayed in Figure 24-7

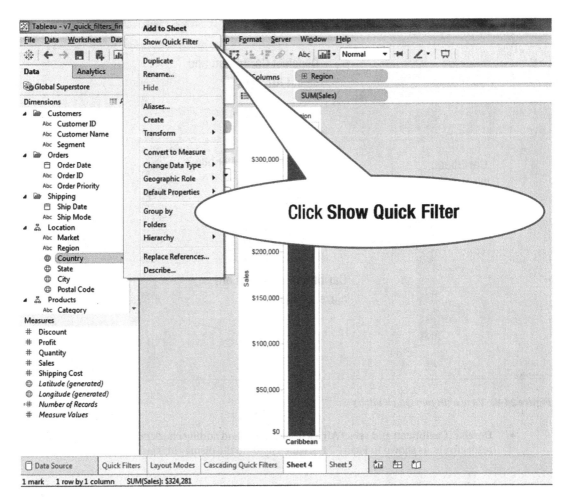

Figure 24-7. Menu tree with Show Quick Filter option

- Click **Show Quick Filter**, as shown in Figure 24-7, which leads to Figure 24-8, where the **Country** Quick Filter has been added to the visualization

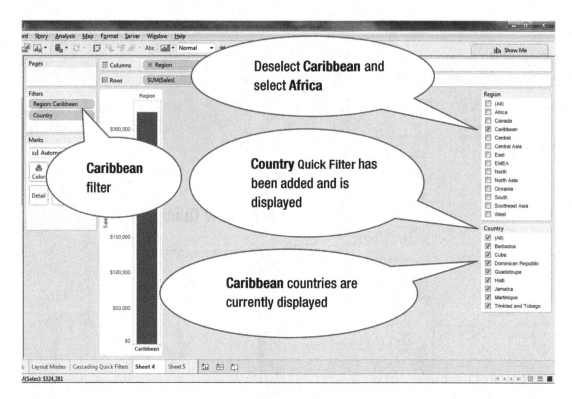

Figure 24-8. *View with two Quick Filters*

- Deselect **Caribbean** and select **Africa** by removing and adding check marks, respectively, as shown in Figure 24-8, which leads to the display in Figure 24-9

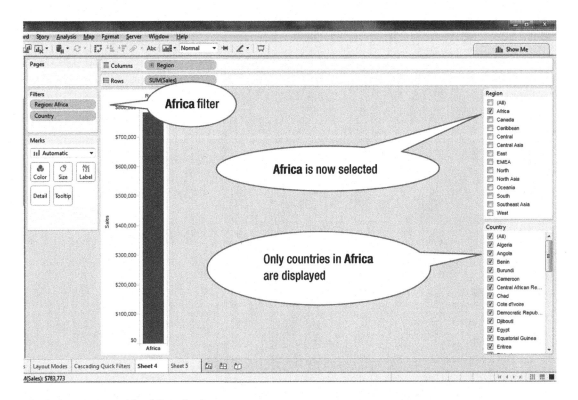

Figure 24-9. *View with Africa selection*

In Figure 24-9, only African countries are being displayed in the second filter (**Country**) because Africa has been selected in the first filter (**Region**), which determines the items to be displayed in the second filter.

CHAPTER 25

■■■

Saving in PDF Format

Objective: This exercise demonstrates how to save a visualization in PDF format
Figure 25-1 shows a chart that needs to be saved in a PDF format.

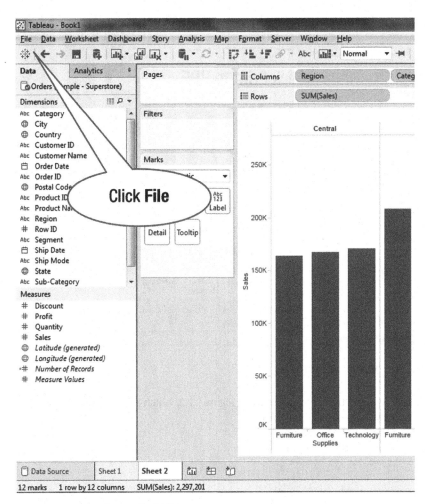

Figure 25-1. *View to be saved in PDF format*

- Click **File** on the **menu bar**, as shown in Figure 25-1, which leads to the menu tree displayed in Figure 25-2

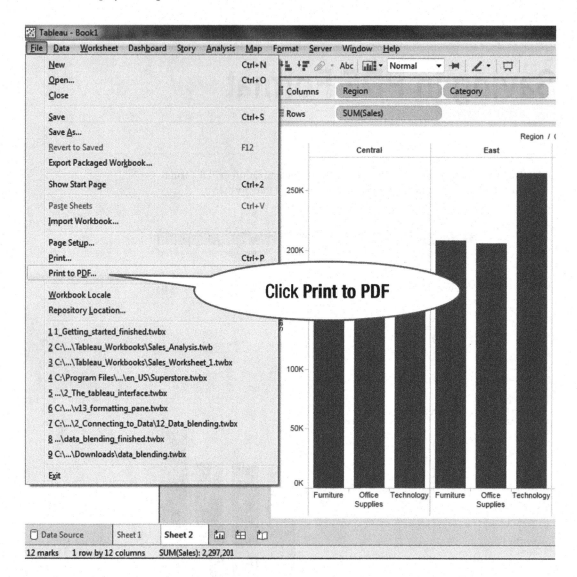

Figure 25-2. *Menu tree with option to save in PDF format*

- Click the **Print to PDF** menu tree item, as shown in Figure 25-2, which pops up the **Print to PDF** window displayed in Figure 25-3

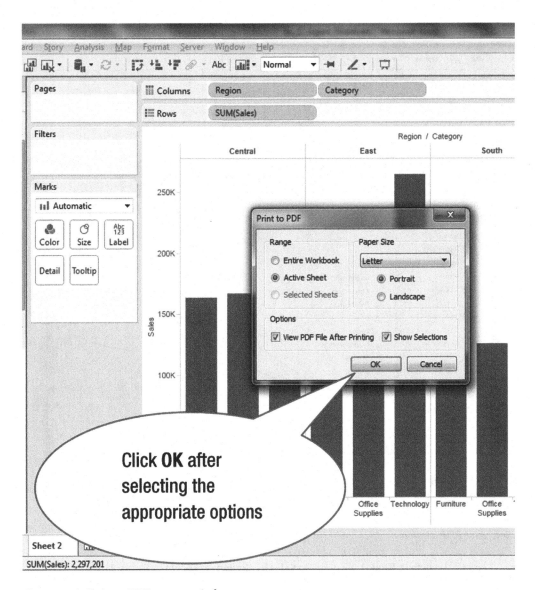

Figure 25-3. *Print to PDF pop-up window*

- Click the **Landscape** radio button, if needed

A drop-down to select the **Paper Size** is also available, as shown in Figure 25-3. If the **View PDF File After Printing** check box is selected, as shown in Figure 25-3, it automatically opens the PDF after it is saved. If the **Show Selections** check box is selected, it retains any selections made on the view when the PDF is saved.

After the desired selections have been made in Figure 25-3:

- Click **OK**, as shown in Figure 25-3, which pops up the **Save PDF** window displayed in Figure 25-4

Figure 25-4. *Save PDF window*

- Rename the default **Book 1** file name to **Sales by Region**, as shown in Figure 25-5

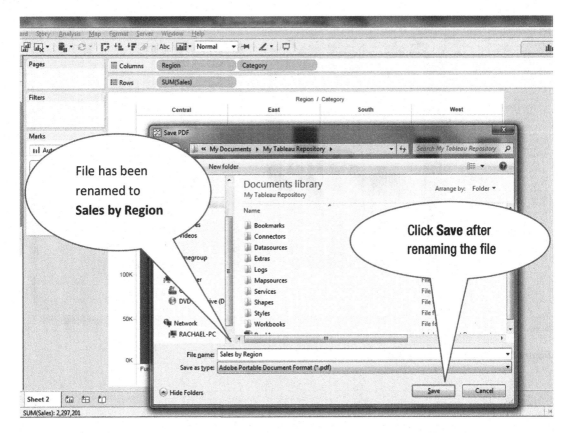

Figure 25-5. *Rename file*

- Click **Save**, as shown in Figure 25-5, which leads to the Figure 25-6 display (which contains the PDF display in a separate window)

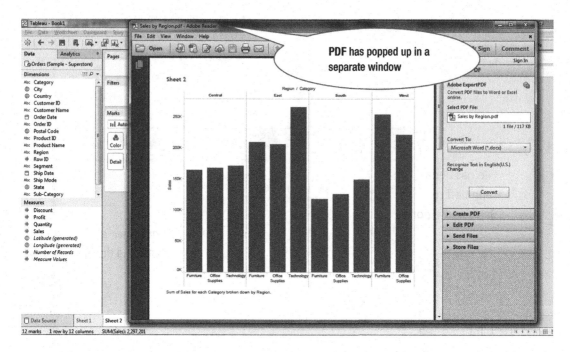

Figure 25-6. *View displaying PDF*

CHAPTER 26

■ ■ ■

Exporting an Image to PowerPoint

Objective: This exercise demonstrates how to copy and export a displayed image
Figure 26-1 shows the visualization that needs to be exported as an image.

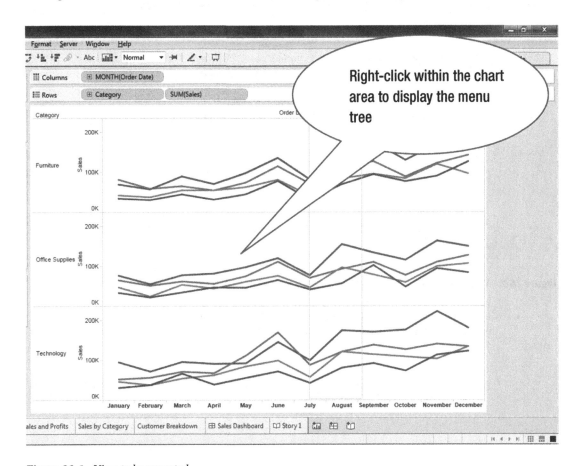

Figure 26-1. *View to be exported*

- Right-click within the chart, as shown in Figure 26-1, which pops up the menu tree displayed in Figure 26-2

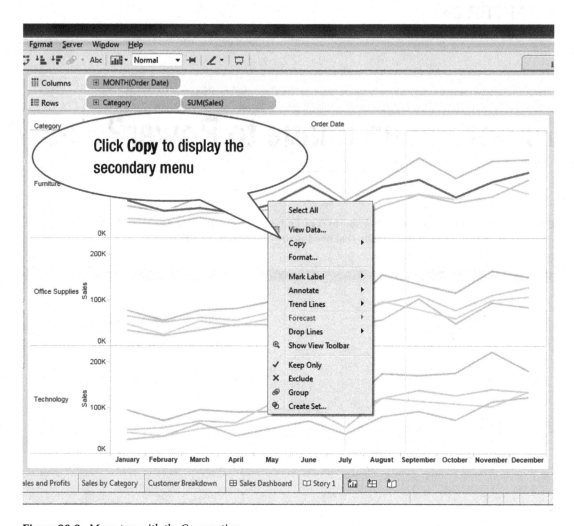

Figure 26-2. *Menu tree with the Copy option*

- Click **Copy**, as shown in Figure 26-2, which leads to the secondary menu tree displayed in Figure 26-3

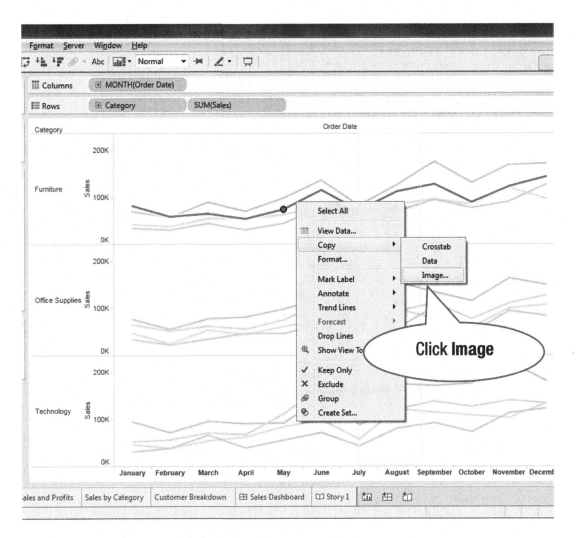

Figure 26-3. *Secondary menu with the Image option*

- Click **Image**, as shown in Figure 26-3, which pops up the **Copy Image** window
  displayed in Figure 26-4

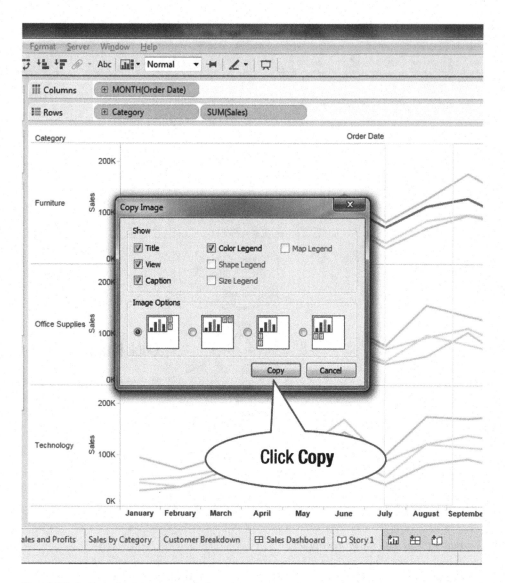

Figure 26-4. *Copy Image pop-up window*

The **Copy Image** pop-up window provides the ability to choose what needs to be copied from the view, such as title and legend, by simply checking or unchecking the selections. It also permits you to specify where the legends should appear.

After making the appropriate selection:

- Click **Copy**, as shown in Figure 26-4, which captures the displayed image

The displayed image can now be exported to another application. To export the image into PowerPoint:

- Launch PowerPoint

- Paste onto the displayed blank PowerPoint slide, as shown in Figure 26-5, where the image is displayed

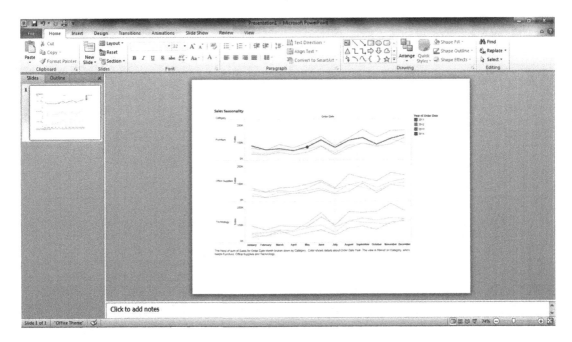

Figure 26-5. *Image displayed in PowerPoint*

CHAPTER 27

■ ■ ■

Exporting Data

Objective: This exercise demonstrates how to display and save the data associated with a displayed visualization

Figure 27-1 shows the visualization whose data needs to be displayed.

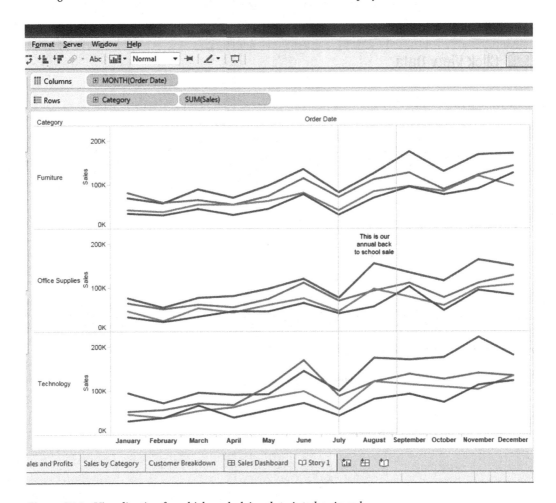

Figure 27-1. *Visualization for which underlying data is to be viewed*

© Arshad Khan 2016

A. Khan, *Jumpstart Tableau*, DOI 10.1007/978-1-4842-1934-8_27

- Right-click within the chart area, which pops up the menu tree displayed in Figure 27-2

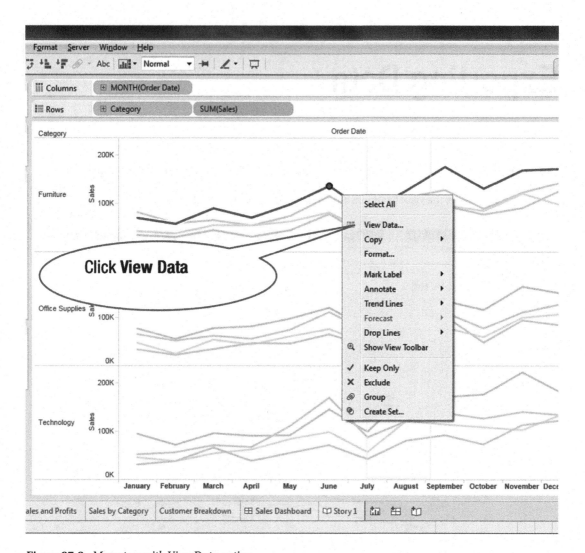

Figure 27-2. *Menu tree with View Data option*

- Click **View Data**, as shown in Figure 27-2, which pops up the **View Data** window displayed in Figure 27-3

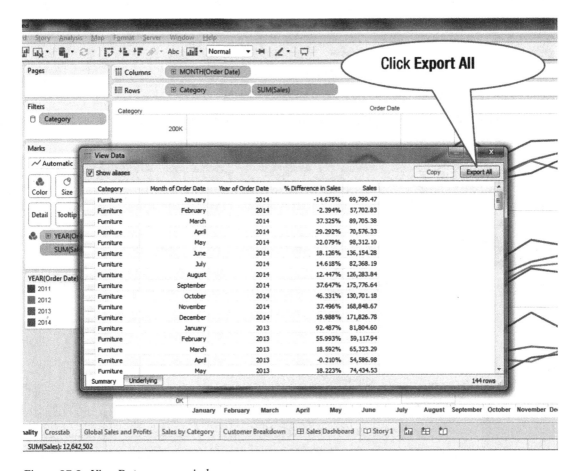

Figure 27-3. *View Data pop-up window*

The **View Data** pop-up window displays the underlying data, which can be analyzed, exported, or saved.

To save the data:

- Click the **Export All** button, as shown in Figure 27-3, which leads to the **Export Data** pop-up window displayed in Figure 27-4

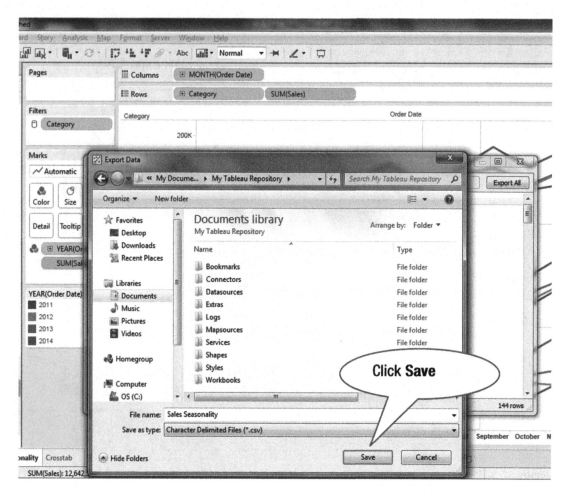

Figure 27-4. *Export Data pop-up window*

In the **Export Data** window, the default folder for saving data is displayed (**My Tableau Repository**). If needed, the folder in which to save the file can be changed.

- Click **Save**, as shown in Figure 27-4, which saves the data

To export data using the Crosstab function:

- Right-click the chart, which pops up the menu tree displayed in Figure 27-5

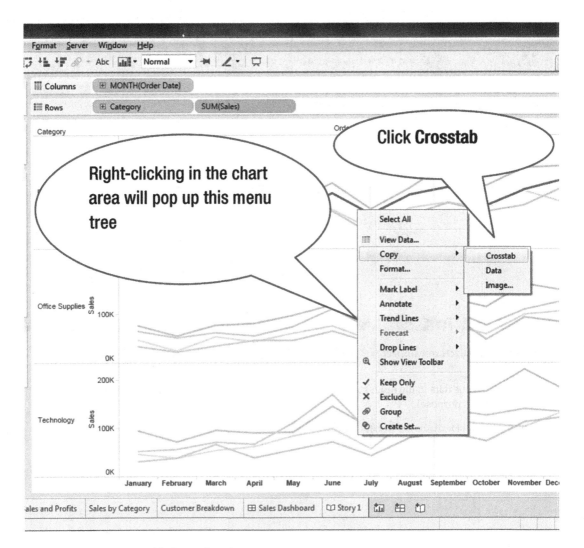

Figure 27-5. *Menu tree with Crosstab option*

- Navigate to the secondary menu tree, as shown in Figure 27-5 (**Copy ➤ Crosstab**)
- Click **Crosstab**, which captures the date for export

The captured data can now be copied onto an Excel spreadsheet. To copy this data:

- Open a new Excel worksheet (see Figure 27-6)

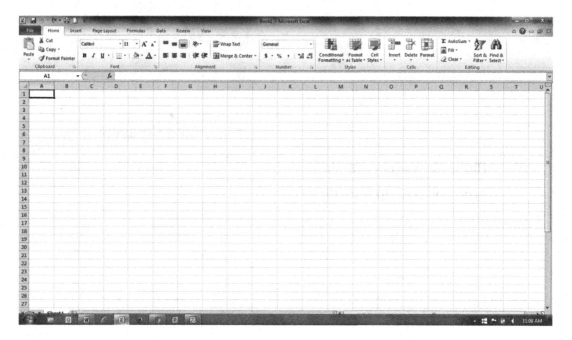

Figure 27-6. *New Excel spreadsheet*

- Paste the data in the open spreadsheet (you can use the Windows **Ctrl+V** function for this purpose)

The pasted data is displayed in Figure 27-7.

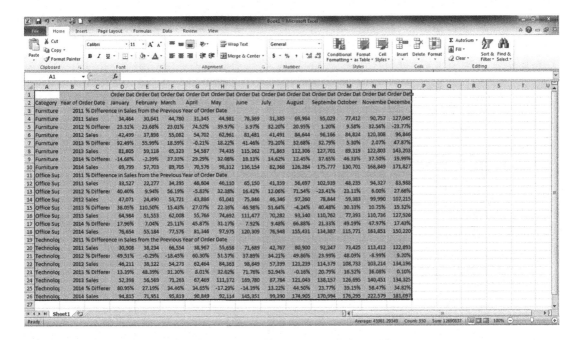

Figure 27-7. *Crosstab data displayed in spreadsheet*

■ ■ ■

CHAPTER 28

Displaying Underlying Data

Objective: This exercise demonstrates how to display and export the detailed underlying data behind a visualization

Figure 28-1 shows a chart with the sum of sales by region by category.

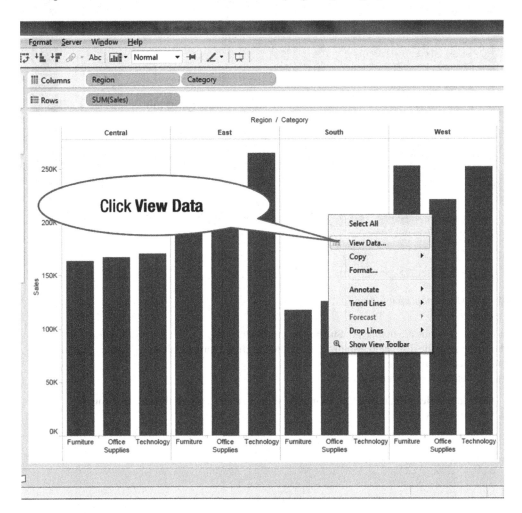

Figure 28-1. *Visualization for displaying underlying data*

© Arshad Khan 2016

A. Khan, *Jumpstart Tableau*, DOI 10.1007/978-1-4842-1934-8_28

- Right-click in the chart area, which pops up the menu tree displayed in Figure 28-1

- Click **View Data**, as shown in Figure 28-1, which pops up the **View Data** window displayed in Figure 28-2

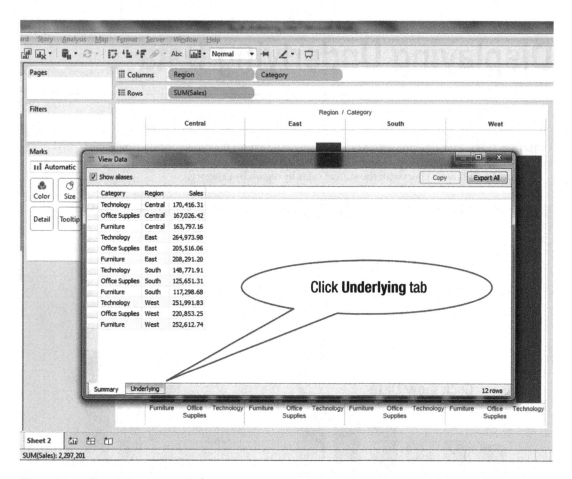

Figure 28-2. *View Data pop-up window*

In Figure 28-2, two tabs are displayed: **Summary** and **Underlying.** The Summary tab shows the aggregated numbers for the displayed visualization, while the Underlying tab displays the raw/underlying data for those aggregated numbers.

To view the detailed underlying data:

- Click the **Underlying** tab, as shown in Figure 28-2, which leads to the display shown in Figure 28-3

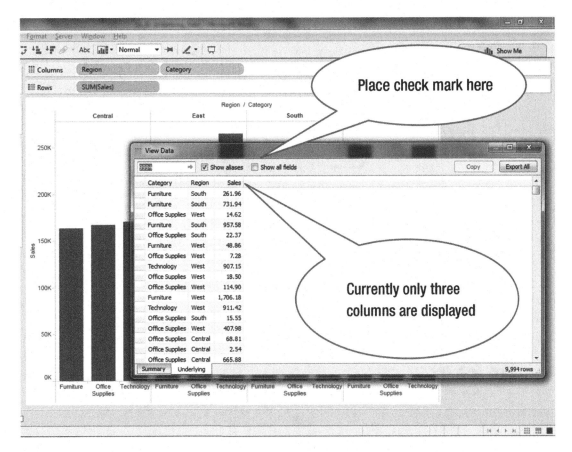

Figure 28-3. Data displayed in View Data window

- Place a check mark in the **Show all fields** field, as shown in Figure 28-3, which causes all fields to be displayed, as shown in Figure 28-4

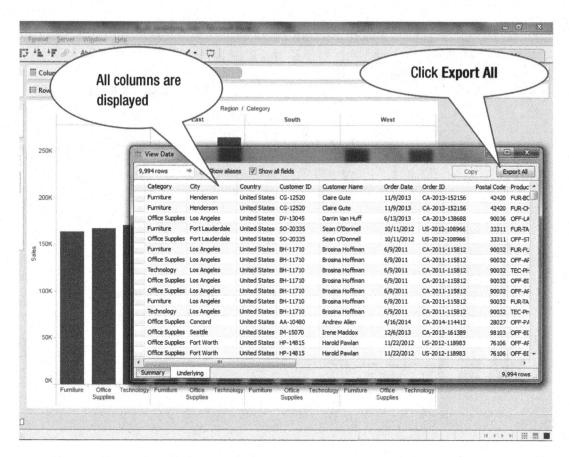

Figure 28-4. *Display with all fields*

To export the displayed data:

- Click **Export All**, as shown in Figure 28-4, which pops up the **Export Data** window displayed in Figure 28-5

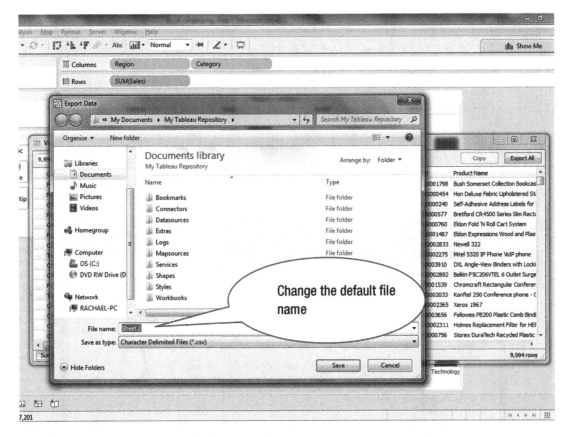

Figure 28-5. *Export Data pop-up window*

To change the default file name provided by the system to **Region_Category_Underlying_Data**:

- Type the new file name, as shown in Figure 28-5, which leads to the display shown in Figure 28-6

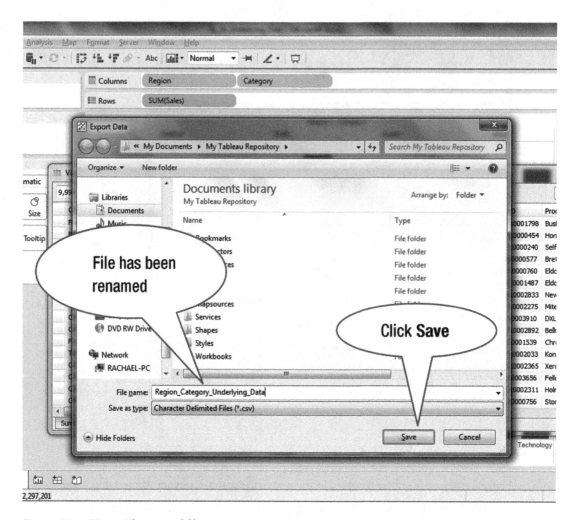

Figure 28-6. *View with renamed file*

- Click **Save**, as shown in Figure 28-6, which saves the file as a .csv file

CHAPTER 29

■ ■ ■

Exporting Crosstab Data

Objective: This exercise demonstrates another method for exporting crosstab data to Excel
Figure 29-1 shows a chart whose data needs to be exported to Excel.

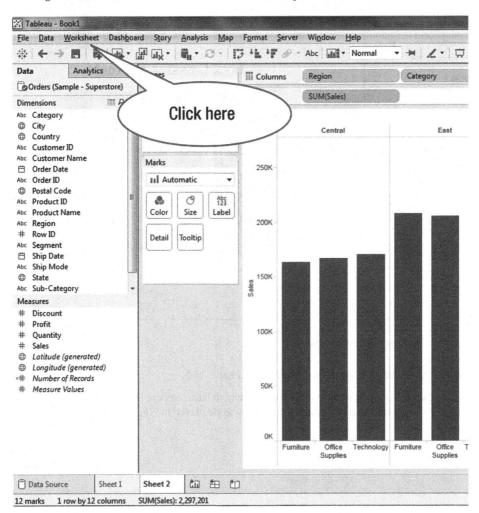

Figure 29-1. *View to be exported*

© Arshad Khan 2016
A. Khan, *Jumpstart Tableau*, DOI 10.1007/978-1-4842-1934-8_29

- Click **Worksheet** on the **menu bar**, as shown in Figure 29-1, which pops up the menu tree displayed in Figure 29-2

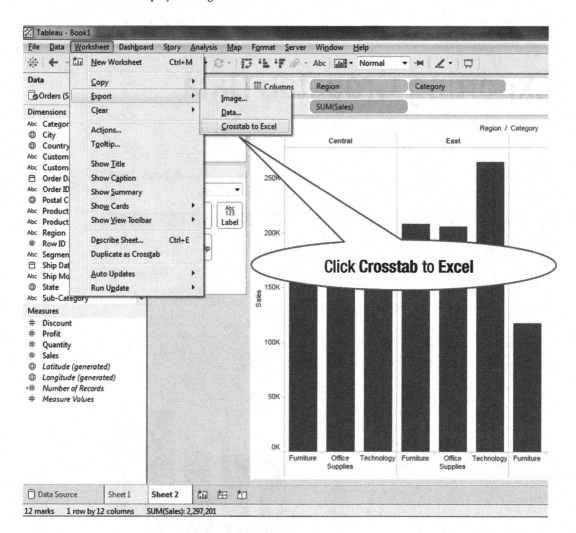

Figure 29-2. *Menu tree displaying option to export*

- Navigate to the secondary menu tree displayed in Figure 29-2

- Click **Crosstab to Excel**, as shown in Figure 29-2, which launches the Excel application and populates it with the relevant data, as displayed in Figure 29-3

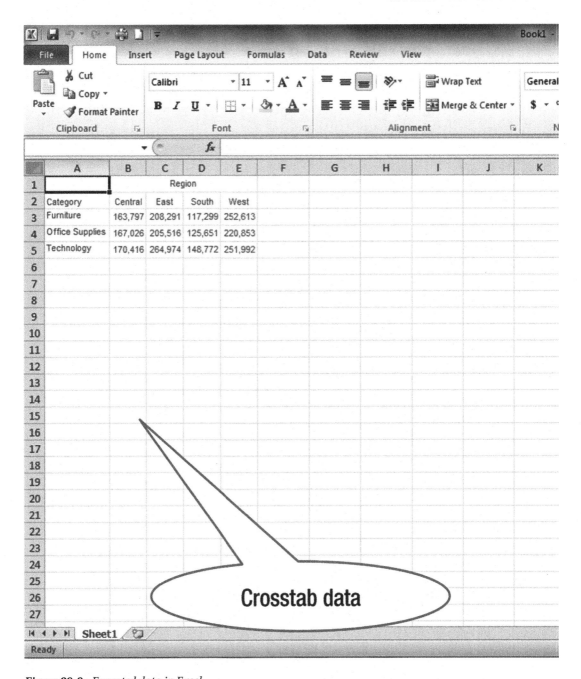

Figure 29-3. *Exported data in Excel*

CHAPTER 30

■ ■ ■

Formatting

Objective: This exercise demonstrates commonly used formatting functions

Figure 30-1 displays a chart used to demonstrate basic formatting functions.

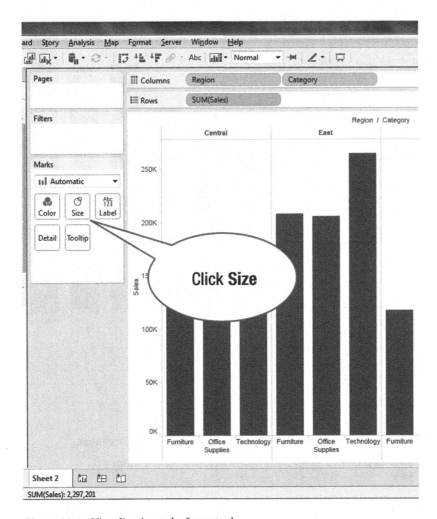

Figure 30-1. *Visualization to be formatted*

© Arshad Khan 2016

A. Khan, *Jumpstart Tableau*, DOI 10.1007/978-1-4842-1934-8_30

To size the width of the bars:

- Click the **Size** icon on the **Marks** card, as shown in Figure 30-1, which leads to Figure 30-2, where a slider is shown

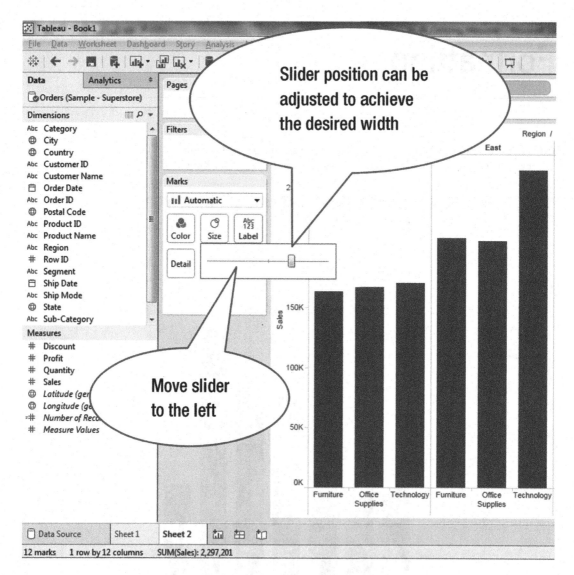

Figure 30-2. *Slider from the Size marks card*

The slider can be used to change the width of the bars simply by adjusting the slider position.

- Move slider to the left, as shown in Figure 30-2, which decreases the bar width, as shown in Figure 30-3

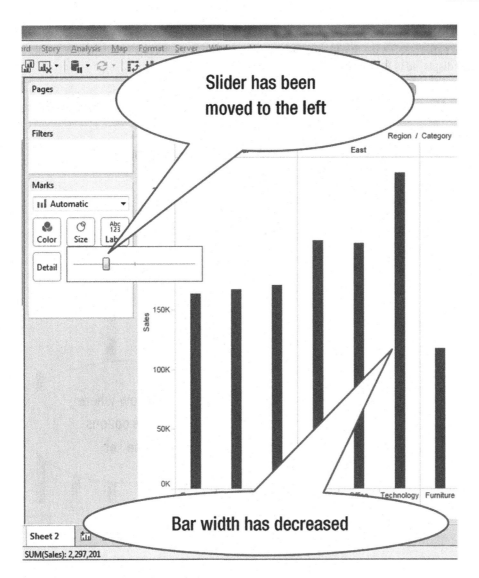

Figure 30-3. *Slider with changed position*

To display the individual values for the bars:

- Click the **Label** icon on the **Marks** card, as shown in Figure 30-4, which pops up the window displayed in Figure 30-4

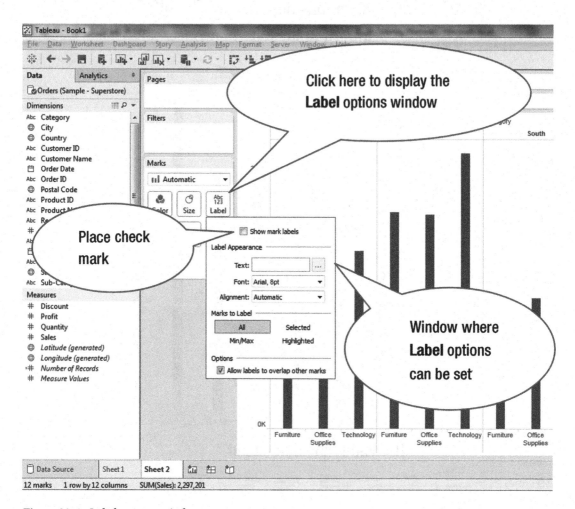

Figure 30-4. *Labels pop-up window*

- Place a check mark in the **Show mark labels** field, as shown in Figure 30-4, which leads to the display shown in Figure 30-5

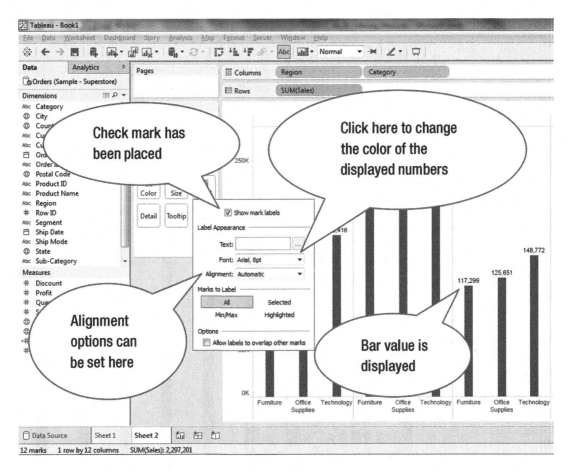

Figure 30-5. *The Show mark labels field is selected*

To change the color of the displayed numbers:

- Click the **Font** pull-down arrow, as shown in Figure 30-5

This pops up another window, which is shown in Figure 30-6, where the font size and color can be selected.

The **Alignment** options can be set from the alignment drop-down, as shown in Figure 30-5. The **Marks to Label** option, shown below the Alignment option in Figure 30-5, enables the user to specify the position of the marks. Using this feature, the user can specify where and when the marks should appear.

- **All**: Shows marks on all the points

- **Selected**: Shows mark label when selected/on click

- **Min/Max**: Shows only the minimum and maximum values

- **Highlighted**: Shows all the values when a particular item is clicked on the color-legend card menu

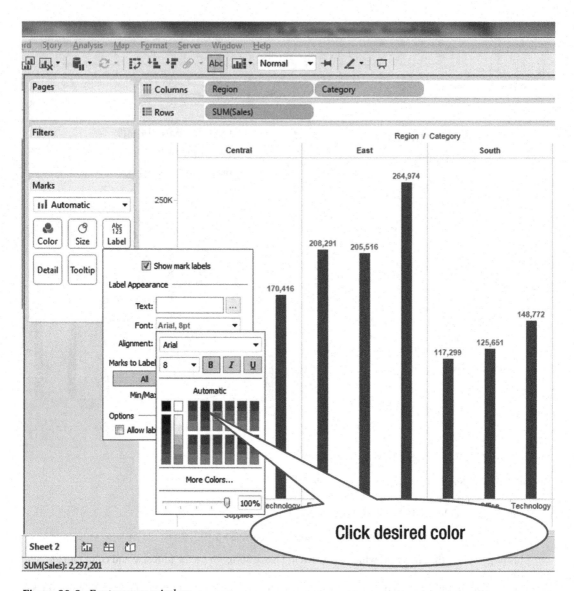

Figure 30-6. *Font pop-up window*

- Click the **Red** color, which changes the color of the displayed numbers to red, as shown in Figure 30-6

To change the color of the bars:

- Click the **Color** icon in the **Marks** card, which pops up the **Color** selection window shown in Figure 30-7

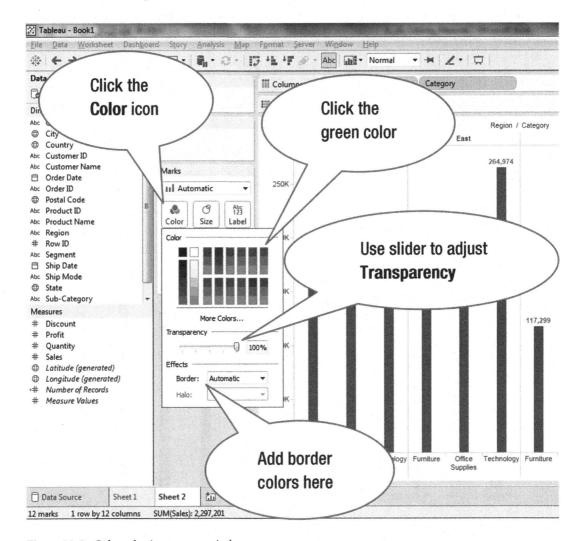

Figure 30-7. *Color selection pop-up window*

- Click the green color in the **Color** pop-up window, as shown in Figure 30-7, which leads to the display in Figure 30-8 (where the bar colors have changed to green)

As shown in Figure 30-7, the transparency of the color can be adjusted by moving the slider to the left. This is useful when you have to view data that is overlapping other marks.

Border colors can also be added to visually distinguish closely spaced marks, as shown in Figure 30-7.

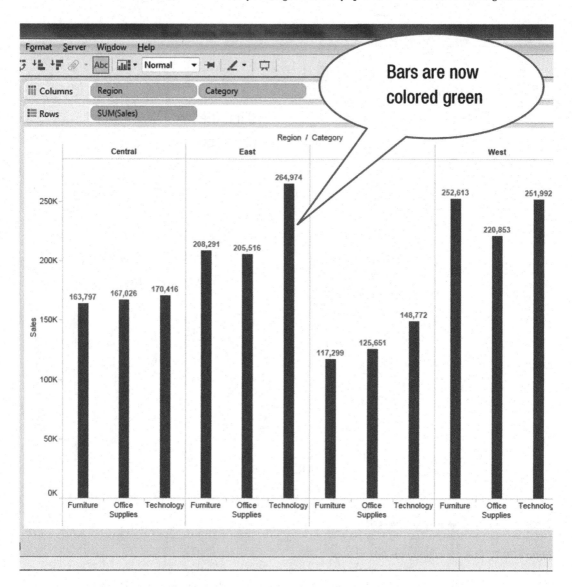

Figure 30-8. *Bars with changed colors*

To access additional formatting functionality:

- Right-click within the chart area, which pops up the menu tree displayed in Figure 30-9

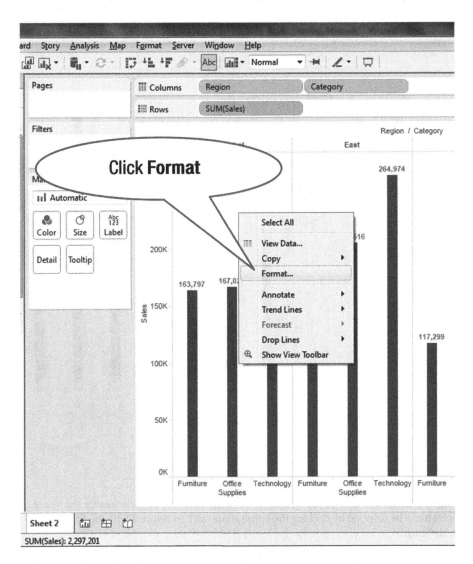

Figure 30-9. *Menu tree displaying Format option*

- Click **Format**, as shown in Figure 30-9, which pops up the **Format Font** window displayed in Figure 30-10

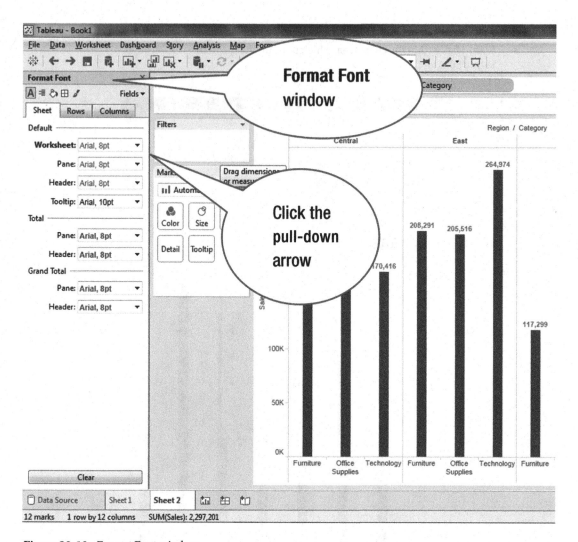

Figure 30-10. *Format Font window*

Various formatting operations can now be performed through the **Format Font** window for the **Sheet**, **Rows**, or **Columns** (which can be selected by clicking the appropriate tab). In Figure 30-10, the **Sheet** tab has been selected (by default).

- Click the **Worksheet** pull-down arrow, as shown in Figure 30-10, which pops up the window displayed in Figure 30-11, where the desired changes can be made

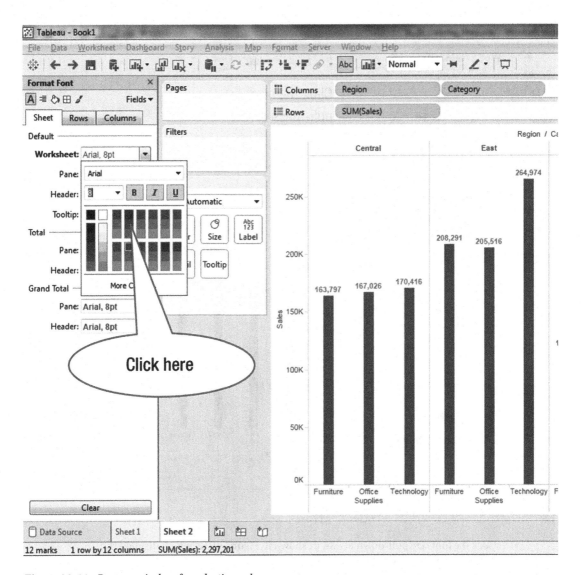

Figure 30-11. *Pop-up window for selecting colors*

- Click the red color, as shown in Figure 30-11, which changes the color of the column and row titles to red, as shown in Figure 30-12

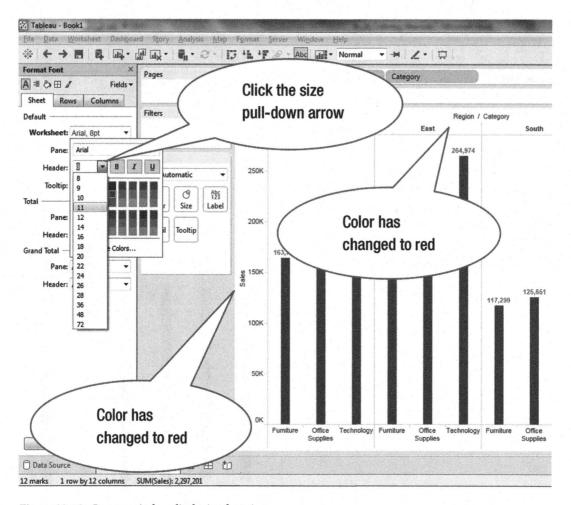

Figure 30-12. *Pop-up window displaying font sizes*

- Click the font size pull-down arrow, as shown in Figure 30-12, which displays the different font sizes shown in Figure 30-12

- Click **11**, as shown in Figure 30-12, which increases the text size to 11 for the row and column headers, as displayed in Figure 30-13

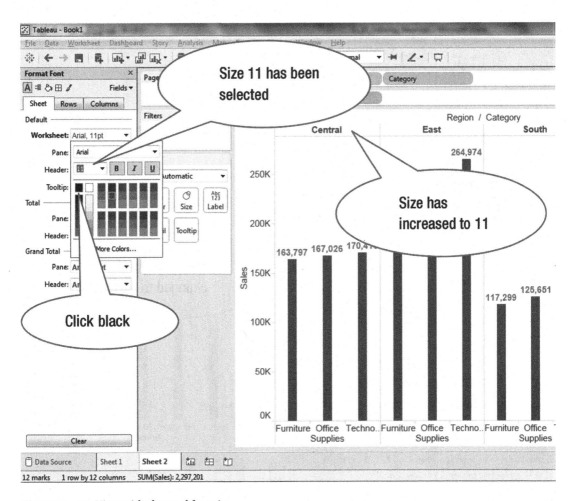

Figure 30-13. *View with changed font size*

To change the color for the column and row headers to black (from green):

- Click the black color in the color selection box, as shown in Figure 30-13, which leads to the display shown in Figure 30-14 (where the headers have changed to black)

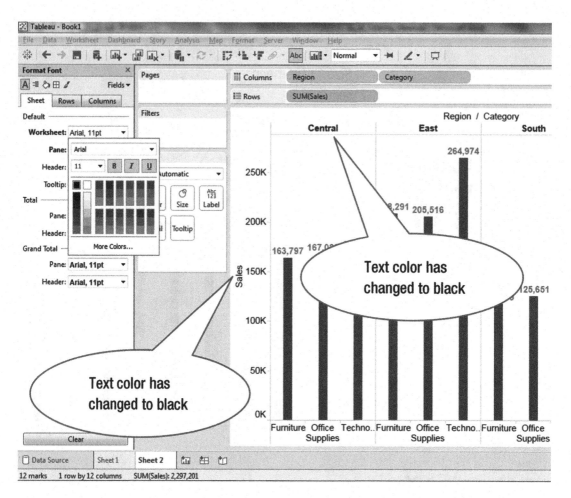

Figure 30-14. *Headers with changed color*

Annotations are text boxes used to highlight a specific mark, point, or the entire area of a view.

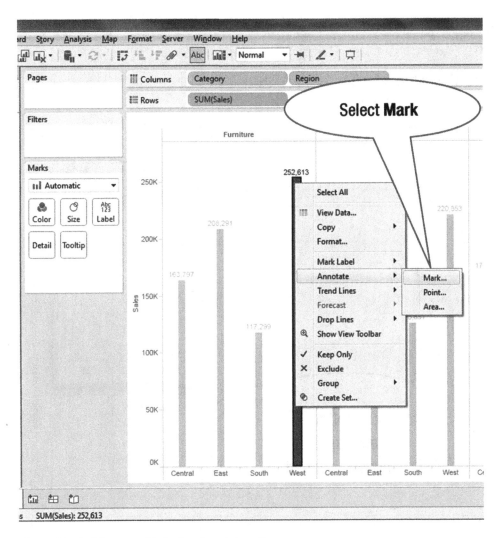

Figure 30-15. *Menu tree displaying Annotate option*

To add an annotation for highlighting a chart:

- Right-click the bar for the **West**, as shown in Figure 30-15, which pops up the menu tree displayed in Figure 30-15

- Navigate to **Annotate ➤ Mark**, as shown in Figure 30-15, which pops up the **Edit Annotation** window displayed in Figure 30-16

Figure 30-16. *Edit Annotation pop-up window*

The default annotation can be accepted as-is or it can be modified by typing in the desired text in the **Edit Annotation** box, as shown in Figure 30-16. In this case, we will not add any custom text.

- Click **OK**, as shown in Figure 30-16, which adds the annotation, as shown in Figure 30-17

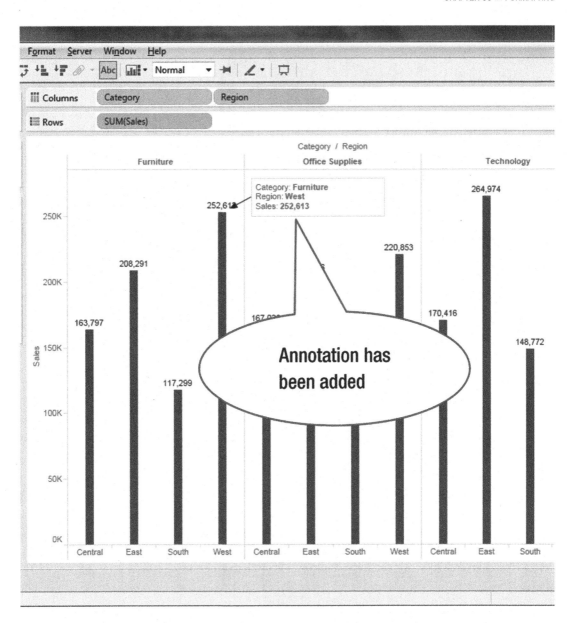

Figure 30-17. *View with annotation*

■ ■ ■

CHAPTER 31

Highlighting with Colors

Objective: This exercise demonstrates how to highlight the data in the visualization using color
We start this exercise with Figure 31-1, which displays crosstab data.

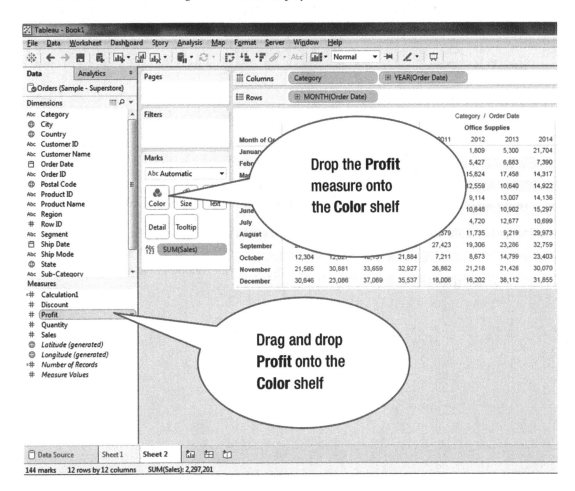

Figure 31-1. *View with crosstab data*

To analyze the profits:

- Drag and drop **Profit** onto the **Color** shelf in the **Marks** card, as shown in Figure 31-1, which leads to the display shown in Figure 31-2

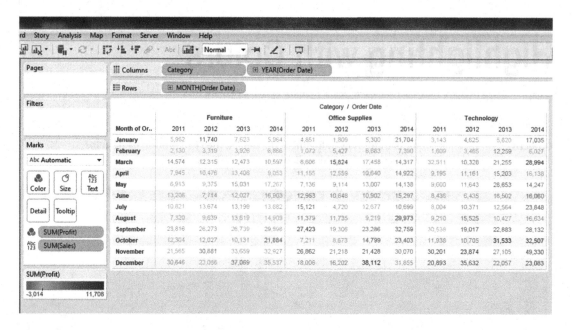

Figure 31-2. *Numbers displayed in color*

When aggregated measures are dropped on the **Color** shelf, a quantitative legend with a continuous range of colors is created.

In Figure 31-2, the red and green colors indicate the relative profitability or loss for the relevant item. The displayed colors are not bright and some enhancement is desired. To enhance the colors:

- Click the **Color** icon in the **Marks** card, which pops up the window displayed in Figure 31-3

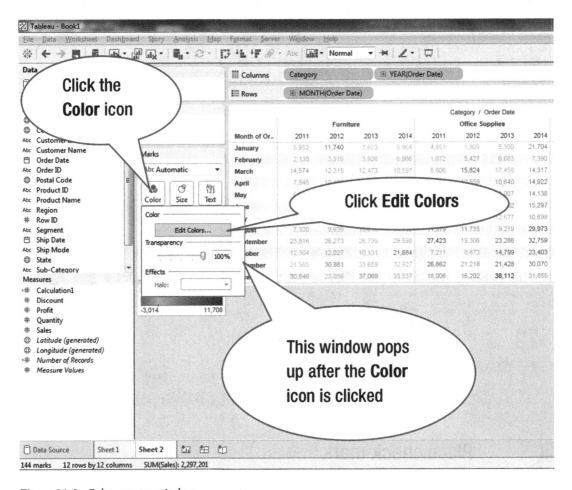

Figure 31-3. *Color pop-up window*

- Click **Edit Colors**, as shown in Figure 31-3, which leads to the display shown in Figure 31-4

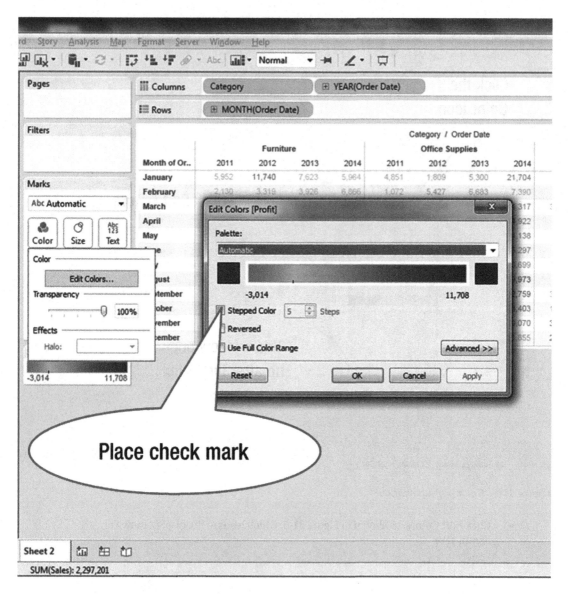

Figure 31-4. *Edit Colors pop-up window*

- Place a check mark in the check box located to the left of **Stepped Color**, as shown in Figure 31-4

- Increase **Steps** from 5 to 6 (which specifies how many steps/bins or buckets are being created)

Figure 31-5 shows the display after the changes have been made.

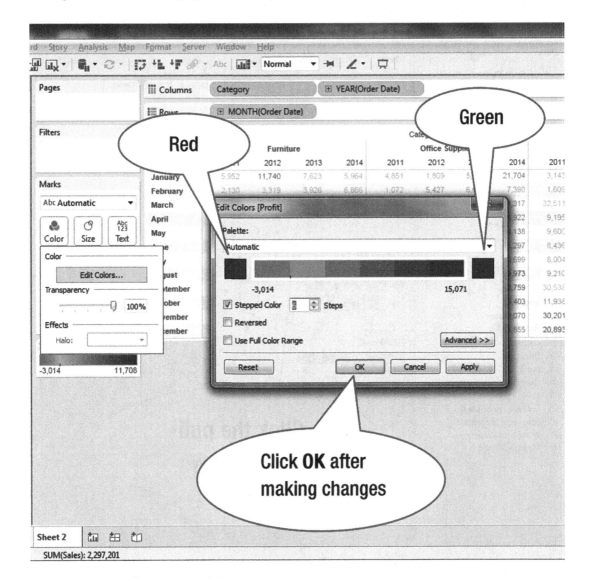

Figure 31-5. *Stepped color modified view*

- Click **OK**, as shown in Figure 31-5, which leads to Figure 31-6, where the changed highlighting is displayed

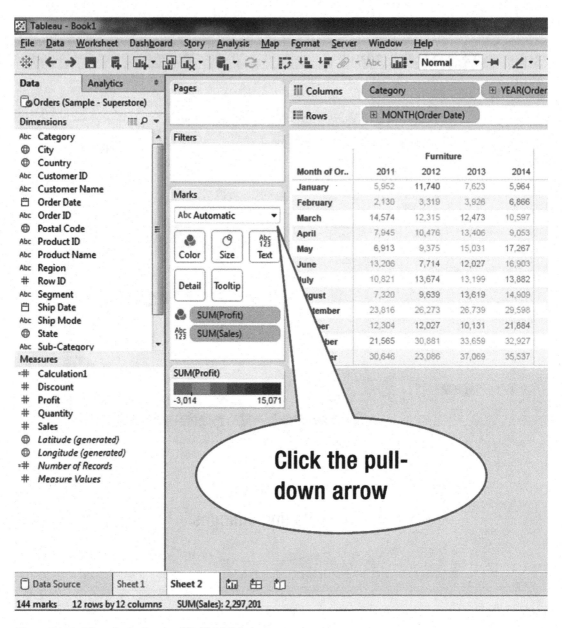

Figure 31-6. *View displaying modified highlighting*

The default red and green colors can be changed by clicking the color selector, as shown in Figure 31-5. These can be reversed by checking the **Reversed** check box.

- Click the **Automatic** pull-down arrow, as shown in Figure 31-6, which leads to Figure 31-7, where the available options are displayed

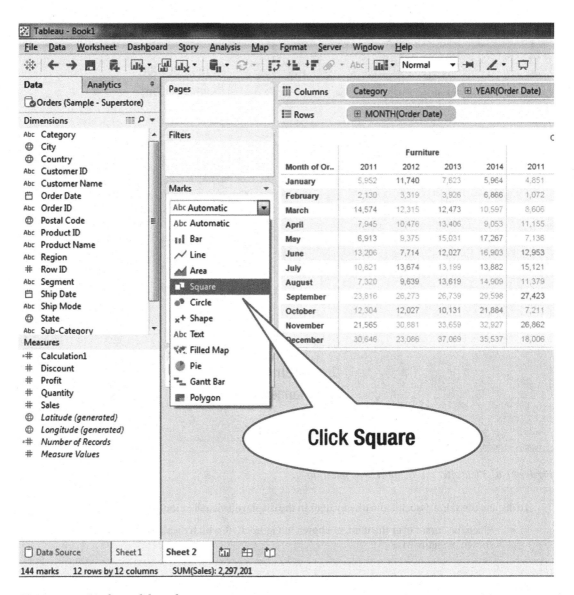

Figure 31-7. *Marks card drop-down menu*

- Click **Square**, as shown in Figure 31-7, which leads to the display shown in Figure 31-8

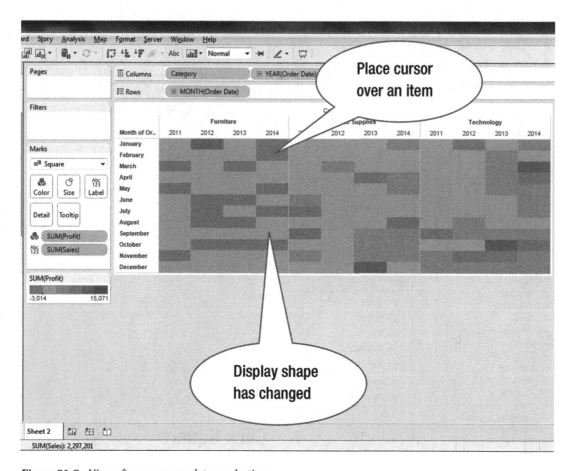

Figure 31-8. *View after square mark type selection*

To display the value associated with any item in the displayed visualization:

- Place the cursor over the item, as shown in Figure 31-8, which displays its value, as shown in Figure 31-9

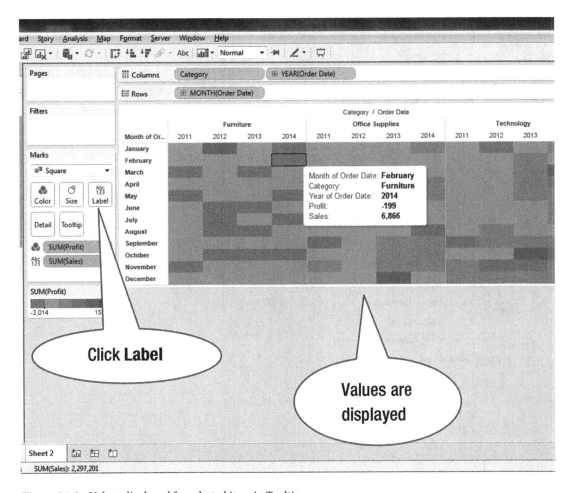

Figure 31-9. *Values displayed for selected item in Tooltip*

The visualization in Figure 31-9 would be more intuitive if the value labels were shown. This is done as follows:

- Click the **Label** icon, as shown in Figure 31-9, which pops up the window displayed in Figure 31-10

285

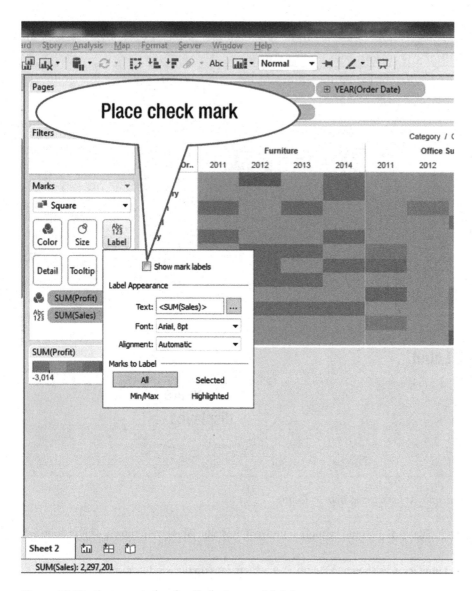

Figure 31-10. *Pop-up window for displaying mark labels*

- Place a check mark next to **Show mark labels**, as shown in Figure 31-10, which leads to Figure 31-11, where the values are displayed

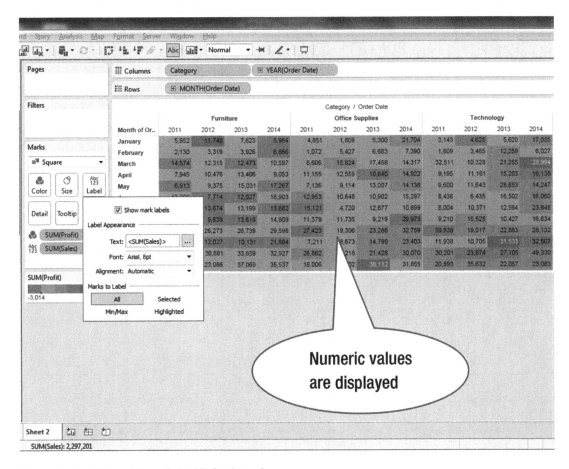

Figure 31-11. View with marks highlighted in color

CHAPTER 32

■ ■ ■

Axis Formatting

Objective: This exercise demonstrates how to format the chart axes and display labels

Figure 32-1 displays the sum of profits vs. the average shipping cost as a scatter plot. On the **Marks** card, **Order Priority** has been added to the **Color** shelf, while **Market** has been added to **Shape**.

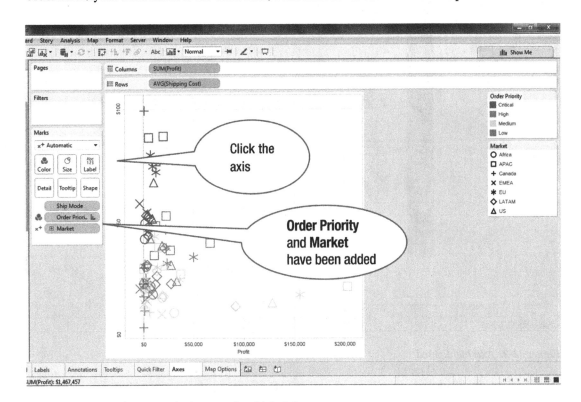

Figure 32-1. *Visualization to be formatted and labeled*

- Click the vertical axis, as shown in Figure 32-1, which leads to the display shown in Figure 32-2, where the axis is highlighted

© Arshad Khan 2016
A. Khan, *Jumpstart Tableau*, DOI 10.1007/978-1-4842-1934-8_32

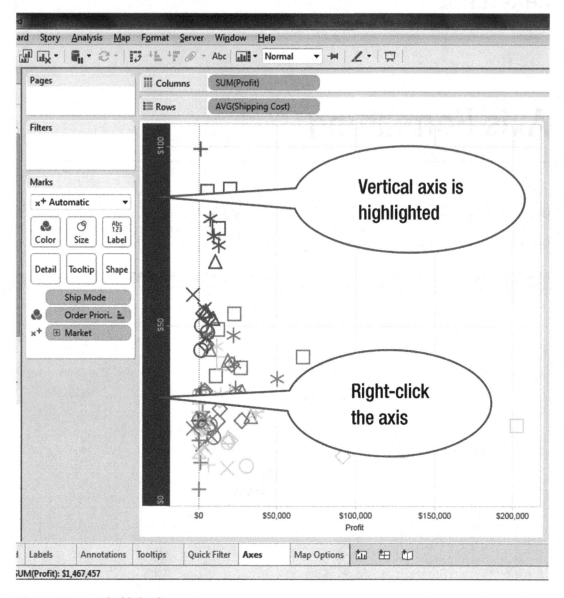

Figure 32-2. *Axis highlighted*

- Right-click the axis, as shown in Figure 32-2, which pops up the menu tree displayed in Figure 32-3

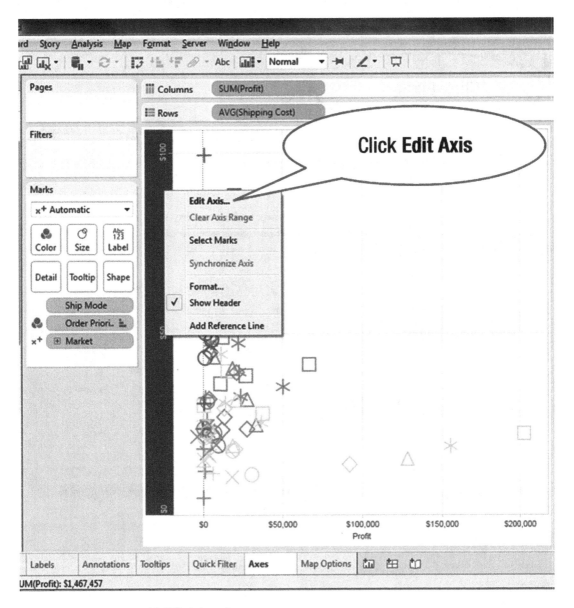

Figure 32-3. *Menu tree with Edit Axis option*

- Click **Edit Axis**, as shown in Figure 32-3, which pops up the **Edit Axis (Avg. Shipping Cost)** window displayed in Figure 32-4

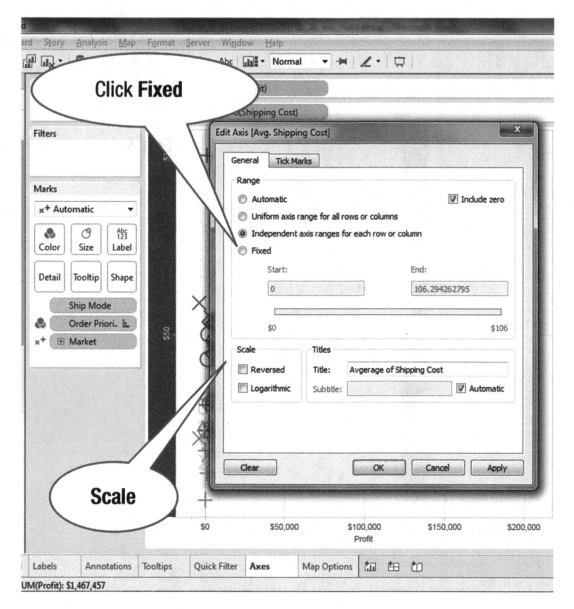

Figure 32-4. *Edit Axis pop-up window*

The following selection options are available in the **Edit Axis** pop-up window (see Figure 32-4):

- **Automatic:** Sets the range on axis automatically, based on the data in the view

- **Uniform axis range for all rows or columns:** Sets the axis range uniformly to the maximum data range for all panes in the view

- **Independent axis ranges for each row or column:** Sets independent axis range for each pane in the view, depending on the range of data in each pane

- **Fixed:** Sets specific start and end values for the axis

Under **Scale**, the two check boxes can be used to reverse the axis and use the logarithmic scale.

- Click the **Fixed** radio button, as shown in Figure 32-4, which leads to the display shown in Figure 32-5

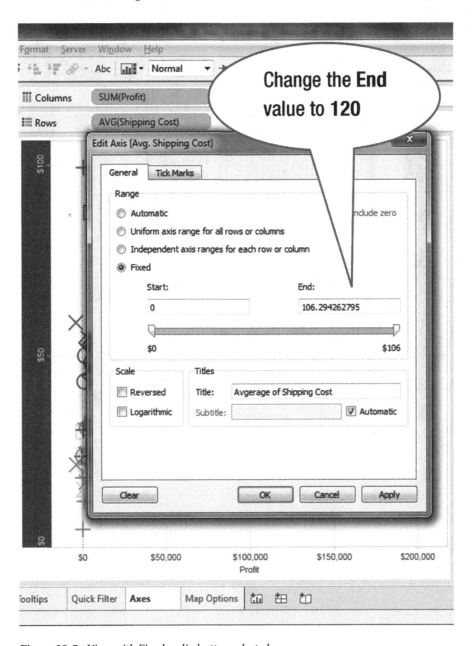

Figure 32-5. View with Fixed radio button selected

- Change the end value for the range to **120**, as shown in Figure 32-5, which leads to the display shown in Figure 32-6

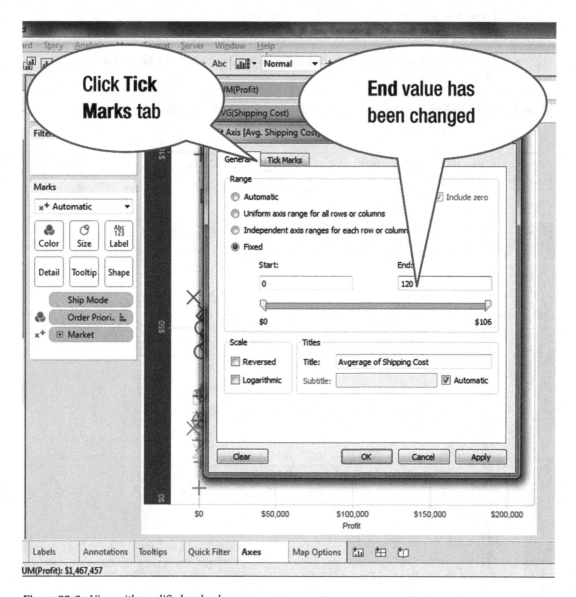

Figure 32-6. *View with modified end value*

- Click the **Tick Marks** tab, as shown in Figure 32-6, which leads to the display shown in Figure 32-7

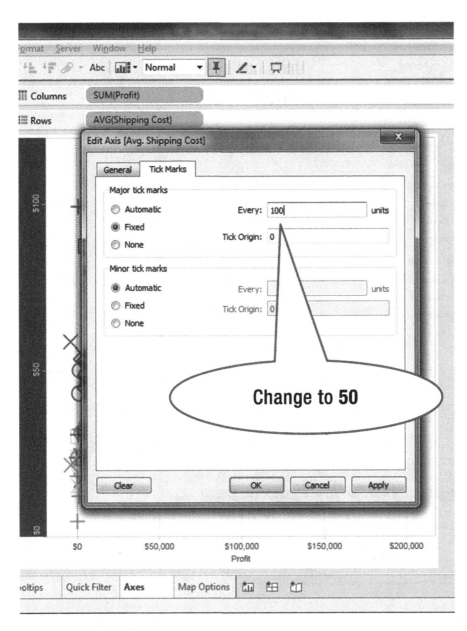

Figure 32-7. *Tick Marks tab*

- Change the **Major tick marks** units from 100 to **50**, as shown in Figure 32-7, which leads to the display shown in Figure 32-8

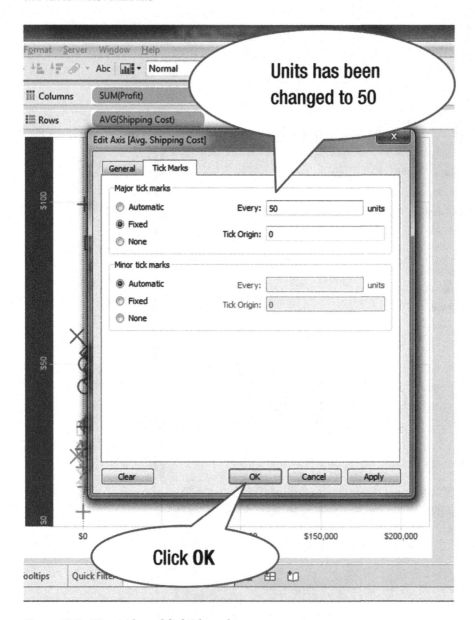

Figure 32-8. View with modified tick marks

- Click **OK**, as shown in Figure 32-8, which implements the changes that were made

The next part of this exercise demonstrates how to display the values/labels. We start with Figure 32-9, which displays a visualization in which the numeric values for the individual bars are not displayed.

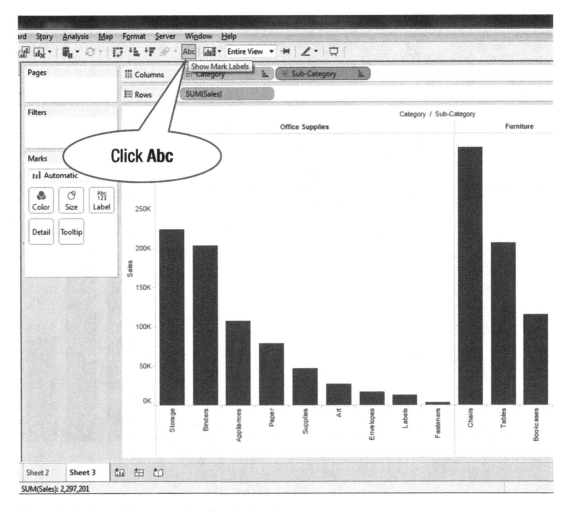

Figure 32-9. *View without numeric values displayed*

To view the values for the bars:

- Click the **Abc** icon on the toolbar, as shown in Figure 32-9, which leads to the display shown in Figure 32-10

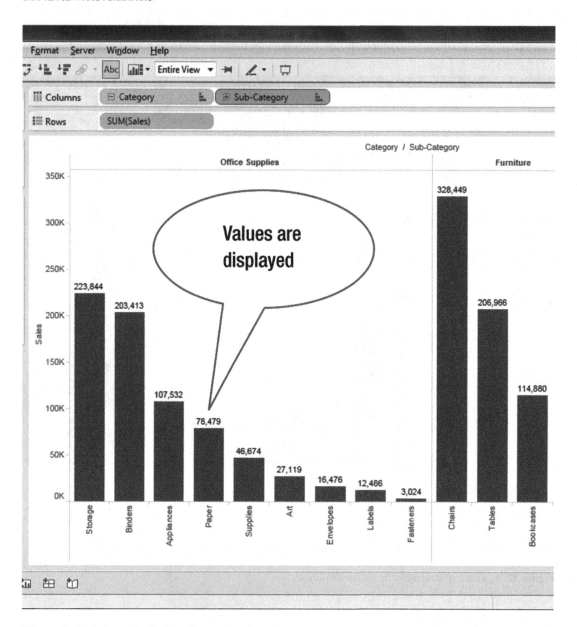

Figure 32-10. *View with displayed numeric values*

CHAPTER 33

■ ■ ■

Formatting Tables

Objective: This exercise demonstrates how to format a table

Figure 33-1 displays a table on which some basic formatting operations will be performed.

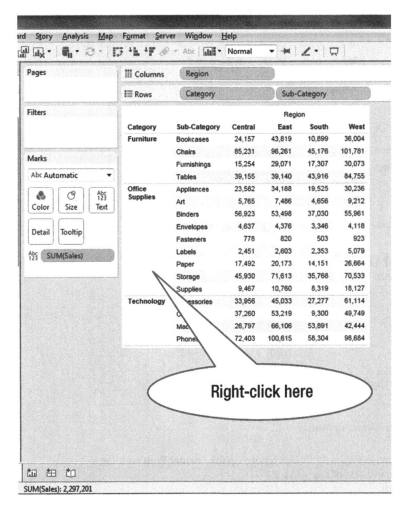

Figure 33-1. *Table to be formatted*

© Arshad Khan 2016

A. Khan, *Jumpstart Tableau*, DOI 10.1007/978-1-4842-1934-8_33

- Right-click the table displayed in Figure 33-1, which pops up the menu tree displayed in Figure 33-2

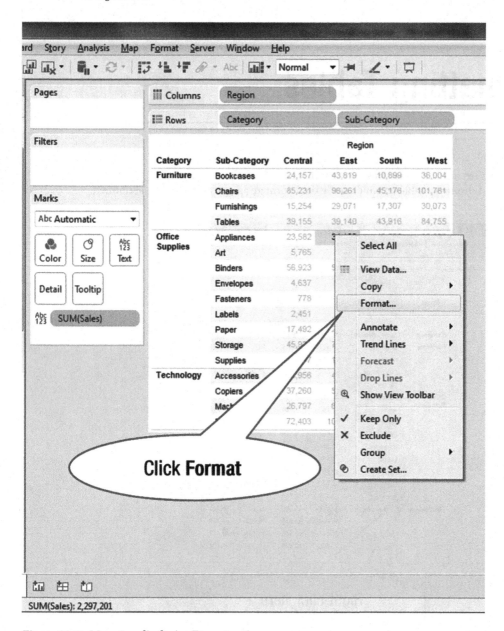

Figure 33-2. *Menu tree displaying Format option*

- Click **Format**, as shown in Figure 33-2, which pops up the **Format Font** window displayed in the left-hand side of Figure 33-3

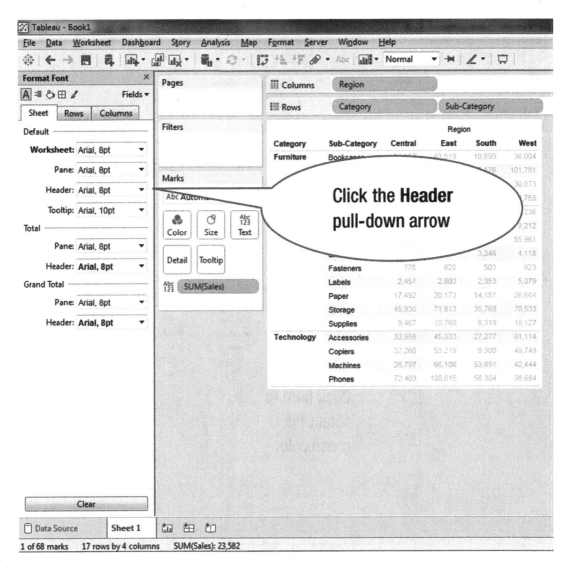

Figure 33-3. *Format Font window*

- Click the **Header** pull-down arrow in the **Format Font** window, as shown in Figure 33-3, which pops up the window displayed in Figure 33-4

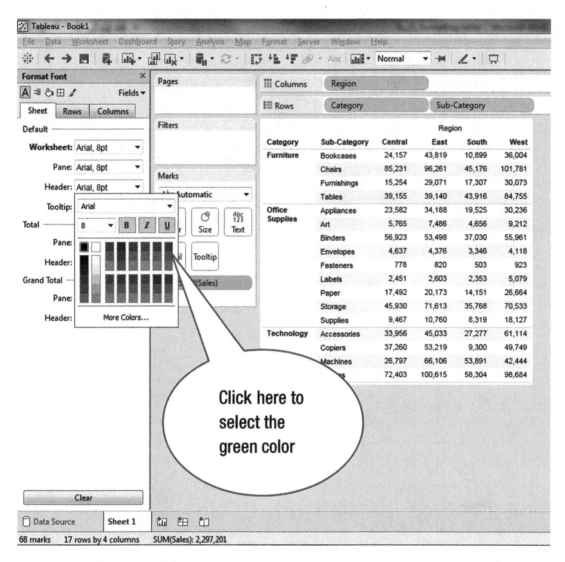

Figure 33-4. *Color pop-up window*

- Click the green color, as shown in Figure 33-4, which leads to the display in
  Figure 33-5 (where the color of the headers has changed to green)

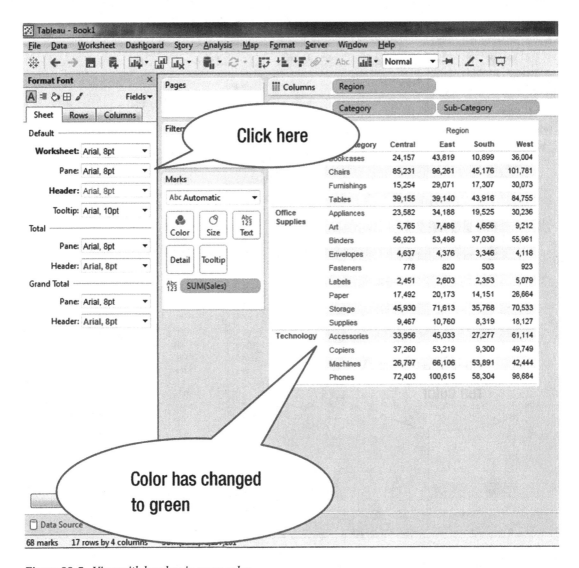

Figure 33-5. *View with headers in green color*

To change the color of the numeric values displayed in the table:

- Click the pull-down arrow for **Pane** in the **Format Font** window, as shown in Figure 33-5, which pops up the window displayed in Figure 33-6

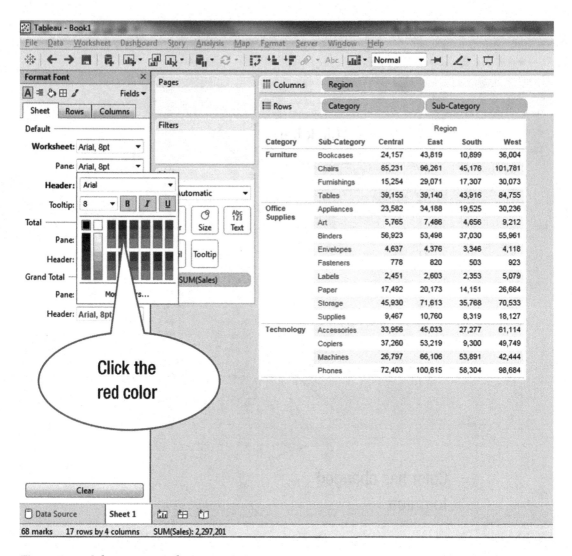

Figure 33-6. *Color pop-up window*

- Click the red color, as shown in Figure 33-6, which leads to the display in Figure 33-7 (where the table data has turned red)

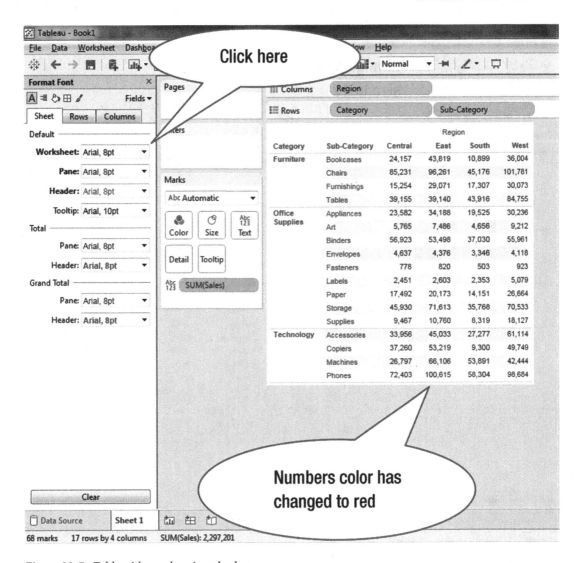

Figure 33-7. Table with numbers in red color

- Click the pull-down arrow for **Worksheet** in the **Format Font** window, as shown in Figure 33-7, which pops up the window displayed in Figure 33-8

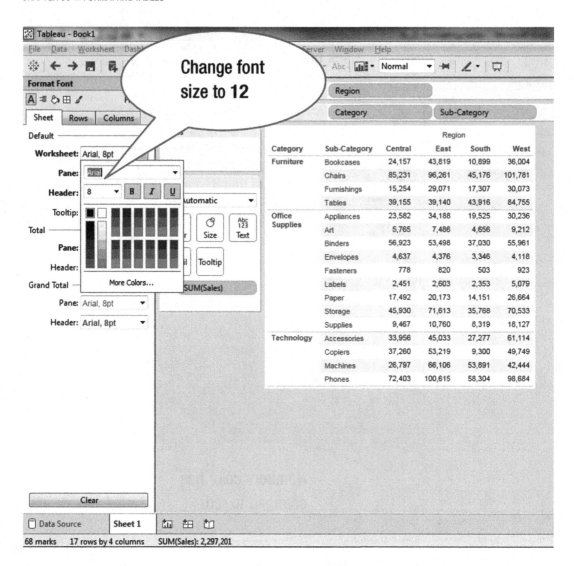

Figure 33-8. *Pop-up window displaying font size*

- Change the font size to **12** (from the default size 8), as shown in Figure 33-8, which leads to Figure 33-9, where the numbers displayed in the table are bigger (size 12)

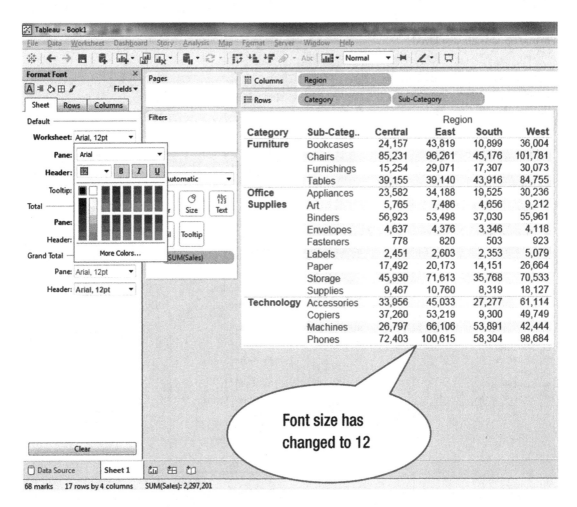

Figure 33-9. *View with numbers displayed in bigger font*

Formatting can also be performed via the menu bar, as shown in Figure 33-10, where the available **Format** options are displayed.

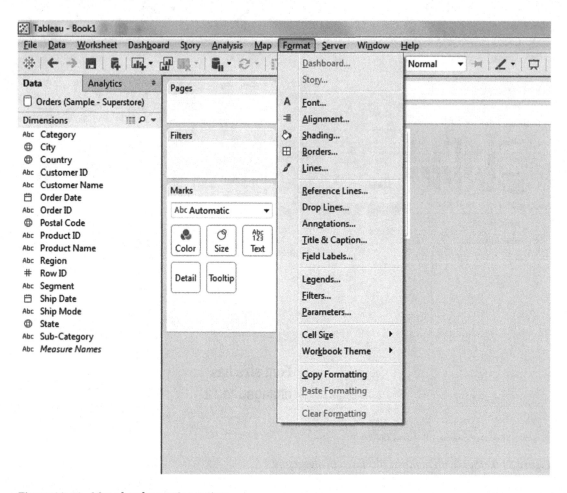

Figure 33-10. *Menu bar formatting options*

■ ■ ■

CHAPTER 34

Top N Function

Objective: This exercise demonstrates how to use the Top N function to determine top performers Figure 34-1 shows a chart with the sum of sales by state.

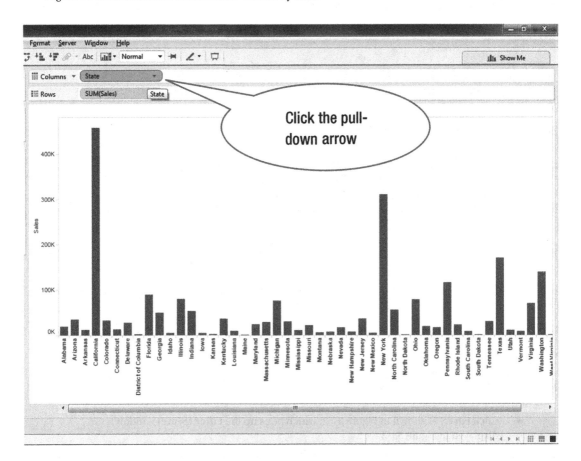

Figure 34-1. Visualization for executing the Top N function

- Click the pull-down arrow for the **State**, as shown in Figure 34-1, which pops up the menu tree displayed in Figure 34-2

© Arshad Khan 2016
A. Khan, *Jumpstart Tableau*, DOI 10.1007/978-1-4842-1934-8_34

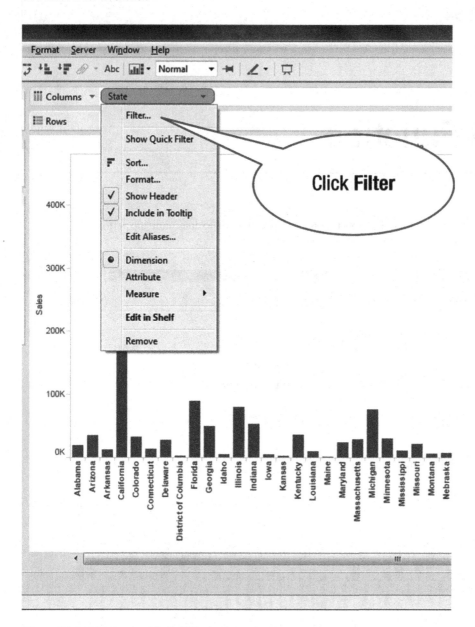

Figure 34-2. Menu tree with the Filter option

- Click **Filter**, as shown in Figure 34-2, which pops up the **Filter (State)** window displayed in Figure 34-3

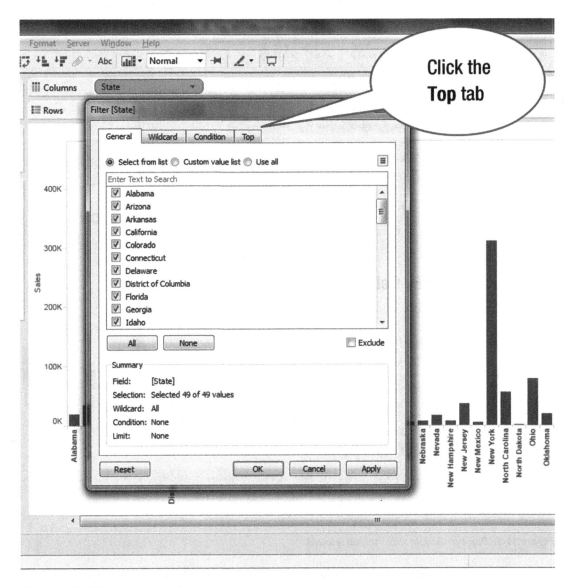

Figure 34-3. Filter pop-up window

- Click the **Top** tab, as shown in Figure 34-3, which leads to the pop-up window displayed in Figure 34-4

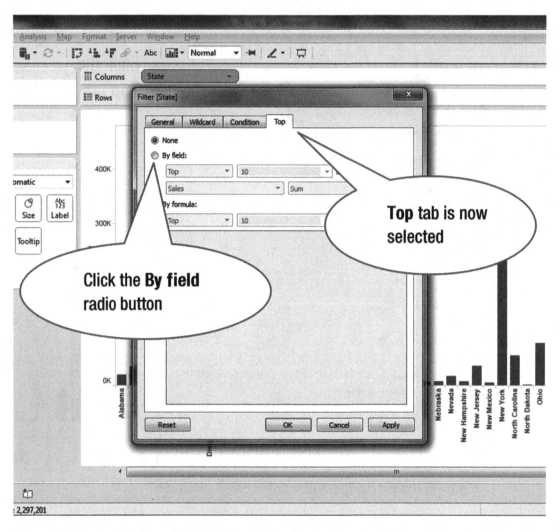

Figure 34-4. *Pop-up window with Top tab selected*

- Click the **By field** radio button, as shown in Figure 34-4, which leads to the display in Figure 34-5

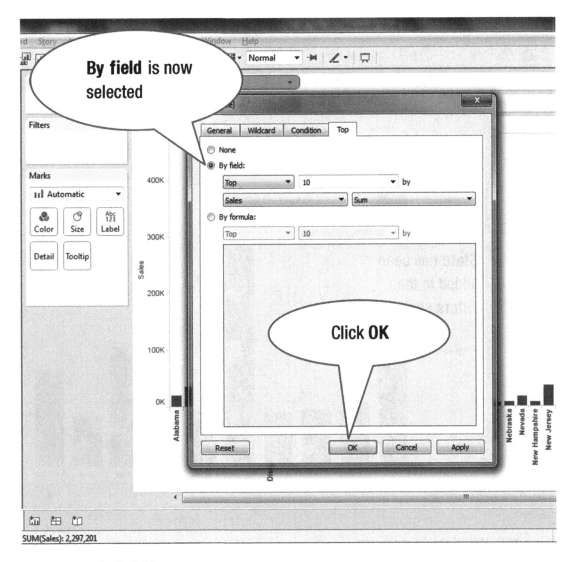

Figure 34-5. *Filter by field*

- Click **OK**, as shown in Figure 34-5, which leads to Figure 34-6, where the ten top states with the highest sales are displayed

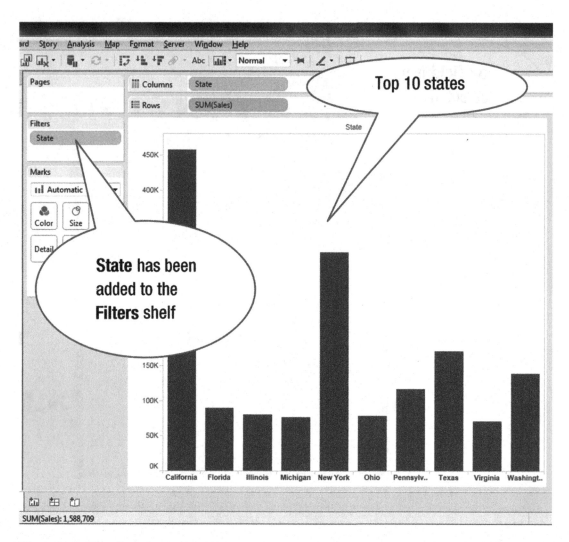

Figure 34-6. *View displaying top ten states*

To view the top ten states by profit rather than by sales:

- Navigate to the **Filter (State)** pop-up window shown in Figure 34-7, which is the same as Figure 34-5, using the procedure demonstrated earlier in this exercise

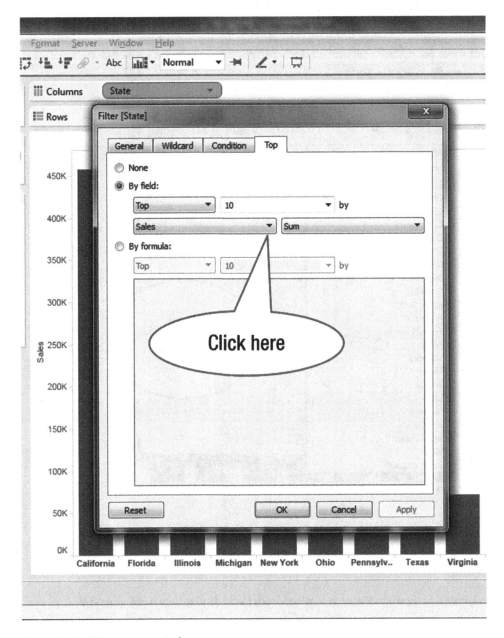

Figure 34-7. *Filter pop-up window*

- Click the pull-down arrow, as shown in Figure 34-7, which leads to the menu tree displayed in Figure 34-8 (from which the desired field, profit, can be selected)

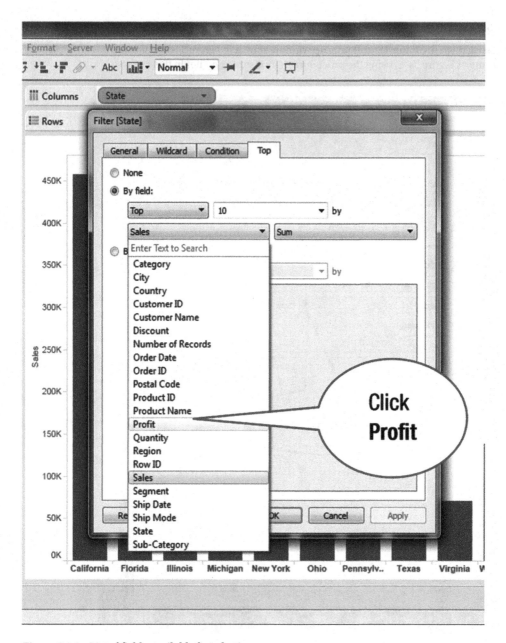

Figure 34-8. List of fields available for selection

- Click **Profit**, as shown in Figure 34-8, which leads to the display shown in Figure 34-9

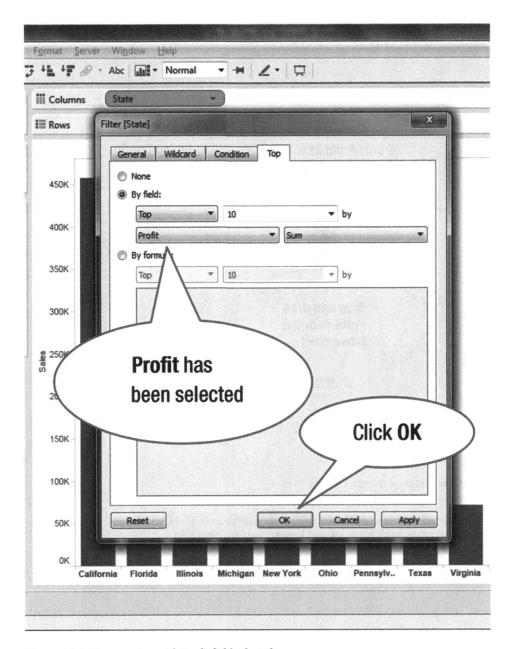

Figure 34-9. *Pop-up view with Profit field selected*

- Click **OK**, as shown in Figure 34-9, which leads to Figure 34-10, where the ten top states with the highest profit are displayed

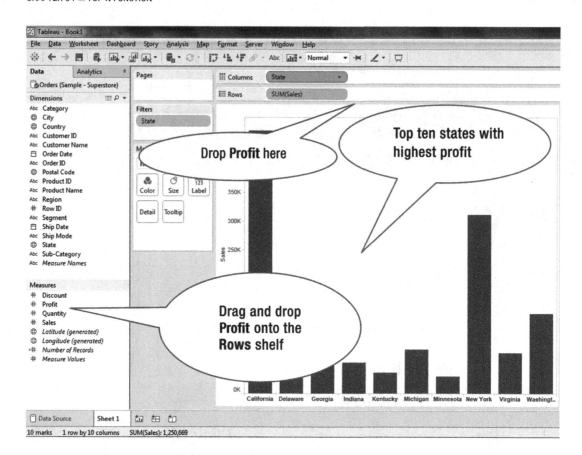

Figure 34-10. *Top ten states with highest profit*

Figure 34-10 displays **Sales** on the vertical axis.
To also view **Profit** on the vertical scale:

- Drag and drop **Profit** onto the **Rows** shelf, as shown in Figure 34-10, which leads to Figure 34-11, where both the **Sales and Profit** charts are displayed

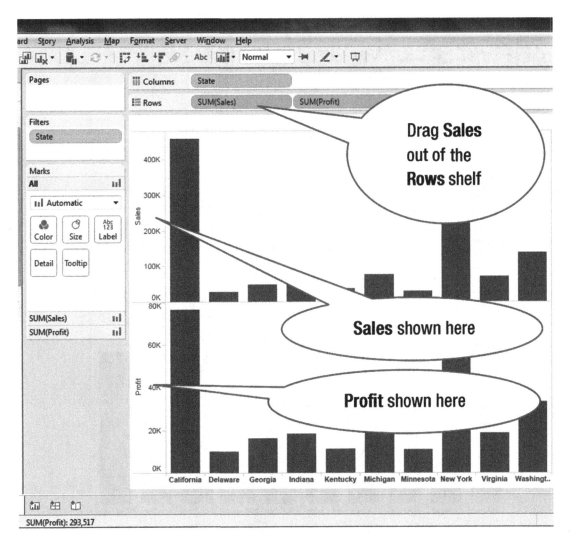

Figure 34-11. *Views showing top ten by sales and profit*

To display only **Profit** on the vertical axis:

- Drag **Sales** out of the **Rows** shelf, as shown in Figure 34-11, which leads to Figure 34-12, where only **Profit** is displayed on the vertical axis

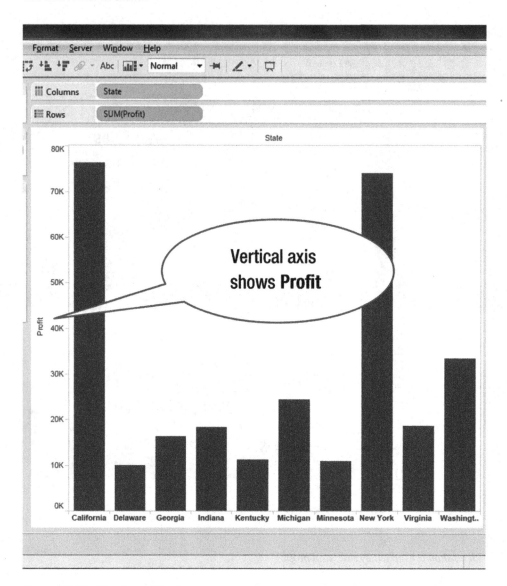

Figure 34-12. *View by profit only*

CHAPTER 35

Trend Lines

Objective: This exercise demonstrates how trend lines are inserted in a chart

Figure 35-1 displays a line chart that shows the sum of sales over a 12-month period.

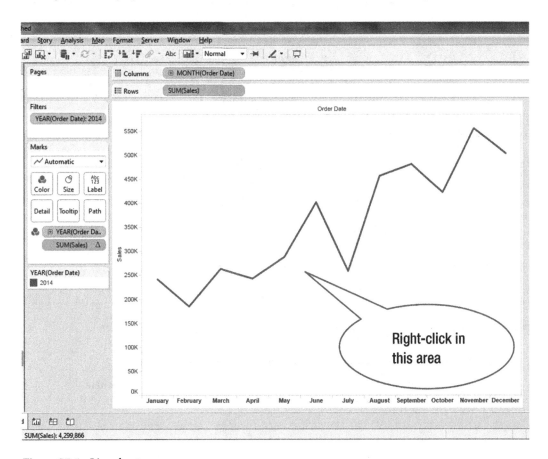

Figure 35-1. *Line chart*

To show a trend line for the displayed data:

- Right-click within the chart area, as shown in Figure 35-1, which pops up the menu tree displayed in Figure 35-2

© Arshad Khan 2016

A. Khan, *Jumpstart Tableau*, DOI 10.1007/978-1-4842-1934-8_35

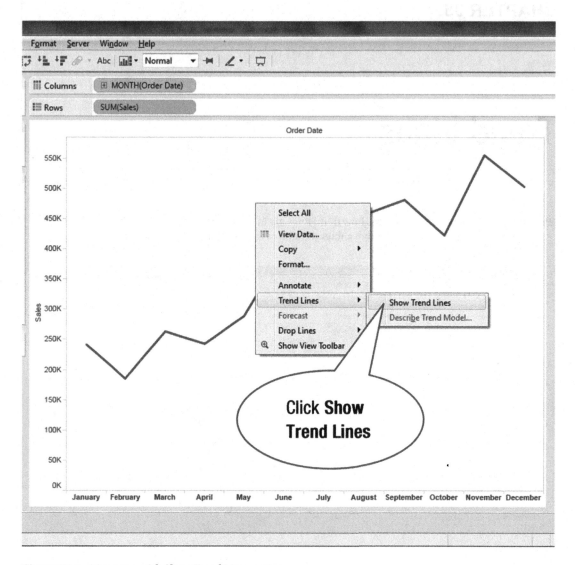

Figure 35-2. *Menu tree with Show Trend Lines option*

- Navigate as follows: **Trend Lines ➤ Show Trend Lines**, as shown in Figure 35-2

- Click **Show Trend Lines**, as shown in Figure 35-2, which leads to Figure 35-3, where the trend line has been inserted

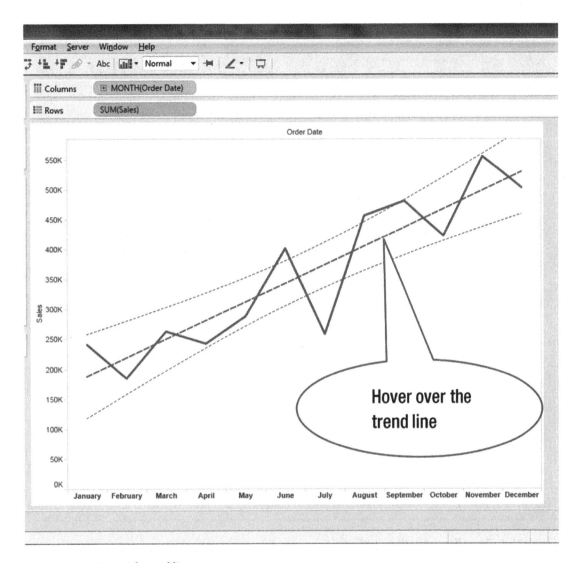

Figure 35-3. View with trend line

- Hover over the trend line, as shown in Figure 35-3, which displays more information about the trend, such as P-value, as shown in Figure 35-4

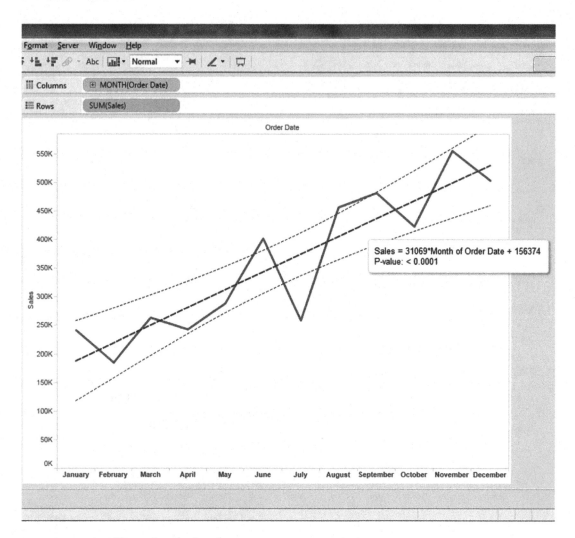

Figure 35-4. *Trend line values displayed*

Figure 35-4 displays the P-value, which indicates the significance of the result. A low value indicates that the results are significant; however, a high P-value can indicate that the trend in the data is due to chance—not due to the model.

If you right-click a trend line, it opens the window displayed in Figure 35-5.

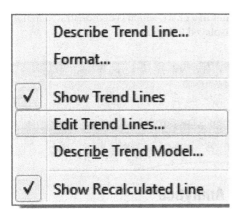

Figure 35-5. *Editing trend lines*

- Click the **Edit Trend Lines** menu item, highlighted in Figure 35-5, which pops up the window shown in Figure 35-6 (where the trend line options are displayed)

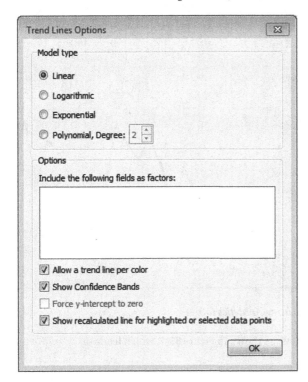

Figure 35-6. *Editing trend lines*

In the **Trend Lines Options** window shown in Figure 35-6, the **Show Confidence Bands** option is selected by default, which can make the window look busy. It can be easily deselected by removing the check mark.

An alternative method can also be used for inserting trend lines in a chart, which is demonstrated in the following steps. For this method, we start with the visualization displayed in Figure 35-7.

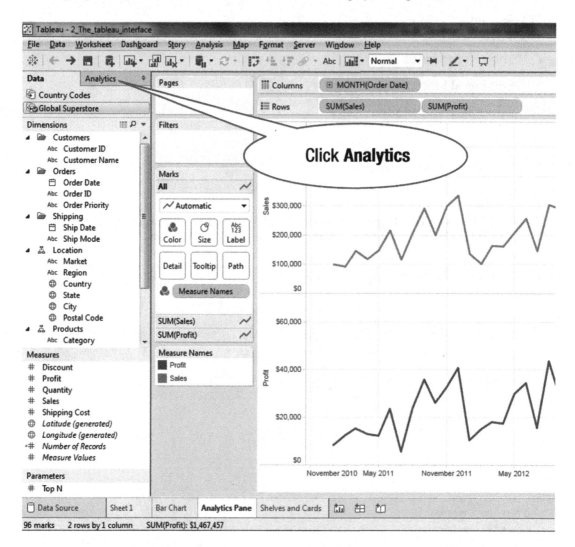

Figure 35-7. *Visualization for displaying a trend line using Analytics tab*

- Click the **Analytics** tab in the **Data** window, as shown in Figure 35-7, which leads to the display shown in Figure 35-8

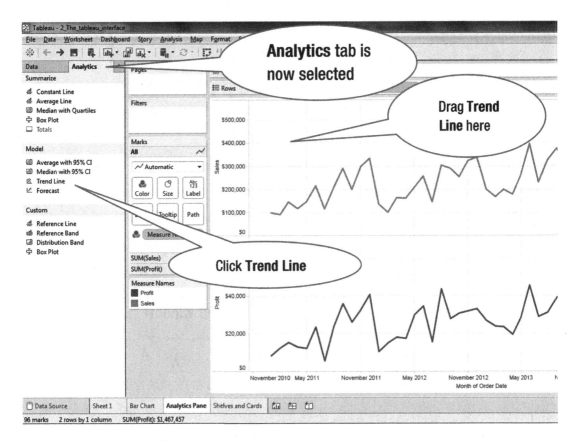

Figure 35-8. *View with Analytics tab selected*

- Click **Trend Line**, as shown in Figure 35-8

- Drag **Trend Line** onto the chart area, as shown in Figure 35-8, which pops up the window displayed in Figure 35-9

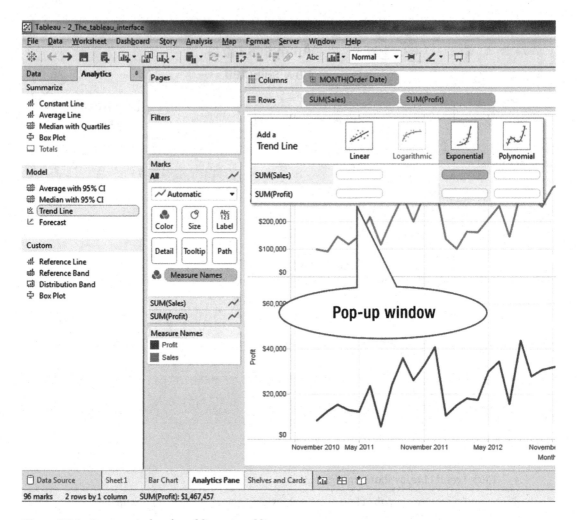

Figure 35-9. *Pop-up window for adding a trend line*

The type of trend line that is desired can be selected in the pop-up window.
To select the exponential model:

- Click the **Exponential** icon, as shown in Figure 35-9, which generates the trend line shown in Figure 35-10

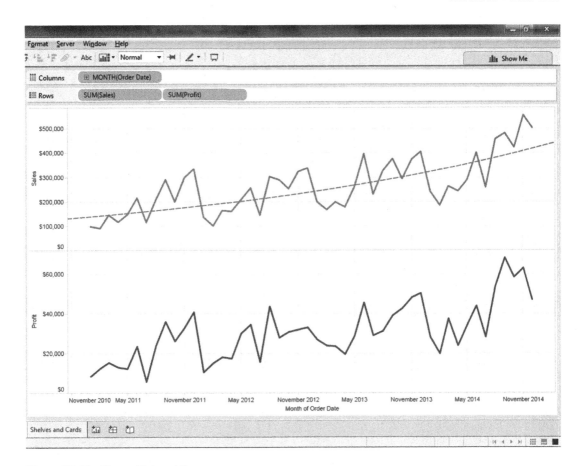

Figure 35-10. *View with trend line*

CHAPTER 36

■ ■ ■

Forecasting

Objective: This exercise demonstrates the forecasting feature in Tableau
Figure 36-1 shows the sales by year and month.

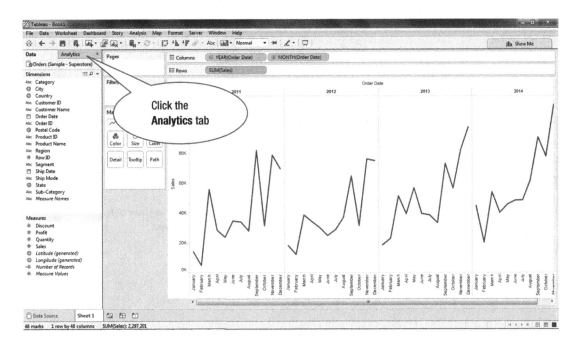

Figure 36-1. *View with historical data*

- Click the **Analytics** tab, as shown in Figure 36-1, which leads to the display shown in Figure 36-2

© Arshad Khan 2016
A. Khan, *Jumpstart Tableau*, DOI 10.1007/978-1-4842-1934-8_36

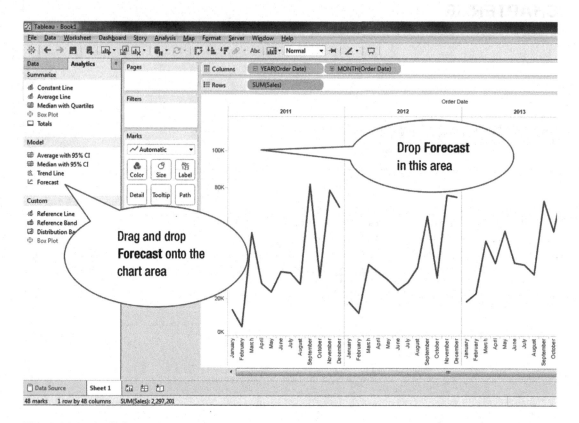

Figure 36-2. Analytics pane

- Drag and drop **Forecast** from the **Analytics** tab onto the chart area, as shown in Figure 36-2, which leads to Figure 36-3, where the forecast is displayed

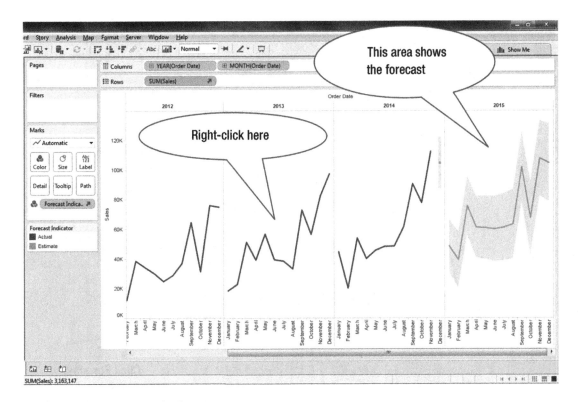

Figure 36-3. *Forecast displayed*

- Right-click the chart, as shown in Figure 36-3, which pops up the menu tree displayed in Figure 36-4

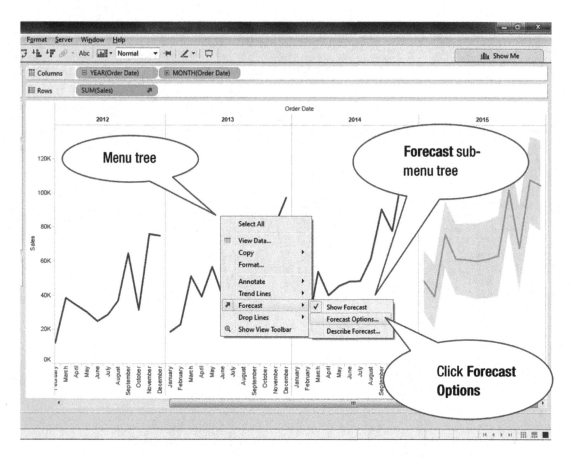

Figure 36-4. *Menu tree displaying forecast options*

- Navigate to the **Forecast** sub-menu tree, as shown in Figure 36-4

- Click **Forecast Options**, as shown in Figure 36-4, which opens the **Forecast Options** window displayed in Figure 36-5

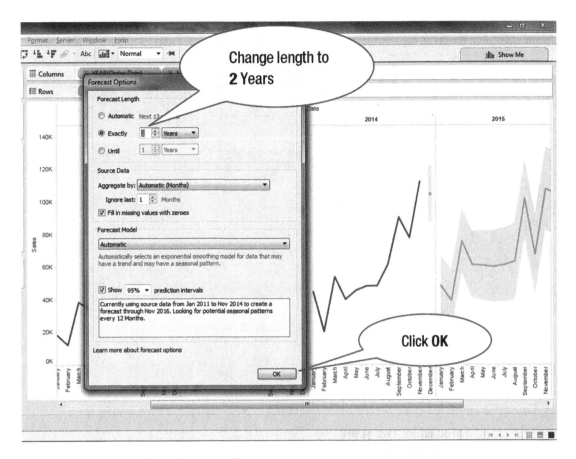

Figure 36-5. *Forecast options pop-up window*

- Change the **Forecast Length** to **2** Years, as shown in Figure 36-5

- Click **OK**, which leads to the display shown in Figure 36-6, where the forecast for two years is displayed

The Forecast Model has three options: Automatic, Automatic without Seasonality, and Custom. The Automatic option selects an exponential smoothing model for data that has a trend and a seasonal pattern.

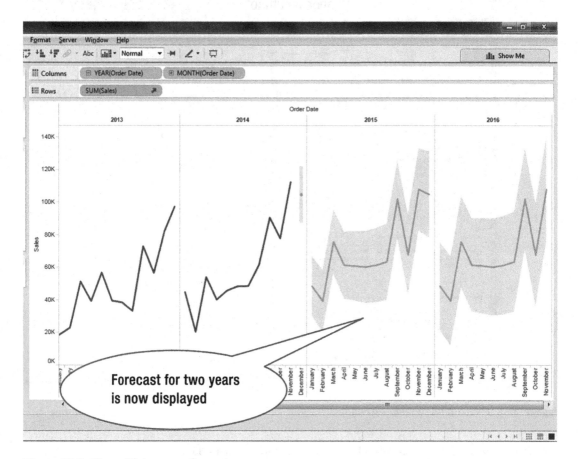

Figure 36-6. *View with two years forecast*

CHAPTER 37

■ ■ ■

Creating a Dashboard

Objective: This exercise demonstrates how to create a dashboard

Dashboards can present one or more views, so that a consolidated view is provided. A view incorporated into a dashboard is just a window to the underlying worksheet. Dashboards tie together different views and frequently offer filters, legends, and interactivity. They can include worksheets, images, text, and web pages. Stories are walk-throughs of one or more dashboards or sheets. Dashboards answer "What?" whereas stories answer "Why?".

Figure 37-1 shows the following five sheets that can be incorporated into a dashboard:

- Sales Seasonality

- Crosstab

- Global Sales and Profits

- Sales by Category

- Customer Breakdown

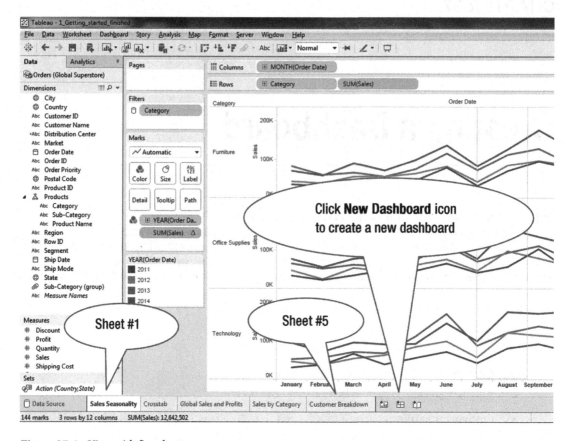

Figure 37-1. *View with five sheets*

- Click the **New Dashboard** icon, as shown in Figure 37-1, which leads to the display shown in Figure 37-2, where a new dashboard sheet (**Dashboard 1**) has been added

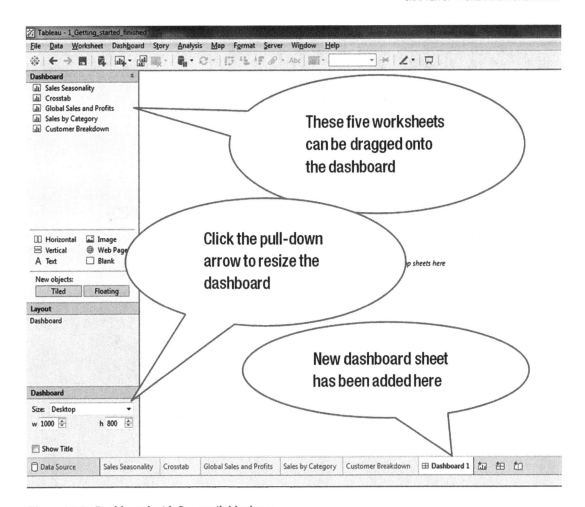

Figure 37-2. *Dashboard with five available sheets*

To resize the dashboard display:

- Click the **Dashboard** pull-down arrow, as shown in Figure 37-2, which pops up the menu tree displayed in Figure 37-3

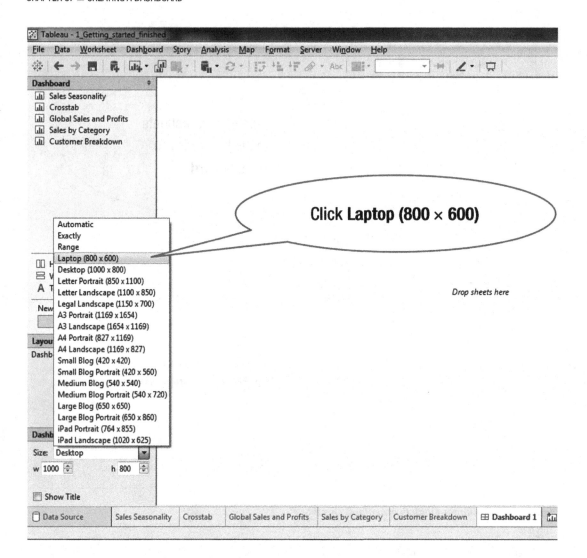

Figure 37-3. *Size options*

The size to be selected depends on the device(s) used for viewing the dashboard, which includes devices as diverse as desktops, laptops, tablets, and smartphones.

- Click **Laptop (800 × 600)**, as shown in Figure 37-3, which leads to the display shown in Figure 37-4

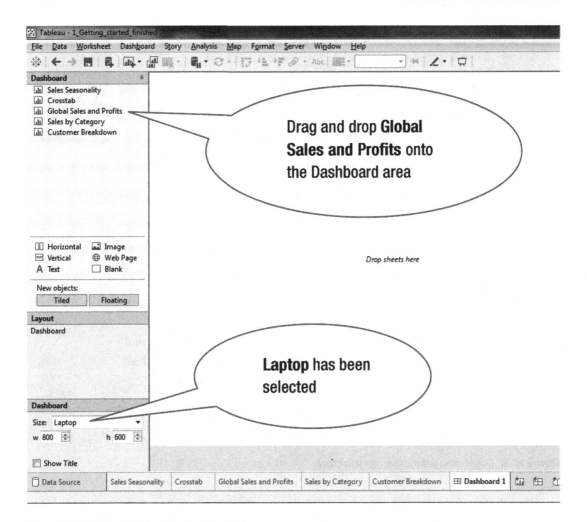

Figure 37-4. *View with Laptop size selection*

- Drag and drop the **Global Sales and Profits** worksheet onto the dashboard as shown in Figure 37-4, which leads to the display in Figure 37-5

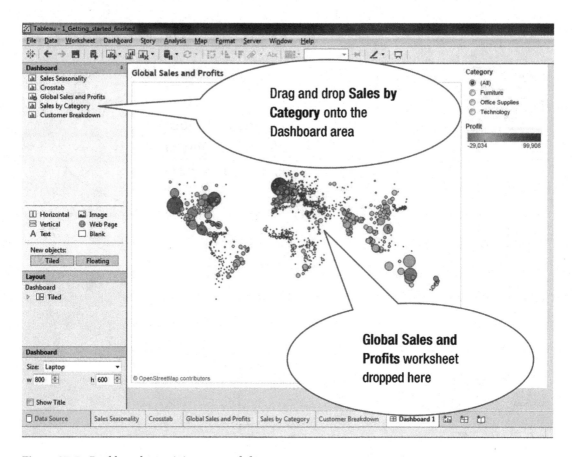

Figure 37-5. *Dashboard containing one worksheet*

When the first view is brought into a dashboard, it automatically takes up the entire view. However, any subsequent worksheet can be placed in specific areas of the screen. If the mouse button is held down as it is moved around the dashboard, gray areas indicate where the dragged view will be located when the mouse button is released. If the view is brought all the way down to the bottom of the screen, it fills the entire width.

- Drag and drop the **Sales by Category** worksheet onto the Dashboard area, as shown in Figure 37-5, which leads to the display shown in Figure 37-6

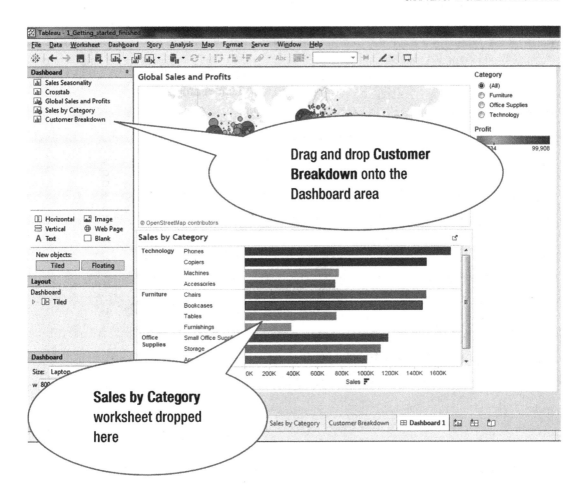

Figure 37-6. *Dashboard containing two worksheets*

- Drag and drop the **Customer Breakdown** worksheet onto the Dashboard area, which leads to the display shown in Figure 37-7

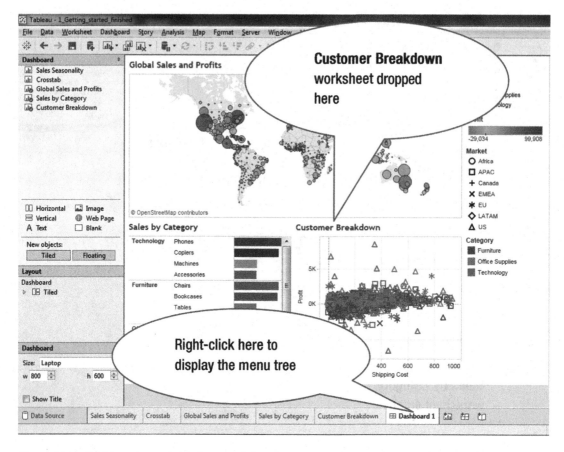

Figure 37-7. *Dashboard containing three worksheets*

- Right-click the **Dashboard 1** sheet, as shown in Figure 37-7, which leads to the menu tree displayed in Figure 37-8

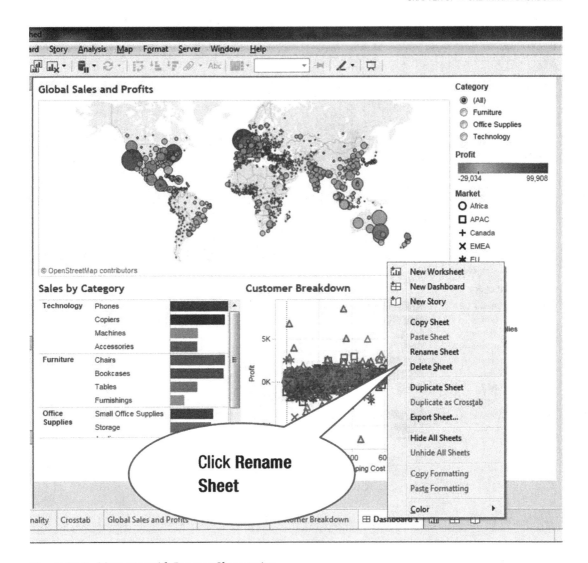

Figure 37-8. Menu tree with Rename Sheet option

- Click **Rename Sheet**, as shown in Figure 37-8, which enables **Dashboard 1** to be renamed

- Rename **Dashboard 1** as **Sales Dashboard**, which leads to the display shown in Figure 37-9, where the new dashboard name is displayed (**Sales Dashboard**)

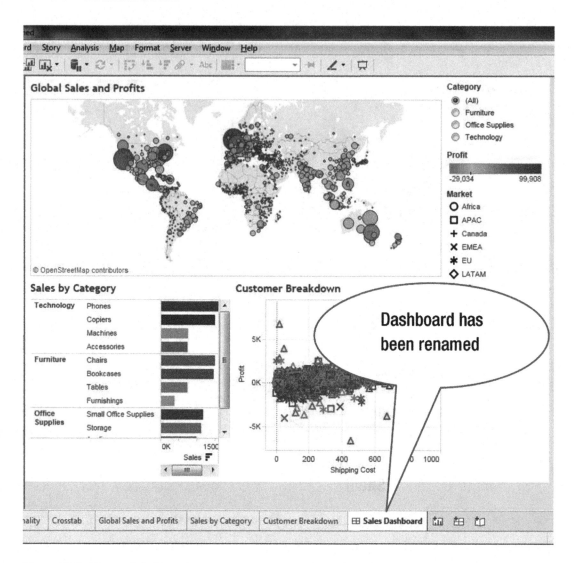

Figure 37-9. *Renamed dashboard*

The individual worksheets on a dashboard and the dashboard itself are customizable. Clicking a worksheet displays a pull-down arrow, through which various options can be accessed.

To customize the **Customer Breakdown** worksheet in the dashboard:

- Click within the **Customer Breakdown** window, as shown in Figure 37-10, which displays its pull-down arrow

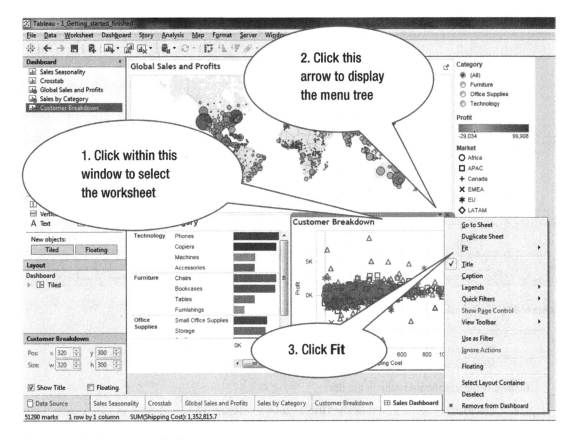

Figure 37-10. *Menu tree with Fit option*

- Click the **Customer Breakdown** pull-down arrow, which leads to the menu tree displayed in Figure 37-10

As the menu tree options indicate, there are many options for customizing the worksheet.

- Click **Fit**, as shown in Figure 37-10, which pops up the secondary menu tree displayed in Figure 37-11

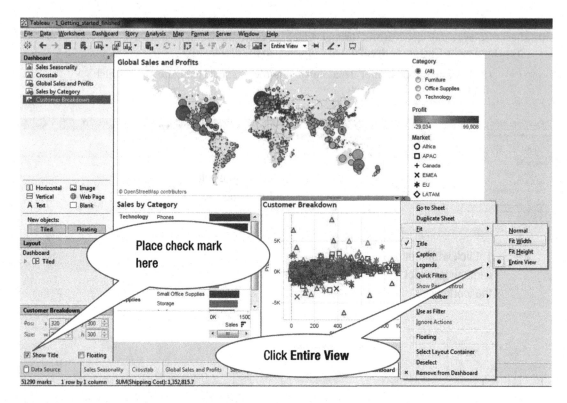

Figure 37-11. *Secondary menu tree with Entire View option*

- Click **Entire View**, as shown in Figure 37-11, which only applies to the **Customer Breakdown** worksheet

To display the dashboard name in the title:

- Place a check mark next to **Show Title**, as shown in Figure 37-11

This places the dashboard name (**Sales Dashboard**) in the title, as shown in Figure 37-12.

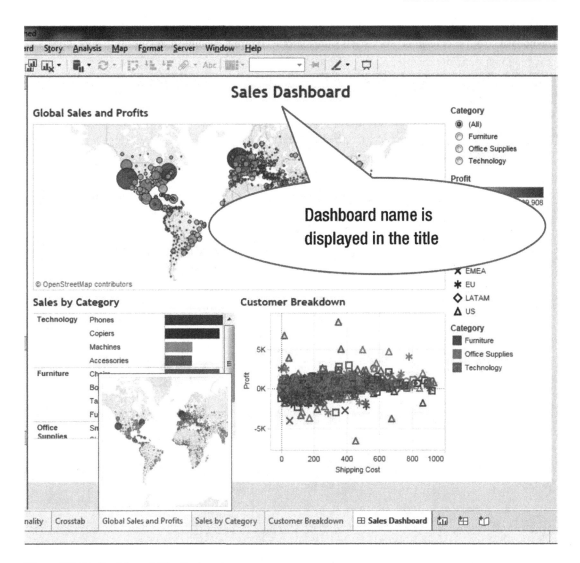

Figure 37-12. Dashboard title displayed

Dashboard items can be rearranged and/or resized as desired. Figure 37-13 shows the new **Sales Dashboard** layout after its three worksheets were rearranged through simple drag-and-drop operations.

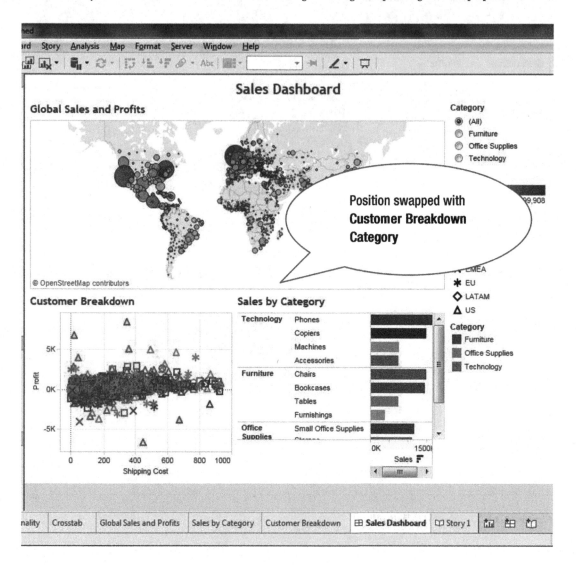

Figure 37-13. *Swapping the location of two worksheets*

CHAPTER 38

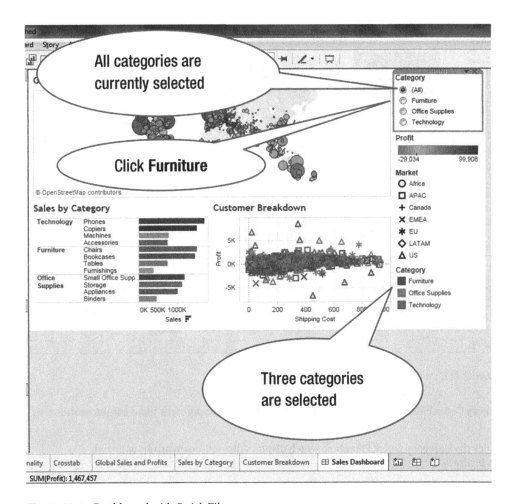

Dashboard Quick Filters

Objective: This exercise demonstrates how to apply Quick Filters for selected worksheets on a dashboard

In Figure 38-1, the **Sales Dashboard** contains the **Category** Quick Filter, where the **All** radio button has been selected.

Figure 38-1. Dashboard with Quick Filter

© Arshad Khan 2016

A. Khan, *Jumpstart Tableau*, DOI 10.1007/978-1-4842-1934-8_38

- Click the **Furniture** radio button, as shown in Figure 38-1, which leads to the display shown in Figure 38-2, where the data is restricted to the **Furniture** category for all three worksheets in the **Sales Dashboard**

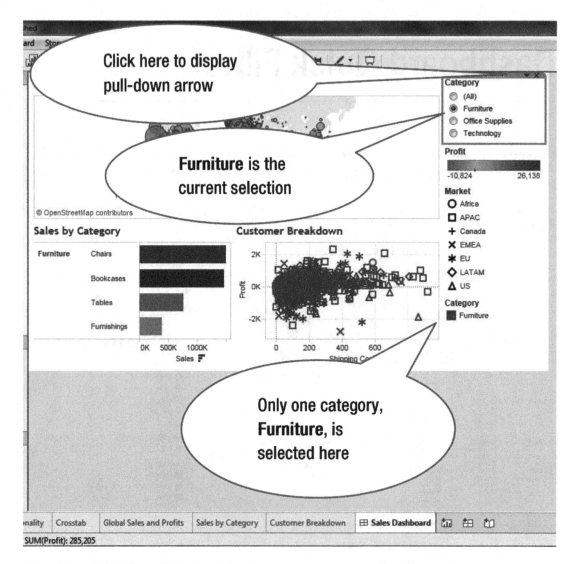

Figure 38-2. *Quick Filter with furniture selected*

The **Category** Quick Filter box displays a pull-down arrow in the upper right-hand corner, as shown in Figure 38-2.

- Click the **Category** Quick Filter box, which displays the pull-down arrow, as shown in Figure 38-3

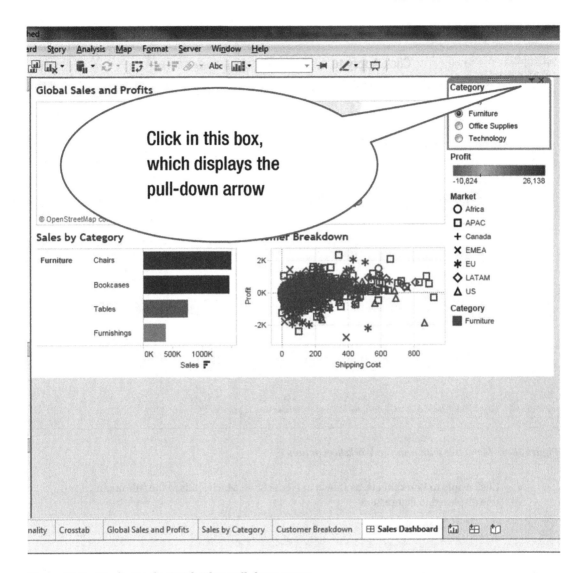

Figure 38-3. *Displaying the Quick Filter pull-down arrow*

- Click the pull-down arrow, as shown in Figure 38-3, which pops up the menu tree displayed in Figure 38-4

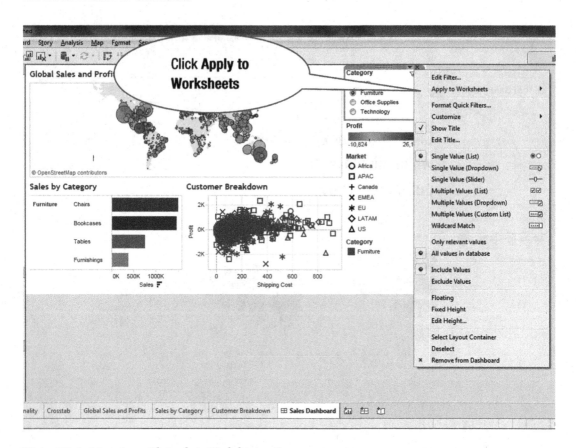

Figure 38-4. *Menu tree with Apply to Worksheet option*

- Click **Apply to Worksheets**, as shown in Figure 38-4, which leads to the sub-menu tree displayed in Figure 38-5

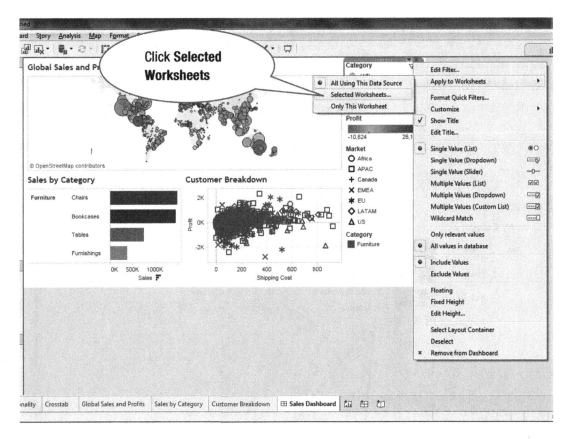

Figure 38-5. *Secondary menu tree with Selected Worksheets option*

- Click **Selected Worksheets**, as shown in Figure 38-5, which pops up the window
  Apply Filters to Worksheets (Category) displayed in Figure 38-6

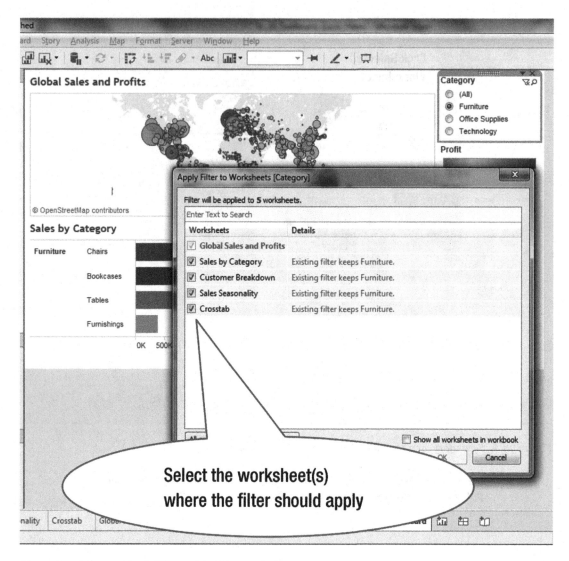

Figure 38-6. *Pop-up Apply Filter to Worksheets window*

By default, all the worksheets on the dashboard are selected.
To deselect a worksheet:

- Remove check mark to the left of the worksheet (to which the filter is not to be applied)

In Figure 38-7, a check mark has only been retained for the **Sales by Category** worksheet. Hence, the filter will only apply to that worksheet.

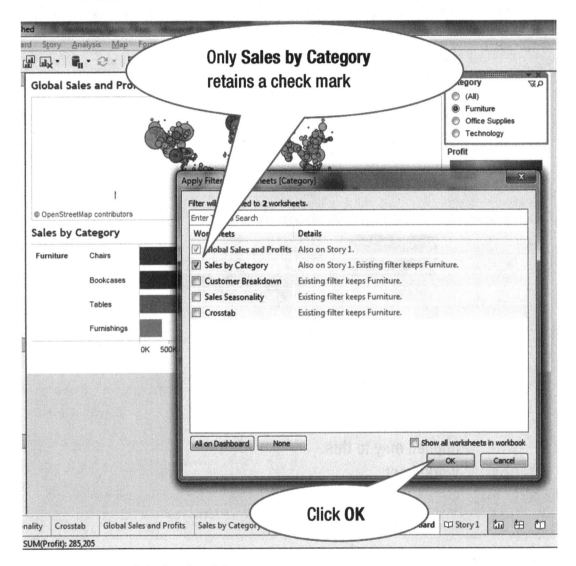

Figure 38-7. *View with deselected worksheets*

- Click **OK** after the desired deselection is done

Figure 38-7 displays the Quick Filter from the Global Sales and Profits sheet. In this figure, the filter is applied to two sheets (there are two check boxes selected for two sheets—**Global Sales and Profits** and **Sales by Category**).

Figure 38-8 displays the dashboard where the filter applies to only one worksheet (**Sales by Category**).

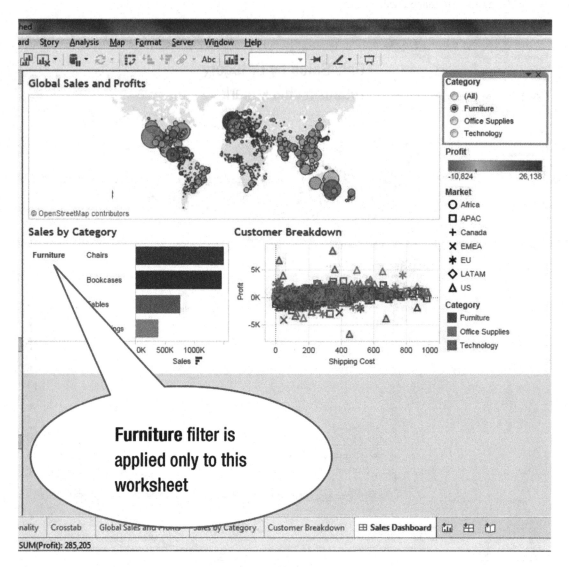

Figure 38-8. *View with filter applied to a single worksheet*

CHAPTER 39

■ ■ ■

Cascading Worksheet Changes in a Dashboard

Objective: This exercise demonstrates how changes to a worksheet cascade in a dashboard

Figure 39-1 shows a chart that plots the sum of sales against the sum of profits.

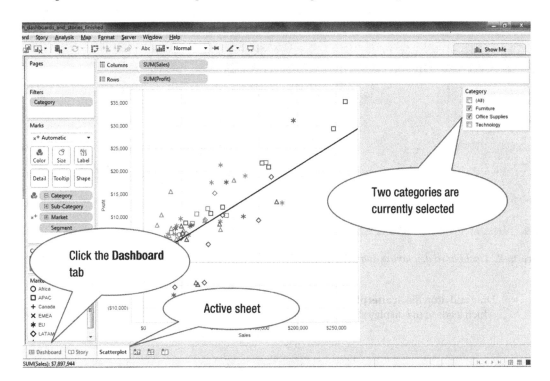

Figure 39-1. Scatterplot sheet

The **Scatterplot** sheet is currently active. In the **Category** Quick Filter, two items currently have check marks: Furniture and Office Supplies.

To go to the dashboard:

- Click the **Dashboard** tab, as shown in Figure 39-1, which leads to the display shown in Figure 39-2

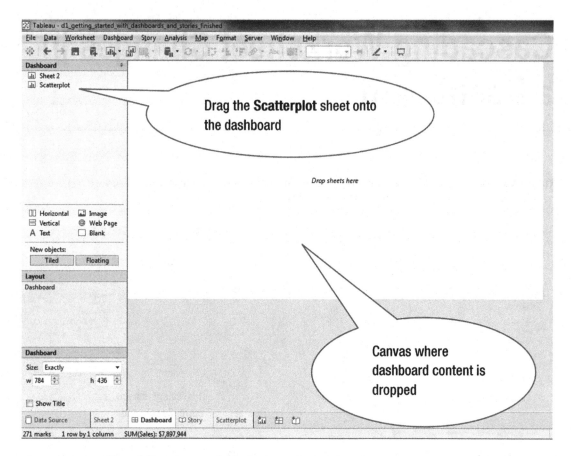

Figure 39-2. *Dashboard displaying available sheets*

- Drag and drop the **Scatterplot** sheet onto the Dashboard, as shown in Figure 39-2, which leads to the display shown in Figure 39-3

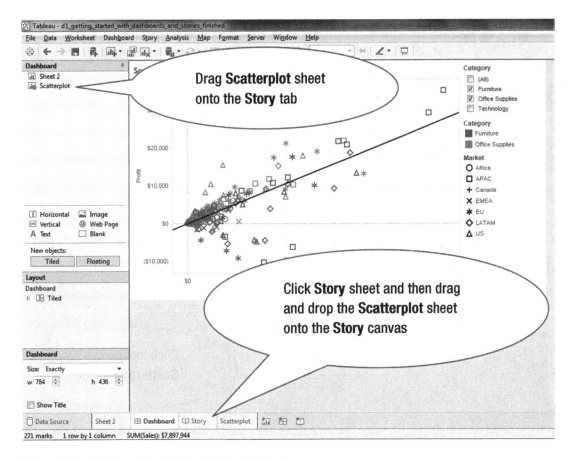

Figure 39-3. Dashboard containing Scatterplot sheet

A worksheet can be dropped onto a **Story** sheet in the same way that it is dropped onto a **Dashboard** sheet, as explained in the previous steps.

To drop the **Scatterplot** sheet onto the **Story** tab:

- Click the **Story** sheet, which makes it the active sheet

After the **Story** sheet is displayed:

- Drag and drop the **Scatterplot** sheet onto the **Story** canvas, as shown in Figure 39-3, which leads to the display shown in Figure 39-4

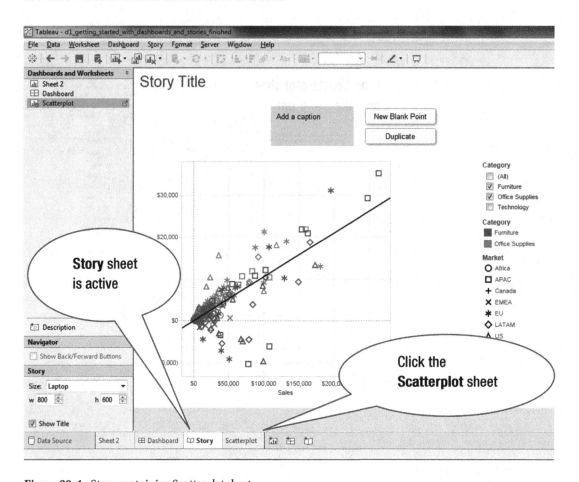

Figure 39-4. *Story containing Scatterplot sheet*

- Click the **Scatterplot** sheet, as shown in Figure 39-4, which leads to the display shown in Figure 39-5

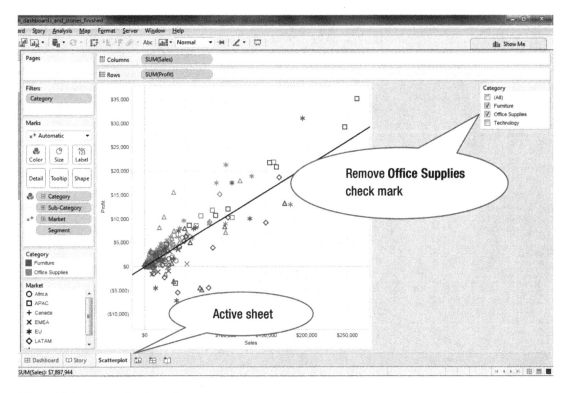

Figure 39-5. *Scatterplot sheet view*

- Remove the check mark from **Office Supplies**, as shown in Figure 39-5, which leads to the display shown in Figure 39-6

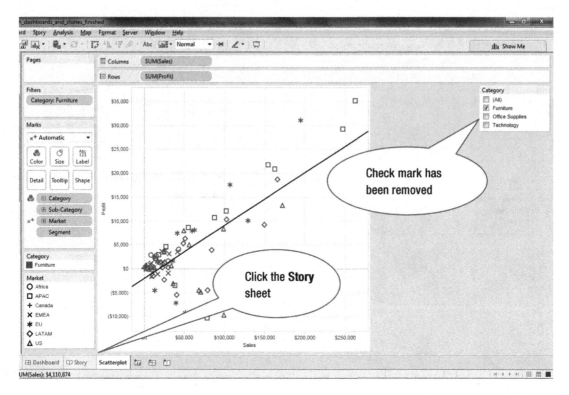

Figure 39-6. Scatterplot after single Category selection

- Click the **Story** sheet, as shown in Figure 39-6, which leads to the display shown in Figure 39-7

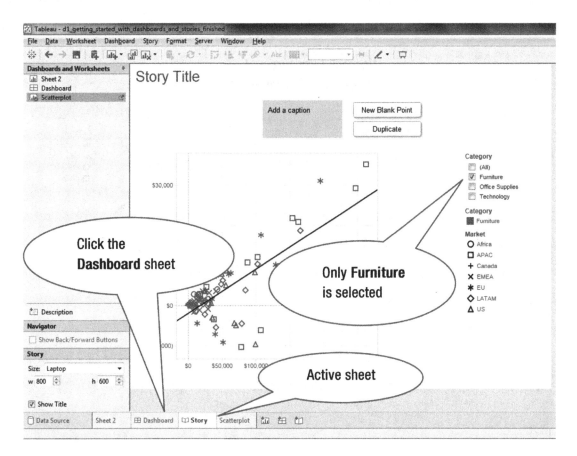

Figure 39-7. *Story view*

Note that the change made to the **Scatterplot** sheet in Figure 39-6 (where **Office Supplies** was deselected and only **Furniture** was retained) is now reflected in the **Story** sheet as well, where only the **Furniture** category remains selected.

To check if the change to the **Scatterplot** sheet is reflected on the **Dashboard**:

- Click the **Dashboard** sheet, as shown in Figure 39-7, which leads to the display shown in Figure 39-8

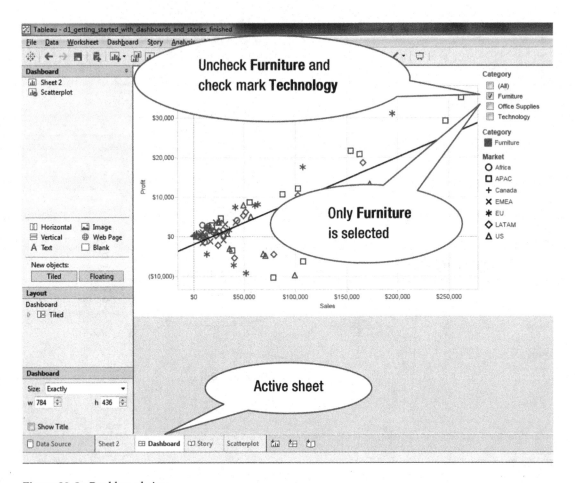

Figure 39-8. *Dashboard view*

Note that the change that had been made to the **Scatterplot** sheet in Figure 39-6 (where **Office Supplies** was deselected and only **Furniture** was retained) is now reflected on the **Dashboard** sheet as well, where only the **Furniture** category remains selected.

On the **Dashboard** sheet shown in Figure 39-8:

- Uncheck **Furniture**

- Place a check mark for **Technology**, which leads to the display shown in Figure 39-9

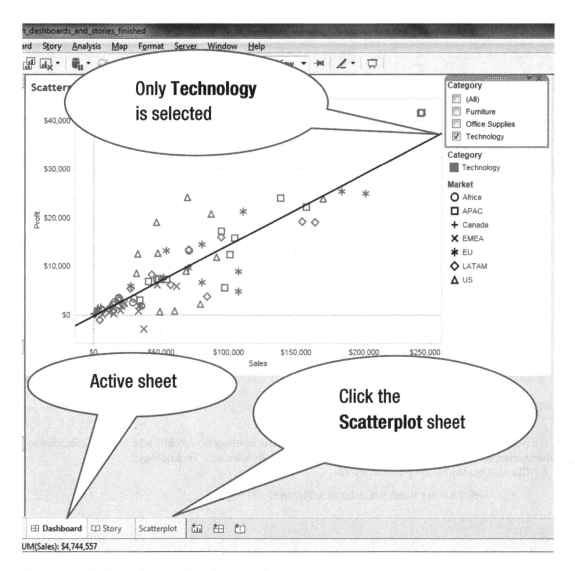

Figure 39-9. *Dashboard view with Technology selection*

- Click the **Scatterplot** sheet, as shown in Figure 39-9, which leads to Figure 39-10

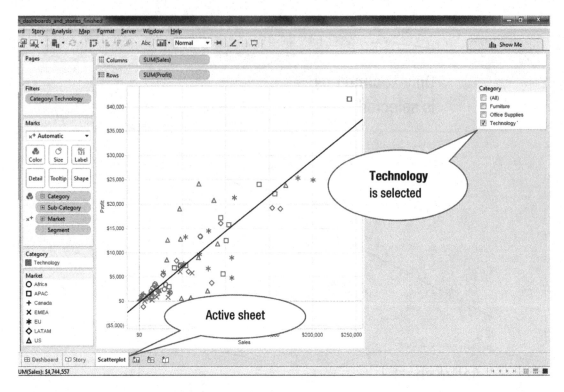

Figure 39-10. *Scatterplot sheet with Technology selection*

Note that the change to the **Dashboard** (where only **Technology** is currently selected) has cascaded to the **Scatterplot** sheet (which also has only one item currently selected—**Technology**).

Changes made to a **Story** do *not* cascade.

- Click the **Story** sheet, which leads to Figure 39-11

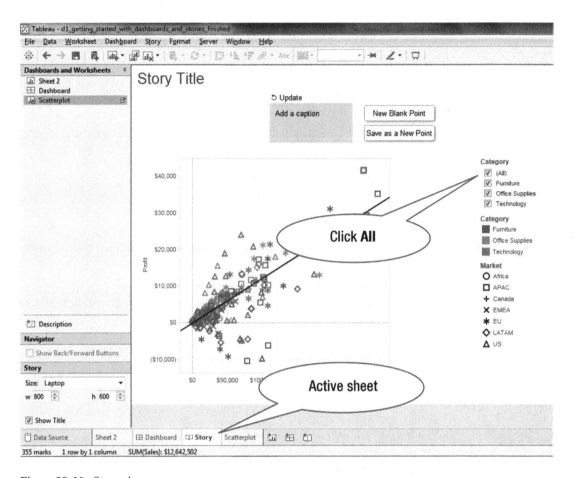

Figure 39-11. *Story view*

To select all categories:

- Click **All**, as shown in Figure 39-11, which selects all categories (Furniture, Office Supplies, and Technology)

If you now go to the **Scatterplot** sheet or the **Dashboard** sheet, the change made on the **Story** sheet (i.e., selecting **All** categories in Figure 39-11), will not be reflected on those sheets.

CHAPTER 40

■ ■ ■

Working with Dashboard Content

Objective: This exercise demonstrates how to modify the dashboard and views display through layout and formatting changes and by adding content

Formatting a Dashboard

Figure 40-1 shows a dashboard with two embedded visualizations:

- Running Total Shipping Costs
- Average Cost for Same Day, Second Class, and Standard Class Shipping

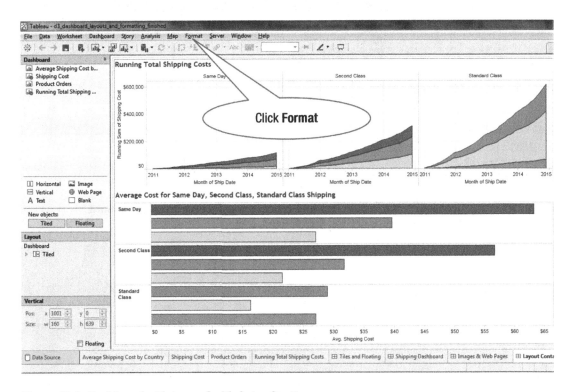

Figure 40-1. Dashboard with two embedded visualizations

© Arshad Khan 2016

A. Khan, *Jumpstart Tableau*, DOI 10.1007/978-1-4842-1934-8_40

To format the dashboard:

- Click **Format** on the **menu bar** as shown in Figure 40-1, which pops up the menu tree displayed in Figure 40-2

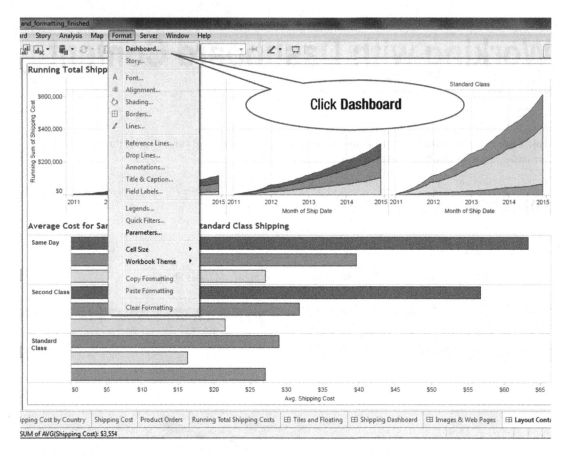

Figure 40-2. Format menu tree

- Click **Dashboard**, as shown in Figure 40-2, which pops up the **Format Dashboard** pane displayed in Figure 40-3 (on the left-hand side)

The **Format Dashboard** pane enables adjustment of the font, alignment, background shading, and borders on the dashboard title, subtitles, and text objects.

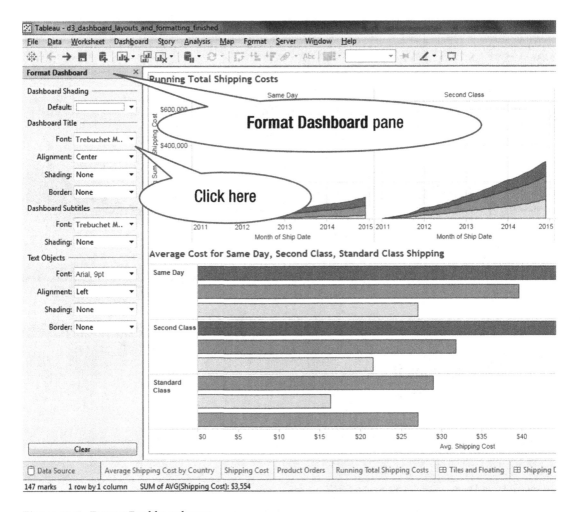

Figure 40-3. *Format Dashboard pane*

- Click the **Font** pull-down arrow, as shown in Figure 40-3, which pops up the window displayed in Figure 40-4

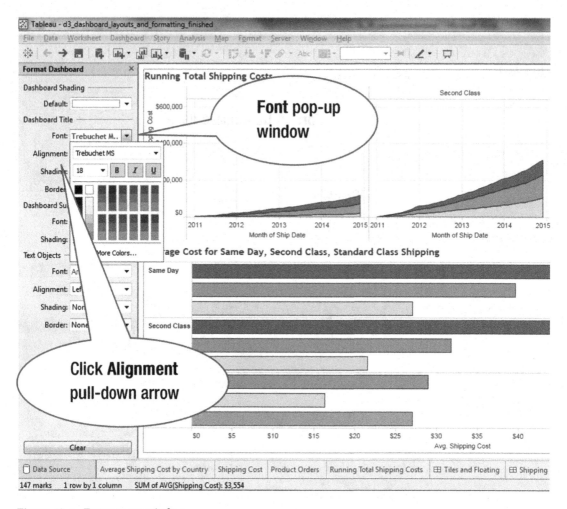

Figure 40-4. *Font pop-up window*

The **Font** pop-up window enables any desired changes to be made to the dashboard title (font type, size, and colors). No font changes have been made in this step, which is for information purpose only.

To change the **Alignment**:

- Click the pull-down arrow for **Alignment** (which is hidden behind the **Font** pop-up window), as shown in Figure 40-4, which leads to Figure 40-5, where the alignment options are displayed

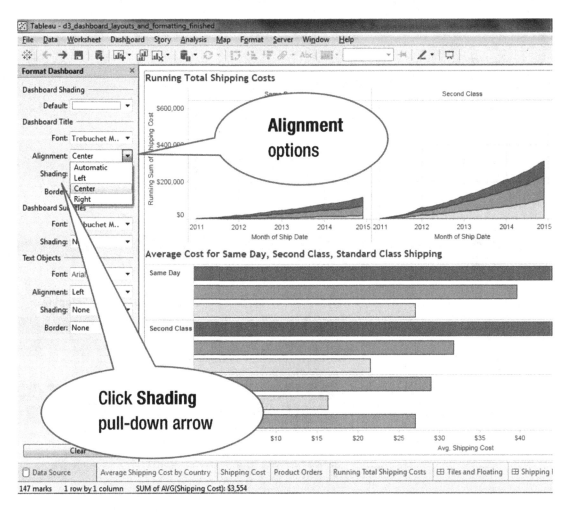

Figure 40-5. Alignment options

No alignment changes have been made in this step, which is for information purposes only. To change the **Shading**:

- Click the **Shading** pull-down arrow (hidden behind the **Alignment** pop-up window shown in Figure 40-5), which leads to Figure 40-6, where the shading options are displayed

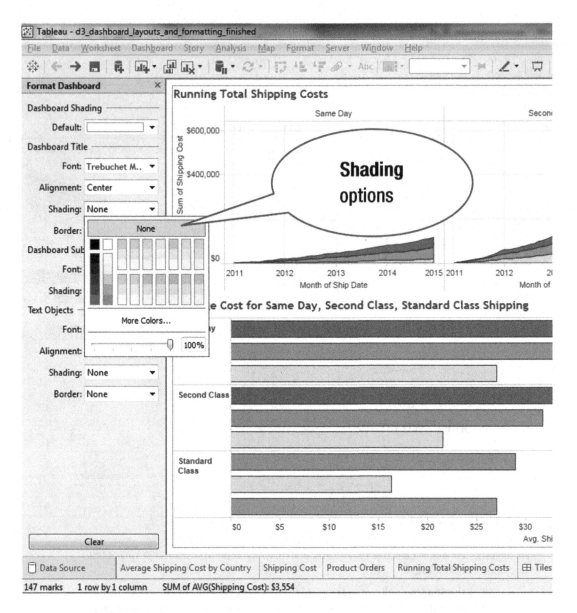

Figure 40-6. *Shading options*

No shading changes have been made in this step, which is for information purposes only.

Formatting Views

Figure 40-7 displays a dashboard, with two views, which needs to be modified. To reformat a view:

- Right-click in the view to be modified (**Average Cost for Same Day**, **Second Class**, or **Standard Class Shipping**), which pops up the menu tree displayed in Figure 40-7

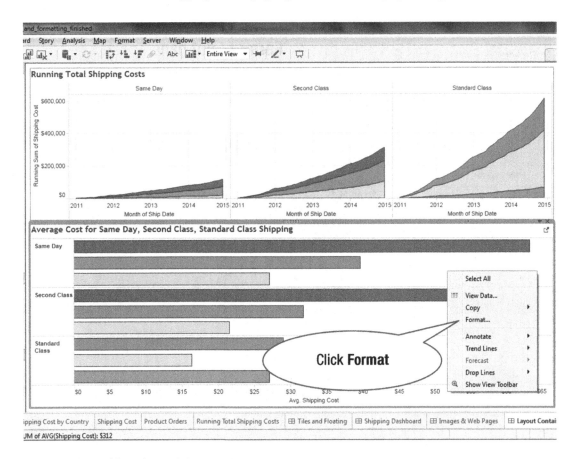

Figure 40-7. *Dashboard containing two views*

- Click **Format**, as shown in Figure 40-7, which pops up the **Format Font** pane displayed in Figure 40-8 (on the left-hand side)

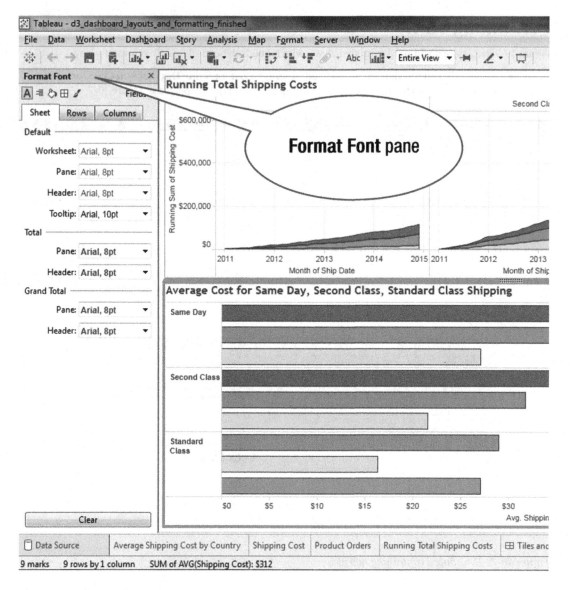

Figure 40-8. *Format Font pane*

Notice the window on the left, where formatting is made. This pane provides the option to make changes for a **Sheet**, **Rows**, or **Columns**, which are selected by clicking the appropriate tab.

Adding a URL to a Dashboard

Web pages, which provide easy access to external web sites, can be easily added to a dashboard.

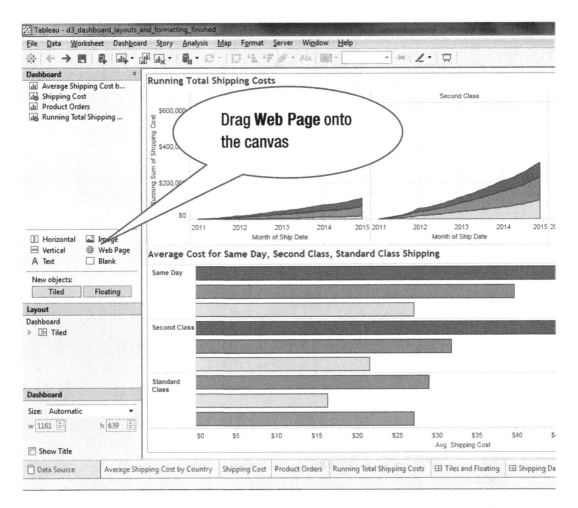

Figure 40-9. *Web Page option*

To add a web page to a sheet:

- Drag the **Web Page** item onto the canvas, as shown in Figure 40-9, which pops up the **Edit URL** window displayed in Figure 40-10

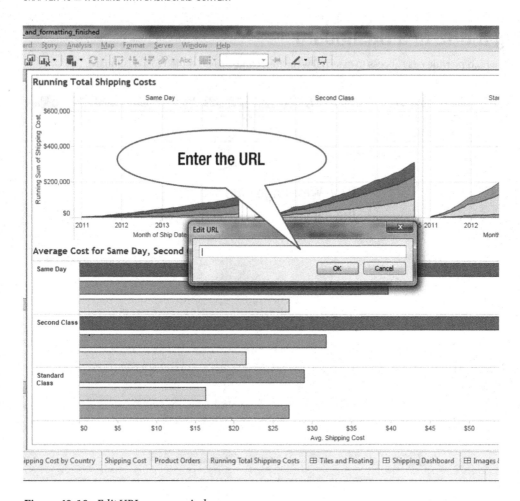

Figure 40-10. *Edit URL pop-up window*

- Enter **www.fedex.com** in the **Edit URL** pop-up window, as shown in Figure 40-10, which leads to Figure 40-11

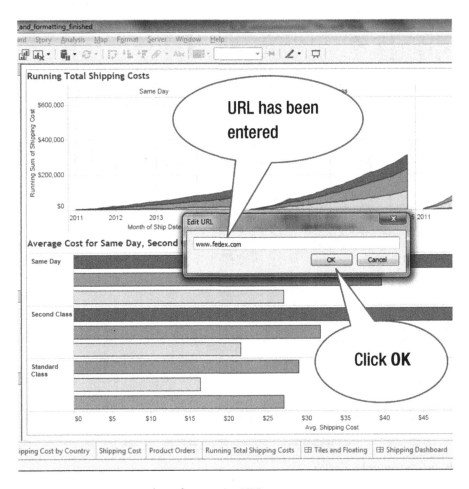

Figure 40-11. *Pop-up window after entering URL*

- Click **OK**, which adds the URL and leads to Figure 40-12, where the FedEx web site is displayed

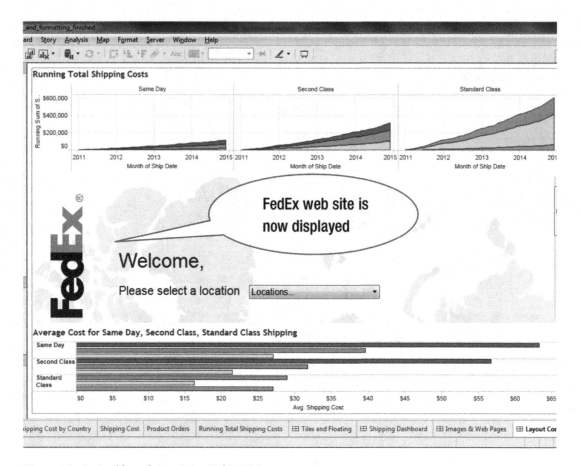

Figure 40-12. Dashboard containing FedEx URL

The individual views in a sheet can be sized or moved, as desired.

Index

Printed in the United States
By Bookmasters